AF323551

Beyond Columbine

Violence Studies

Felix Ó Murchadha
General Editor

Vol. 1

This book is a volume in a Peter Lang monograph series.
Every volume is peer reviewed and meets
the highest quality standards for content and production.

PETER LANG
New York • Bern • Frankfurt • Berlin
Brussels • Vienna • Oxford • Warsaw

Julie A. Webber

Beyond Columbine

School Violence and the Virtual

PETER LANG
New York • Bern • Frankfurt • Berlin
Brussels • Vienna • Oxford • Warsaw

Library of Congress Cataloging-in-Publication Data

Webber, Julie A.
Beyond Columbine: school violence and the virtual / Julie A. Webber.
Pages cm. — (Violence studies; vol. 1)
Includes bibliographical references and index.
1. School violence—United States. 2. Violence—Social aspects.
3. Violence in mass media. 4. Digital media—Social aspects.
5. War and society—United States. 6. United States—Military policy. I. Title.
LB3013.3.W427   371.7'82—dc23   2013020002
DOI 10.3726/978-1-4539-1176-1
ISBN 978-1-4331-2041-1 (hardcover: alk. paper)
ISBN 978-1-4539-1176-1 (ebook pdf)
ISBN 978-1-4331-3836-2 (epub)
ISBN 978-1-4331-3837-9 (mobi)
ISSN 2161-2668

Bibliographic information published by **Die Deutsche Nationalbibliothek**.
Die Deutsche Nationalbibliothek lists this publication in the "Deutsche
Nationalbibliografie"; detailed bibliographic data is available
on the Internet at http://dnb.d-nb.de/.

The paper in this book meets the guidelines for permanence and durability
of the Committee on Production Guidelines for Book Longevity
of the Council of Library Resources.

© 2017 Peter Lang Publishing, Inc., New York
29 Broadway, 18th floor, New York, NY 10006
www.peterlang.com

Printed in Germany

Contents

Acknowledgments

This book has been a long time coming. I'm glad it's done. Thanks to my family and friends for support.

Added value was achieved by the brilliant suggestion of Marie Thorsten that we attend Timeline Theatre's production of *Harmless*, a play about questionable creative writing at a small Midwestern university by a returning Iraq soldier. Thanks also goes out to Brett Neveu, the playwright, for making scripts to *Harmless*, as well as *Eric LaRue*, immediately available to me upon request.

Thanks to Jim Thomas for making time to reflect with me. Also, thanks to Tomi Kiilakoski and Atte Oksanen for their brilliant work on school violence in Finland. Nathalie Paton's work on school violence and social media is invaluable.

I am motivated by reviews of my work and several reviewers of the first book on this theme, *Failure to Hold: The Politics of School Violence*, deserve mention since their careful criticism and their endorsement of certain themes in the book formed in my mind the great bulk of what the reader will find here. Thanks to Dennis Cooper for his selection of my book and use of the insight about equality as the drive to violence on his blog, where he examines school shootings in interesting detail. This project would not have been possible without the support of two summer university research grants provided by the Illinois State University. Organization, proofing and bibliographic work was completed with the assistance of an undergraduate research assistant, Steve Reising. Thanks also to Courtney

Johnson for assisting with preparing the manuscript for submission to my publisher, as well as critical discussion of the book with me.

Thanks to the provost's office staff at Illinois State University for helping me to locate demographic data on student attendance at universities.

Thanks to Ali Riaz, Marie Thorsten, Diane Rubenstein, and John Weaver for providing feedback on final drafts of the project.

Thanks to Felix Ó Murchadha, for feedback and support.

This book is for my dad.

Mass Attacks (1999–2016) Included in This Analysis

Incident	Date	Location	Perpetrator's Name(s)
Columbine High School massacre	1999, April 20	Columbine, Colorado, U.S.	Eric Harris and Dylan Klebold
Gutenberg-Gymnasium	2002, April 26	Erfurt Germany	Robert Steinhäuser
Red Lake massacre	2005, March 21	Red Lake Minnesota, U.S.	Jeffrey Weise
Emsdetten school shooting	2006, November 20	Emsdetten, Germany	Sebastian Bosse
Virginia Tech massacre	2007, April 16	Blacksburg, Virginia, U.S.	Seung-Hui Cho
Jokela school shooting	2007, November 7	Jokela, Tuusula, Finland	Pekka-Eric Auvinen
Northern Illinois University shooting	2008, February 14	DeKalb, Illinois, U.S.	Steven Kazmierczak
Kauhajoki school shooting	2008, September 23	Kauhajoki, Western Finland	Matti Juhani Saari

Winnenden school shooting	2009, March 11	Winnenden, Germany	Tim Kretschmer
Fort Hood shooting	2009, November 5	Fort Hood, Texas, U.S.	Nidal Malik Hasan
Rio de Janeiro school shooting	2011, April 7	Realengo Rio de Janeiro, Brazil	Wellington Menezes de Oliveira
Norway attacks	2011, July 22	Oslo and Utøya, Norway	Anders Behring Breivik
Aurora shooting	2012, July 20	Aurora, Colorado, U.S.	James Eagan Holmes
Sandy Hook Elementary School shooting	2012, December 14	Newtown, Connecticut, U.S.	Adam Lanza
Boston Marathon bombing	2013, April 15	Boston, Massachusetts, U.S.	Tamerlan and Dzhokhar Tsarnaev
Washington Navy Yard shooting	2013, September 16	Washington D.C.,	Aaron Alexis
Inland Regional Center attack	2015, December 4	San Bernardino, California, U.S.	Rizwan Farook and Tashfeen Malik
Orlando massacre at Pulse Nightclub	2016, June 12	Orlando, Florida, U.S.	Omar Mateen

Introduction—Virtual Violence

Beyond the "Columbine Thesis"

Most rampage shootings are a form of retaliatory violence; they are revenge for perceived past wrongs. Columbine gave new meaning to school rampage shootings, especially to disaffected outcast students not only in the United States but throughout Western society. Rampage shootings were no longer the provenance of isolated, loner students who were psychologically deranged. Columbine raised rampage shootings in the public consciousness from mere revenge to a political act. Klebold and Harris were overtly political in their motivations to destroy their school (Larkin, 2007). In their own words, they wanted to "kick-start a revolution" among the dispossessed and despised students of the world (Gibbs & Roche, 1999). They understood that their pain and humiliation were shared by millions of others and conducted their assault in the name of a larger collectivity. Klebold and Harris identified the collectivity—outcast students—for which they were exacting revenge. That is what distinguishes Columbine from all previous rampage shootings (Larkin 2009, 132).

To the one who wishes to flee this world, how do the insults that the world promises to heap on his corpse matter? He sees therein only another act of cowardice on the part of the living. In fact, what kind of society is it wherein one finds the most profound loneliness in the midst of many millions of people, a society where one can be overcome with the urge to kill oneself without any of us suspecting it? This society is no society, but, as Rousseau said, a desert populated by wild animals.

—Marx (1999, 50)

When my hope is gone, people die.

—Kip Kinkel

Journalism is the first draft of history.

—Unattributed

Introduction

Sitting at a Coney Island restaurant in suburban Detroit preparing a dissertation prospectus on John Dewey's *Experience and Nature*, I overheard the newscast about Kinkel's shooting spree, and I began writing about school shootings. This event provoked my interest in what has become over the past decade a research program. It led me to wonder about the use of writing yet another dissertation on the history of political theory that would no doubt be shelved for decades without the binding so much as cracked in the Purdue University archives. What was so wrong, I asked myself, with schools and American society that students wanted to murder their classmates? As I delved deeper into my topic in the spring of 1999, Columbine occupied my television screen for nearly a week, proving to me that my choice had not been in vain. Indeed, in many ways the news media coverage of Columbine was so unbelievable to me because I had been spending so much time looking at school shootings that occurred prior to it in the nineties. For instance, it was clear to me that such a thing as a Trench Coat Mafia could not possibly have the social relevance at any American high school ascribed to it by the media that were no doubt searching for some kind of ideological source for Harris and Klebold's evil act.[1] I also knew from my examinations of the media coverage of Springfield that each and every interpretation for Kinkel's motivations (antidepressants, guns, video games and *South Park*) made for interesting television but that no proof for them from the event itself ever materialized, and the media, done with that particular tragedy, moved on without a second thought, leaving each of those interpretations standing to be co-opted by reporters during the days-long coverage on 20 April 1999 (as Glenn Muschert points out, Columbine came in 2nd only to the O.J. Simpson trial in terms of media coverage during the nineties). Each of these explanations spent time as the "Columbine thesis" in the news. The most enduring one thus far has been about video games, no doubt because the political establishment is knee deep in both the gun lobby and big Pharma for support. The idea of a single thesis that explains school shootings, as well as other shootings in presumed to be *spaces of civility* (high schools, universities, cinemas, malls, parliament buildings, elementary schools) is seductive, but illusory. We must move outside these spaces to understand that the problem of civility is filtered through all of them by the corporation, which, as Deleuze once argued, "constantly presents the brashest rivalry as a healthy form of emulation, an excellent motivational force that opposes individuals against one another and runs through each" (Deleuze 1992, 5). This is the control society that characterizes the late twentieth and early twenty-first century that follows the disciplinary one of the late nineteenth and early twentieth. The crucial difference is that institutions of that disciplinary civil society still exist (family, school, hospital, military); the problem is that we confuse their constant need for "reform" as a democratic improvement when in reality the reform happens in order to "[sic]deliver the school over to the corporation" (ibid.). Thus, we find well-meaning calls for perpetual training to deal with "bullying" alongside increasing modes of surveillance, wiretapping, Internet monitoring—especially cameras—that track movement and sociality within these spaces. As an example, what was the first reform measure called for after the two young Tsarnaev brothers detonated a pressure cooker bomb at the finish line of the Boston Marathon in the spring of 2013? The city of Boston asked for more cameras.[2] Isolating the problem to the school or even to a particular logic of security at a physical site, or contagion by terrorist ideologies on the Internet obscures the fact that the problem exceeds our disciplinary focus: we are in a control society. This means any attempt to formulate or rehabilitate a political civility to counter corporate inspired "rivalry" within this globalized milieu of social media and transnational capital (as we shall see in Chapter 3, of outsourced discipline) will have to confront the vicious conformity (Nietzsche might have called it a herd mentality) produced across all these spaces (the cinema, the mall, the school, the marathon, the military hospital, the parliament building, etc.) that, when confronted with an attack, blinks, and calls it "senseless."

So, how does corporatism socialize? Even when we admit that there might be a multi-causal explanation for school violence, or rampage violence, or however we wish to limit or define it in order to explain it, we are still searching in the wrong place because we begin with the fact of the social as it existed for the disciplinary society: passing from one enclosure to another, as Deleuze says, "first, the family; then to the school ('you are no longer in your family'); then the barracks ('you are no longer at school'); then the factory" (ibid., 3). By contrast, corporatism urges us to, at every turn, depoliticize antagonisms that interrupt the flow of perpetually "reformed to extinction" institutions (welfare, unionization, tenure, pensions, universities, public schools) and instead see these as part of an inevitable flow of capital. These perpetrators are indeed our canaries, as Jackson Katz and Sut Jhally said in the wake of Columbine: it's just that the coal mine is much broader than they had anticipated. Instead we should begin at the exit: suicide or psychotic break. The intention is to end one's life, either through a bullet or separation from reality. The decision to stylize it can then be read as the suicide note or the ramblings of the psychotic. One of the major ideas for preventing random violence episodes is that somehow the plan will "leak" through into the community of peers who will then warn authorities about it. With the exception of Columbine, there has never been a successful *conspiracy* to commit homicide on the way to suicide. Columbine stands unique in this regard.

Alexander Galloway introduces the term *methexis* to understand how game play works in the control society. Galloway sees this methexis in its broader usage for video gaming and even playful socializing. For Galloway, methexis is self-conscious imitation with creative addition. I am using it here to discuss how it is used in ritual forms of violence like mass attacks. In contrast to the way the media and others use "copycatting" as a descriptive term, I use "citation," meaning that these perpetrators self-consciously copy certain key aspects of the script, then add their own additions to it. So, it is not strictly mimetic but methectic. Columbine can be seen as a model for methectic violence as a way to stylize one's exit from reality as the singular, existential act itself is not properly political. If we compare mimesis (what most critics allege about popular culture from film to video games is really critical, alongside the realist representations in them) to methexis, we see that the individuals who engage these acts, especially when they reference past acts, are in game play in the sense that they are a form of "group sharing" where the "the audience participates, creates and improvises the action of the ritual" (according to *Merriam Webster*, a theatrical ritual). However, Gadamer further complicates this notion through a reinterpretation of Plato's deployment of the term in philosophy when he writes that it is different from but often confused with "mimesis" (or what people like to call "copycatting" in the media). Gadamer writes, "When the stars bring the numbers to representation through their paths, we call this representation 'mimesis' and take it to be an approximation of actual being. In contrast to this 'methexis' is a wholly formal relationship of participation, based on mutuality" (Gadamer 2007, 311). They are not copycatting each other; they are improvising the basic ritual established (mainly) at Columbine and also prior to that in the rampage aspect of the event established by Kip Kinkel in 1998 who failed to exit (he taped a bullet to his chest in case he ran out of ammunition at the scene, yet was tackled before he could end his own life).[3] I borrow this term *methectic* from Alexander Galloway who, following Huizinga, uses it to describe games in general, and video games in particular, which are "realism in action" because, "being based on actions rather than images, games quite naturally would turn around a different problematic, something like message sending or 'correspondences' where the core issue is not about mimesis or realistic depiction but about the fidelity of action to image, of motion to outcome" (Galloway 2006a, 72; 133, f.n. 2). Consider the way Bastian Bosse, the perpetrator of the school shooting in Emstadden, Germany, put it in his blog:

> I am not a copy of REB, VoDKa, Steini, Gill, Kinkel Weise or whoever else! Is a village priest just a 'copycat' of the Pope? No! Of course not! He believes the same thing as the Pope, but he's not emulating him. He has the same take on things. He is, like the shite Pope, a part of the whole [...] I want to do my bit for the revolution of the dispossessed. (qtd. in Böckler & Seeger 2012, translated from Böckler & Seeger 2012, 123–4)

This was in 2006. What is political is the way we relate to the spaces of civility in their role as object cause of the desire to commit suicide *in this way*. Nearly every one of the perpetrators of "the violence of extermination" (Balibar), where I take it to mean literally: "to deprive something of its own end" (Baudrillard 2005, 62), examined in this book have been over-modulated, as Deleuze writes, in societies of control: "one is never finished with anything—the corporation, the educational system, the armed services being metastable states coexisting in one and the same modulation, like a universal system of deformation" (ibid., 5). Where did Seung-Hui Cho, the young man who attacked Norris Hall at Virginia Tech, find an end to his modulation? In the IEP (individualized educational program), college, separate tutoring, the 24-hour psych hold (which entrenched his reputation as "?")? None of these institutions ever followed up in a meaningful way, pronounced him "cured" or even "diagnosed." This is the nihilism of the control society: the Medusa face that cares so much it is completely indifferent after the threshold of coverage is reached. Yet we cannot blame these institutions individually—it is the modulation between them that seeks to deform existence ever more insistently. In the absence of civil society, and, as we shall see in Chapter 4, through the "failure of the middle-class social contract," individuals already strained react violently to what they consider to be artificial systems of justice and therapeutic containment. What was the primary policy recommendation by the Justice Department's report on the Virginia Tech shooting? Eliminate "information silos" between mental health, police and educational institutions.

I find it curious that so many sociologists are interested in school violence, yet forget both Marx and Durkheim's warning that sometimes society produces strain on individuals who cannot withstand it. It would be an affront to our democratic, capitalist present to believe that someone might not want to take part in it. This is what is political, is ideological even, and we invent all kinds of ways to avoid acknowledging it, from blaming video games to southern culture. What if, however, the problem is that all these shooters feel stuck in a present; that is, a time when things are not allowed to change according to the passage of time, or to provide a new milieu? As repugnant as it may seem to avow such an insight, wouldn't admitting it give a starting point for truly understanding it? As Galloway says, "It is a central prohibition of capitalism: never to think the present as second best. As Jameson wrote recently (2006) it is "our imprisonment in a non-utopian present without historicity or futurity" (4). What capitalism teaches us is that the present moment *is* the best of all possible worlds, that stasis *is* utopia" (Galloway 2006b). Think about that for a minute.

We are willing to admit that the perpetrators are "canaries in the coal mine" for all kinds of ready-made explanations: masculinity in crisis, violent masculinity, failure to intervene psychiatrically, a simple, unelaborate idea of bullying. One thing that I find truly frightening about this: if young men from relative affluence find no reason to live, what does that say for the rest of us? Certainly, we cannot say that women and other kinds of persons whose religion or race excludes them from full and meaningful participation in liberal democratic institutions have been emancipated, can we? How are we lying to ourselves about the crisis of the future we now face? What exactly do they "identify" with when they plan to participate in this ritual game? I will explore this through the concept of civility further in the next chapter using Étienne Balibar's ideas. Briefly put, Balibar sees civility as a political problem. Civility "regulates the conflict of identifications" (both "total" and "free floating") (Balibar 2002, 29). As we saw above, the current mode of civility is control itself which asks the subject to move from one identification to the next without the promise of an end or discrete starting point for a progressive and autonomous life path. We have one endless chain of diversions. ...

An Attempt to Explain the "Senseless"

> The very fact that ethnic cleansing is not only *practised* but *theorized*—that again and again, the violence of extermination appears as a *passage à l'acte*, becomes implemented as an 'acting out' of a theoretical script which is obviously also fantasmatic (albeit deeply rooted in the substratum of the nation or the nation-form)—could be considered, I think, to be an imprint of an outbreak of cruelty—that is, a violence which is not completely intelligible within the logic of *Gewalt*.
>
> —Balibar (2002, 143)

Étienne Balibar attempts to explain extreme forms of violence in recent work, calling it "ultra subjective" or "ultra objective" in that it is framed in a universalist logic, one that works much like contemporary forms of capital. His phrase above indicates two important points. First, that for something like ethnic cleansing to need to be theorized signifies that we are missing something in our politics (and perhaps also our journalism) in order to explain why these events are happening. Second, his use of the term "cruelty" signifies a kind of evolution of violence that moves away from rationalization, whether it's justified in terms of fighting back against the state or other powerful institutions. School violence and by extension most forms of mass violence that occur in spaces of civil society resist rational interpretation. There is no obvious social or political movement behind them demonstrating that they are fighting against a higher power to achieve a significant goal. This is why so many theorists either resist labeling them political or do so with trepidation, and little by way of explanation. I too have experienced this problem.

In 2003, I published my first book, *Failure to Hold: The Politics of School Violence*, and it was the polished version of the dissertation that I had struggled to write long before Columbine. In it, I devoted much time to detailing the media inconsistencies and related the Columbine event to a larger American cultural quest to securitize youth and public schools through a widespread denial of a hidden curriculum of schooling, the unsaid, unnoticed aspects of existence of students, schooling and American ideologies of so-called "progress." I did not "read" Columbine in that book. I mistakenly hoped it (and 9/11) would signal the end of all such tragedies and left it as a "disaster" in the sense of the type of event that Maurice Blanchot warns us against memorializing. None of my cases in that book had successfully committed suicide. Moreover, at the time in 2003, the events of September 11, the subsequent U.S. and allied military forays into Afghanistan, and then Iraq all but eclipsed the problem of school violence for the American public. Newman's book, *Rampage: The Social Roots of School Shootings* was published in 2004 and quickly its title became the meme for all future acts of mass attacks. Newman's interpretations of the "roots" of shootings being social were problematic as she asserted that school shooters were "failed joiners." Here is Newman's synopsis of the process:

> Sadly, the shooter is usually trying to solve what he (and it is virtually always a he) sees as a serious problem: social acceptance. Rampage shootings are generally the last act, not the first, in a series of attempts to change a damaged reputation. The shooter is rarely a loner. He is, rather, a "failed joiner," someone who has tried, time and again, to find a niche, a clique, a social group that will accept him, but his daily experience is one of rejection, friction and marginality. These experiences are amplified by social media: Facebook and its electronic cousins speed the damage done by teasing, stigma or outright bullying. (Newman 2012)

All of this seems true, until you reach the part about "someone who has tried, time and again, to find a niche, a clique, a social group that will accept him," and it really falls apart. Newman's problematic assumption here is that the person believes a "damaged reputation" can be reversed. I do not believe that any of the shooters believe this; in fact, they have already found a "niche" in marginality. They know they are fated to be objects, and they exact their revenge. The only way that they can see to avoid the terrible outcome is to be given an opportunity to create a new identity in a different environment. In the case of Michael Carneal, Newman's own research confirms this important existential part of the problem:

> What is it about these towns where no one locks their doors that generates these deadly outbursts? We argued the very thing most Americans celebrate about small-town life— close-knit neighbors, friendly families, adults engaged in the schools and churches— become sources of stultifying depression for marginal boys. We interviewed kids who were attending the same high school as their grandparents, in communities where very few left town for college, preferring to stay home and attend the local community college or state institution. For most people, this is a sign of social solidarity. For Michael Carneal, the shooter in a 1997 attack at Heath High School (outside Paducah), that solidarity felt like a life sentence of exclusion. (Newman 2012)

Newman would like us to believe that this only happens in small, rural towns. Her solution to this problem might be increased enlightenment for small towns, bring in diversity, expand capital to these spaces: make it so someone like Carneal might disappear into the dark recesses created by the reach of globalization. Yet, this is what has already happened. If it wasn't a problem for the loners of Carneal's grandfather's generation, why is it a problem at present? Something *has changed* in these towns. They are not any less affected by corporatism than large cities with their Starbuck's diversity; it's just that the pre-existing social formations were different from one another prior to the influence of corporatism, so their transformation will not be identical. In these towns, the trend is toward social *conformity* with the most marketable aspects being celebrated as what Larkin calls the "moral elite," usually those heavily invested in sports and some version of the Christian religion. The whole world is becoming homogeneous—a homogeneous social so that value can continue to be extracted from it. The truth is that it happens in every school that is treated as an island experiment in democracy, in all 98,000 of them in the U.S. The conformity bred in American schools is unrelenting and uninteresting; it is, as Arendt argued, a Rousseauian experiment in socialization. And it would be *even* worse if the standardized testing were removed.[4]

Administrators, teachers and parents (read: authorities) connected to the schools cannot admit that they see the peer group conformity because it disrupts a profound imaginary belief that we carry around identified by Hannah Arendt, that our children are liberated by education: "Children cannot throw off educational authority, for that would mean they were playing the role of the oppressed—though even this absurdity of treating children as an oppressed minority in need of liberation has actually been tried out in modern educational practice. Authority has been discarded by the adults, and this can mean only one thing: that the adults refuse to assume responsibility for the world into which they have brought the children" (Arendt 1961, 190). This is primarily because children are "new" in the sense that they have no way to interpret the world they are inheriting without the guideposts provided by those who built it, the adults. Instead, in American schools (and perhaps elsewhere) authority is shunned and students are left to form their own forms of socialization, without any reference to culture or tradition or even authority. As a default, they form them according to the logic of corporatization, what Balibar calls in an updating of Hegelian/Nietzschean/Foucaultian phrasing, "the normality of morals" (Babibar 2009, 11). What Hegel referred to as the "morality of custom," that is, the state's way of legitimizing moral norms needed to produce civil society, was to make them consonant with (national) culture. Nietzsche, critical of this cultural phenomenon, likened it to creating a "herd mentality," and Foucault, following Nietzsche, saw it as a normalizing tendency; that is, through science and clinical observation, that we have come to produce civility no more through distinctive religious/national culture(s) but now *reroute* these through strategies of normalization that borrow their moral force from positivist science and clinical focus. Hence, the locus of action for civility becomes the "self."

Balibar mentions how destructive the educational portion of normalization can be, "dismembering" even as part of the "crisis of the modern school system" in "both its 'authoritarian' and 'libertarian' forms": "Sometimes the libertarian forms are the most violent, because they put the burden of dismembering and remembering upon the child him- or herself, thereby asking him or her to be his or her own surgeon and engineer and torturer, the *heautontimoroumenos*" (Balibar 2002, 140). Self-torture. In American schools, but also in others where the purpose of education has been redefined to mean achieving a level of normality determined by corporatization (e.g., having the right attitude, being saved, citing the correct consumer fads, cheering the right team, etc.). It's all relentless in its positivity.

Are Balibar and Arendt conservatives? By no means, they simply understand the violence of education in the socialization process. Arendt argues that children need a form of "security of concealment"; that is, to not be exposed to public forms of culture without at least some mediation by authorities. This is not because children are innocent (the current favorite term), but because they are "new," and Arendt calls this condition "nativity." This juxtaposition between authority and nativity can be elucidated by explaining Arendt's view on ideologies of conservatism and liberalism, for she argues that it is not fruitful to be consistent ideologically and take on one position or another, but to use these ideologies in their appropriate contexts. Adults should be conservative when it comes to children; liberalism and the progressive social policies that may be formulated out of enlightenment thought, should only be active in relations between adults. As she further argues, not following this distinction leads to great problems with authority and with the preservation of civilization itself because adults are forgoing authority and tradition by having new people (children) "moving forward in a world unstructured by authority and not held together by tradition." As a result, children inherit an old world that they can never fully understand. Thus, for Arendt, no matter how hard the progressives try to erase the past to begin anew with children as agents who will forge a progressive agenda for the world, the remnants of the old will be met with confusion and terror by them. Nativity is a force to be reckoned with, and Arendt does not do it the injustice of underestimating it. There are three main problems with progressive education that Arendt predicted would lead to the future crisis we now witness.

First, by abandoning authority over children, adults sever the relationship between themselves and children, abandoning them to self-government. This leaves children on their own, in an independent world, that abolishes the important relationships between generations that move history forward and makes adults impotent when guidance is necessary. Newman expands on this notion when she argues that Carneal found "friends" in the goth subculture who urged him to shoot at the prayer circle in order to become part of their marginal group. Furthermore, she notes that no one "knew" what was going on with him at school, at home or elsewhere. Even though there had been many signs, people were unable to put them together with a troubled existence. This kind of neglect is ruthlessly protected by inappropriately applied progressive philosophies of education and socialization. Frank DeAngelis, the principal at Columbine, had no idea who Harris and Klebold were before Columbine, yet he presided over a school where jocks got lesser sentences for acts of brutality while marginalized students were penalized with the full force of school policy and the law. Another set of students, those "saved" by Christ, were allowed to pass moral judgment on the marginalized without question (it might have violated their personal beliefs!) while they drank, smoked and had sex on the sly. What is behind this urge to leave the children to themselves is the desire or hope that they will change the world, instead of asking us to think about how to do it. This is ideological: the children are our future.

Second, in the profession of teaching this also has disastrous consequences because progressive education, by combining insights from modern psychology and pragmatism, has made methods superior to expertise in subject matter. As a result, teachers in the classroom can only resort to method fetishes or brute dictatorial rule to gain students' attention and make authoritative claims. Teachers are not individuals who possess high quality knowledge that students want to gain (making them respectable; authoritative; instead they are more like fast-food workers, executing their time on task, Taylorist models of information delivery anyone can do it, therefore it is devalued). The move on the moderate Right in the United States is to have education delivered by phone applications, and increasingly there are challenges to university policies about who owns the content of professorial lectures, online or otherwise. Professors may increasingly be referred to as "university content providers" under the new regime of MOOCs (massively open online courses). This also means the student herd, or homogeneous social that forms there, knows it has complete social power and that teachers are impotent.

Third, Arendt says Americans have a fetish for pragmatism in their educational philosophies which asserts that one can only truly understand through doing (experience) (Arendt 1961, 182–83). This has negative outcomes because it abolishes the important distinction between play and work. Doing school as a preparation for the adult world of work blurs the boundaries between playfulness and seriousness, making the experience of each less important and pleasurable on its own terms. Furthermore, abolishing the distinction makes it impossible to tell in which situations one is necessary over the other. Moreover, as will become clear later in my analysis of games and control, the blurring of work and play, indeed, the preference for play to become subsumed under work, creates the ideal conditions for forming the "flexible" subject so necessary under globalization. Galloway discusses how play has been co-opted by the new economy as well, arguing that we need a critical analysis of how this works with the flexibility demanded of workers by the market and makes them feel good about work becoming a space of never-ending but redefined kind of play.

All three of these negative outcomes grace our present educational horizon. What Arendt means by "progressive" should not be confused here or opposed to contemporary ideas of conservatism. Arendt indicts the entire enterprise of American education with this critique: no conservative attempt at reform has touched the core of this critique. Left and Right are in agreement on all three aspects above. Newman's approach to being a "failed joiner" does not approach the structural problem outlined above. Therefore, her analysis can only take us so far. Her research (with a consortia of colleagues commissioned by the National Research Council) studied only West Paducah (Carneal) and Jonesboro, Arkansas (Johnson & Golden). Both of these shootings took place in rural, small towns (prior to widespread, quotidian use of the Internet), and in neither case did the shooters plan to commit suicide. They hoped these acts would bring them infamy and they were in both cases very young people (14, 11 and 13, respectively). Newman retains the thesis by December 2012, *after* Newtown, that these shootings only happen in small, rural communities, but this can only make sense if we take Blacksburg (the town itself) as the social milieu. Virginia Tech's students (Seung-Hui Cho included, hereafter Cho) are mainly from urban D.C., while Newtown, Connecticut, is a short train ride (60 miles) from New York City. In order for this to continue to make sense, we must exclude most shootings outside the U.S. from our viewpoint (which is impossible to do after Columbine). To use this logic, practically the only places where we would not expect shootings to happen would be in large cities. Finally, the problem with the 2012 article that Newman wrote surrounding Newtown, Connecticut, and Adam Lanza is that none of these features are present: Lanza shot his mother beforehand, committed suicide, did not plan to see his infamy produce social inclusion, admired several prior shooters on the Internet, and was absolutely ruthless in his execution of the killings. We are not going to find, as Newman surmises, "a boy trying to find acceptance." Lanza is the degree zero of school shooters. Later in 2014 his father he told *The New Yorker*, "With hindsight, I know Adam would have killed me in a heartbeat, if he'd had the chance." "I don't question that for a minute. The reason he shot Nancy four times was one for each of us: one for Nancy; one for him; one for [his brother] Ryan; one for me" (Huffington Post 2014).

For those shooters following Columbine (with few exceptions), suicide is the trademark of the act. They no longer falsely believe that they will gain attention or infamy if they survive the attack. They are willing to die, with no hope for a future. In the control society, they would only move through to the next modulation, without any kind of acknowledgment that their suffering ever had any meaning. Harris and Klebold were the first to figure this out and make it into an action, to forge "the fidelity of action to image, of motion to outcome" (ibid. Galloway). It is not so much that Columbine was so huge or so "successful," but that it repurposed rampage violence to become a game, an action that corresponded to their reality that is of these marginalized young men. The only interesting thing about Harris and Klebold doing it together is that they were able to transliterate it to the "symbolic" from the "imaginary." That its message has not been received by the larger symbolic world (it is "senseless," "meaningless" violence) does not mean it hasn't been identified with by other (future) members of the marginalized, heterogeneous social. In fact, all those following Columbine have been solitary players, satisfied to stay within the non-diegetic script, even perfecting its elements to the exclusion of all others. Where Harris and Klebold left diaries and videos, subsequent actors would "add" or "enhance" the script as technology and insight allowed.[5]

There is also a catch here: they must be able to start over in an environment that is structured, so that they can heal the traumas inflicted in the past. This is nearly impossible for any of them to do anywhere in the developed world outside of the military. And often they are rejected by the military because of evidence of psychiatric assistance, usually a result of the trauma of bullying and social exclusion itself. This was certainly the case of Eric Harris, who was initially accepted into the Marines, then rejected because they found he had been prescribed Luvox, an antidepressant, following his enrollment in a diversion program after being arrested for vandalism.[6] So too, with Steven Kazmierzcak, the successful criminology graduate of Northern Illinois University who returned to his alma mater, to the very classroom where he first attended a course that would decide his major, and shot 21 people, killing 6. Kazmierzcak was discharged from the Marines once they found out he had been institutionalized during and after high school in a psychiatric facility. This occurred on February 13, the day before the anniversary date of his shooting six years later. As Pekka-Erik Auvinen, the shooter in Jokela, Finland, said in his online writings, an "individual, who is going through his/her natural power process and trying to live naturally, but is being told that the way he acts or thinks is wrong and stupid, will usually have some reactions which might be considered as 'psychological disorders' by the establishment. In reality they are just natural reactions to the disruption of natural power processes. They will have some of the following (depending on individual's personality): feelings of inferiority/superiority, hostility, aggression, frustration, depression, self-hatred/hatred towards other people, suicidal/homicidal thought, etc. … and it is completely normal" (Auvinen 2007). It is the constant judgment and the insistence that they be normalized[7] that makes them realize they are never going to experience any kind of autonomy relative to the peer cultures in their schools, or the cultural environments they are expected to advance to in their futures. The environment makes them sick and then their sickness is further used against them in much the same way as before, only this time it is the authorities (e.g., parents, teachers, administrators, psychologists, criminal justice agents) who are using it against them, as a way to define and then normalize them, either through diversion programs and Prozac (Harris & Klebold), incarceration in mental institutions (Kazmierczak), an IEP (Cho), school withdrawal (Weise), and homeschooling (Lanza). Along the way, all of these students (or former students) have been institutionalized in some way; they have been interpellated by failed institutions that let them down: the family, the school and the criminal justice/psychiatric community. The only place they find validation is in online communities that celebrate their views. Newman's analysis is marred by its crisp linearity: they fail at school, fail in social settings, then they fail online. But they often don't fail online. It is there that they find kindred spirits, especially after Columbine. They admire Harris and Klebold, who admired Timothy McVeigh's *acts*, another lonely (and it must be said) "failed joiner." Obviously they all suffer from deep forms of depression and anxiety, but our problem is that dominant media accounts keep feeding the mistaken notion that depression and anxiety have no causes, other than internal ones. More specifically, that depression and anxiety are natural responses to toxic, predatory environments that the threatened person cannot flee (they are in or have been ejected from a compulsory environment). The perpetrators also don't think they "failed" as this would imply that they took a social test that was fair, and due to their own lack of preparation or disfigured social skills "screwed up." How can that be the case when they clearly identify the social structure itself as the problem when they target it, as Newman admits, randomly? If they thought they had failed, they wouldn't have taken revenge. There is a reason why Harris wore a shirt extolling "natural selection," Kazmierczak one that read "Terrorist" and Saari, the Finnish school shooter, chose the screen name "Naturalselektor." If we try to avoid the usual mistake of identifying such choices with Hitler (inarguably the worst attempted natural selector in history) and reinterpret them with an evolutionary concept, we can see that they are not only interested in their own fate, but that of the larger society. They are making a political and social statement through their deaths. If they wanted to get back at targeted individuals, they could do that, or they could leave a note with a detailed explanation of why they did not. They do not do this (leave a personal note; Cho left a sociopolitical note) because they want their acts to incite public scrutiny: of the police, of the school, of their parents, of the psychiatric institutions and of their peers. They leave instead a media package. They foil the assumptions of the authorities through "diversions," and they escape scrutiny. Auvinen was interviewed the day before his shooting by the police. The problem is that there is no willingness on the part of authorities to help them in a truly genuine way. They see very clearly the gap between their own perceptions of what has happened to them and how others view their role in it. So, while Newman and colleagues have provided a vivid conceptual term for a key feature of these episodes in "rampage," there is little here in the way of a phenomenology of violence that can explain what these acts mean for us.

A Gap

We have another curious gap to explain, however. Why are there no rampage shootings between 1999 and 2005 that reached the scale of Columbine, or even came close? The ability to start over in a new setting is a compelling interpretation. Perhaps that explains why there weren't any rampage shootings between those years, since any potentially alienated student would have been recruited (and finally accepted) by the U.S. military or its allies into the fight against the GWOT (Global War on Terror) thus making him, finally, a "successful joiner." Eric Harris had been rejected. Who knows what would have happened if he had applied to the military under lessened post-9/11 standards? Or perhaps as Glenn Muschert argues, the media attention was redirected to terrorism:

> Starting in 2001, the school shooting problem began its decline as a national concern, and incidents were once again most strongly characterized as relevant to the communities in which they occurred (Muschert & Carr 2006). Although school shootings were still newsworthy and do garner media attention, they are somewhat less intensely discussed and the duration of the discussion tends to be brief. In the U.S. terrorism, the economy and foreign military involvement have displaced school shootings as a social problem on the public agenda. When compared to the 1997–2001 period in which the media characterized school shootings as a social problem of national concern, between 2001 and 2006 school shooting events no longer attracted the intense interest from the media. Following the 2007 shootings at Virginia Tech, it is possible that we will see a resurgence in the media focus on issues related to campus crime and safety. (Muschert 2007, 66)

Most analyses avoid the school shooting at the Red Lake reservation in Minnesota. I am including the 2005 incident at Red Lake. This incident was not covered intensely by the media, and whether this was because it occurred on the Red Lake Band of Chippewa (comprised of six tribes in the 1930s under the Objiwe language) reservation and they refused to let the media inside protected territory or because of the more salient issue of race is unclear (Leavy & Maloney, 2009). It is clear that this shooting fits the pattern following Columbine of second generation "school-related massacres" in that they are carefully planned over a period of time, attempt to be "successful" in their execution by achieving certain limits or diversions invented at Columbine (i.e., through improved copycatting/citation) and attempt to be newsworthy. Nearly all of them result in a successful suicide, brought on indirectly by cop (the gap between the time they get to the site and begin shooting and the arrival of the authorities to the scene depends on their planning) which is part of the game. Or they result in a successful psychotic break: Holmes and Breivik come to mind here. Harris, Klebold, Weise, Gill, Bosse, Cho,

Auvinen, Kazmierzcak, Saari, Oliveira, Kretschmer, and Lanza all committed suicide as the authorities closed in on them. All of these shooters either referred to each other or to Columbine alone when referencing and posting claims about their intended acts. All of them have been reported to have been loners at some point, and most of them have been bullied. Whether or not they "failed" to join social communities at their respective schools is never confirmed. In order to write this phenomenology of violence that produces a specific kind of school-related massacre that I will, following Balibar, call "cruelty," we need to describe the social dynamics of what has gone under the heading of "bullying," and we need to analyze the politics of reporting and the academic work surrounding the deployment of this term. This has very real consequences for how we view solutions to this problem, who we see as the agents that can produce policy results and protect student and other civilian populations. This phenomenology has political implications.

The Bully Pulpit

If I can make one intervention in this book, it will be to let other academics who might read it know where the rot is located: in Dave Cullen's *Columbine*. As we can see there's a lot of confusion about bullying among the American literati. As school violence became a growth industry for the media following Columbine, the reporting of it got much worse. I'm not sure it's fair to blame "scholarship," but Cullen is certainly right that sometimes an idea gets solidified in the press that then becomes the uninvestigated truth of the story. The idea that Harris and Klebold were not bullied is one of these "truths." Cullen is now a reporter at the *New York Times*. When Columbine began he was at *Salon* and produced two very important streams of articles for that online magazine, initially in 1999 and again in 2004, that were cited over and over again by academics and others as if they were the truth. One way that Cullen was able to succeed in this was by demystifying all the stories that initially rolled out of Columbine: the martyr story, the Trench Coat mafia, etc. He's been a good foot soldier for clearing up media gossip. By 2009 and the book that was "ten years in the making," Cullen was able to get away with his own truth stretching: a new "demystification" was produced: Harris and Klebold were not bullied, they had friends, etc. Larkin has addressed this hyperreal construction in his book directly in a section parodying Cullen's thesis laid out in 2004, "The Depressive and the Psychopath?" (148–154). He thinks this is not quite the case and probably absolves the administration at the school of some responsibility. By contrast, Cullen and

Det. Dwayne Fuselier's theory about Harris's psychopathology exonerates the entire administration at Columbine, the media, the jocks and the Christians, and wraps it up into a neat little package with Eric Harris's face on it, and served to the American public as "evil." Cullen, in true masculine fashion, is able to call both of them things like "losers" and get away with sounding professional, whereas Katherine Newman must take a different tack and sound understanding: they are failed joiners.

It is this failed joiner issue that is most troubling with Newman's book, because it dovetails so nicely with the growing Columbine fantasy structure created by Cullen (also in 2004). For in "exposing" the myth of the Trench Coat Mafia on *Salon.com*, his book effectively gave legitimacy to Newman's claim about failure to join, as Cullen also asserted that Harris and Klebold were in fact, not bullied (at least by his standards), but had friends and participated in activities at school. So they joined, they just weren't popular (why do we believe they wanted to be popular? This is the unstated assumption of Cullen's analysis). The media's cognitive dissonance that allows a report to quote from Newman and Cullen at the same time is equally perplexing: Cullen claims they were not bullied, but that Harris was a psychopathic Pied Piper leading Klebold down a path of destruction and chaos (the very same thing he would argue about the Tsarnaev brothers); Newman proclaims them officially bullied, but her analysis does not condemn the social structure that reproduces and affirms the cruelty they experience. Together they perform a compromise formation for the American political imaginary: on the one hand, yes, they were bullied, but bullying isn't so bad because you can still have friends (so they must be pathological individuals who do not respond to a normalized part of American civil society). In this the audience never has to look at bullying in its raw and cruel form nor do they have to look at the schools as places where their children might not be protected.

Dewey Cornell, the forensic clinical psychologist who interviewed many of the first generation school violence perpetrators, is more honest about what we can know at this point: they represent a third category of shooter (behind the psychologically ill and antisocial youths, basic criminals who make up 2/3 of youth violence episodes) in that they "appear to be normal well-adjusted kids who suddenly shoot and kill for what appears to be no reason. However, these kids are actually emotionally disturbed, socially alienated, troubled and conflicted, angry and depressed. They may be very intelligent and capable of many things but they are not satisfied with their own achievements and they are often victimized or treated unfairly in some way by their peers. They could have a few friends but still feel alone and isolated from the rest of the world" (qtd. in Roach 2010). What is this world they feel isolated from, and why do they react so violently toward it? Why are they not capable of indifference?

One problem could be with the notion of joining altogether; to say that one fails at it presumes that one wants to join something, like a "social," and has problems doing so. This may be the case with Klebold and Harris, although it may also be that they did not want to join: no one ever places under scrutiny the particular groups they had before them for membership, with the exception of Larkin (2007) whose actual sociological interviewing of Columbine survivors and friends of Harris and Klebold will structure our reading later in this chapter. As Murray Forman has written,

> As the Columbine tragedy revealed, Harris and Klebold were identified by their schoolmates as being inarguably uncool, and once labeled as such they struggled under the symbolic weight of the designation. At some point they evidently gave up on being cool, and, as an emancipatory strategy akin to the survival techniques identified by Gaines, the boys embraced their low social status fully, announcing their attitudinal and taste differences through the "semiotic guerilla warfare" of style accompanied by surly and irreverent social dispositions. Harris and Klebold didn't precisely abandon the reality of a school-based economy of cool, but, rather, prior to their deadly actions, *they redefined their position within the economy, shuffling their point of identification in a manner that drew attention to their marginal status and, in turn, the very existence of a powerful social hierarchy that ostracizes and excludes teens.* (Forman 2004, 72, emphasis mine)

Earlier on in his analysis of the alternative "cool" that has been co-opted by television in the last decade through such shows as *Freaks and Geeks*, Forman gives voice to Gaines's earlier insights about marginalized youth that are eerily forgotten in Cullen's story about Columbine, Newman's analysis of the "social roots" as well as FBI reports and profiles that focus on subsequent school shooters: "Gaines explains that 'transgressive' teens are often caught between the demands and expectations of adult authorities and the 'hegemonic' authority of the school jocks, and, furthermore, they are repeatedly labeled as 'burnouts,' 'losers,' and other pejorative terms. As she determines, what from the outside looks like indifferent self-exclusion or uncaring failure due to chronic social, athletic, and scholastic ineptitude may actually be a deliberate defensive strategy for subsistence" (Forman 2004, 67). Finally, Forman quotes Gaines, "The further away from the mainstream they could get, the greater their self-respect. Whether that meant nonparticipation, obliteration through drugs, or contemplating suicide, it was a matter of psychic survival" (Gaines 1992, 92, qtd. in Forman 2004, 67). Or, as Larkin has found from interviewing friends, classmates and teachers of Dylan Klebold, in the ninth grade he "went from being a nobody to one who was recognized for his negativity" (Larkin 2007, 141). Even a teacher perceived him as "unattractive" (ibid.) With few exceptions, coverage of Columbine and subsequent shootings has been marked by its lack of interest in the shooter's point of view or message. Part of the problem has been that any portrait of school violence perpetrators has been undertaken by the Federal Bureau of Investigation or some other federal agency whose unit of analysis begins with the notion of an already committed criminal act. As a lead investigator for the Red Lake shooting wrote, "Jeffrey's family dynamics are interesting. However, this was a criminal investigation and not a psychological autopsy" (O'Toole 2012, 178). The FBI is the security guard for the control society.[8] Uninterested in looking at the symbolic evidence of what leads these young men to plan, document, mediate and brand events that use bombs, gasoline, tear gas, diversionary tactics and ends in a rampage event that culminates in suicide, whether by cop or by self, both the media and researchers have ignored the rampant social conformity in American schools (and elsewhere) that produces a "heterogeneous social" (Sumiala & Tikka 2011). While Newman's notion of "rampage" is helpful in terms of describing a discrete part of the script that school violence perpetrators act out, it is by no means the whole part of the event. In the case of Columbine, especially Cullen, Kass and Larkin, many have shown it was really an event that was meant to be a bombing. The rampage part only inheres to the indiscriminant shooting, which lasts less than 10 or 20 minutes in each case. It wasn't the main event in Harris and Klebold's pilot.

Unfortunately, more shootings took place as the years went on, including the 2005 shootings in Red Lake, Minnesota, by Jeff Weise, the Virginia Tech shootings by Seung-Hui Cho in 2007 and the Northern Illinois shooting on Valentine's Day in 2008. I prepared to publish a new book incorporating all of the new insights generated by these shootings, as well as the media coverage of them, especially in light of 9/11 and other terror events that generated public acceptance of the various Columbine theses that would substitute for one another on any given day. The three shootings are examined in detail at the end of Chapter 5 for the way they fit into this script.

First, however, I must examine an example of what I consider to be a productive disavowal generated by "critical journalism" of Columbine. In order to do this, I will have to (finally) do my own (partial) reading of the event. This initial reading will serve as the first instance in a series of shootings I will briefly mention in scattered places throughout the rest of the book, including shootings by military personnel as in the case of Ft. Hood, as well as the attempted attack on Ft. Dix, the case of John Walker Lindh and finally the case of Staff Sgt. Roger Bales, who was court marshaled in the shooting deaths of 17 Afghan citizens in March 2012.

As well, I will backtrack into the series to look at the bombing and murder spree undertaken by Anders Breivik on 22 July 2011 and link it back to two shootings in Finland that took place in 2007 and 2008, in Jokela and Kauhajoki respectively, and their connection with post-Columbine events through listservs and web pages devoted to cultural fetish objects, like music and violent videos. Furthermore, I will discuss the role that YouTube may play in creating what Finnish researchers Kiilakoski and Oksanen have called a "brand" for "shootings to come" (Kiilakoski & Oksanen 2011, 247). There are also the mass shootings that took place in Germany in 2002, 2006 and 2009, but my analysis here will focus mainly on 2006 in Emsdetten and 2009 in Winnenden.[9] In 2006 especially, the European media began rethink its previous disavowal that school shootings were an American problem linked to violent culture and gun availability. It is also at this time that research has shown that American right-wing bloggers as well as their Australian-English counterpart Rupert Murdoch began fiercely defending Second Amendment rights. As DeFoster has argued, after Winnenden, European media "turned inward" (DeFoster 2010, 467). Also, in 2009, the U.S. witnessed a mass shooting on an American air force base, Ft. Hood, by none other than one of its own army military psychiatrists, Maj. Nidal Hasan. This shooting initially conjured up fear of a terrorist attack, but quickly turned out to be a case of increased psychological strain, possibly brought on by an impending deployment to Afghanistan, as well as anger that colleagues refused to prosecute several soldiers Hasan had discovered to have committed war crimes. Hasan is included here because many analysts close to the case believe this more closely resembles the shooting in Virginia Tech, and because Hasan "passed up several opportunities to shoot civilians, and instead targeted soldiers in uniform," in other words, his peers (Zucchino 2010). One might also call this a new—democratic—form of fragging. Hasan was later indicted as a terrorist by the right-wing media and several U.S. senators. Hasan was a severely troubled American doctor and soldier working in a veteran's hospital. Like the Tsarnaev brothers, he was Muslim, and like them, he was constantly interrogated for terrorist activities, unlike the other perpetrators we examine here, who were not.

There is no school-related massacre or civil society mass killing that fits this model in 2010.

In April 2011, another mass shooting took place in Rio de Janeiro, Brazil, that more closely resembles the Newton massacres in that the shooter, Wellington de Oliveira, who was also 24-years-old and returned to his grade school to commit his rampage, he burned his hard drive, lined the students against the wall and shot them at point-blank range, and he admired the 9/11 attacks (Sibaja 2011). He is said to have been bullied and an outcast. After killing 12 students, he also committed suicide. By mid-2011, on the date of the onset of the Crusades, 22 July, Anders Bering Breivik exploded a bomb at the Norwegian parliament building in Oslo, killing eight, and then proceeded, dressed as a police officer, to hail a ferry out to Utøya Island (the site of a Labor Party youth camp) and commit a rampage shooting on the ferry, killing close to 60 more people. Unlike all the previous shooters, Breivik surrendered to the police and spent much of his time in court defending his actions. Breivik's "Manifesto" and critical attention to it by scholars discusses the role of multiculturalism in fostering the takeover of Europe by Muslims.[10] I will link Breivik to Columbine and other shootings and read it through his focus on "Eurabia" in his paranoid mind a real place where Muslims take over an authentically Christian Europe (e.g., Norway) through "multicultural relativism" and "feminism" in the next chapter. In March 2012, another military shooting took place, only this time it was by a sniper who killed Afghan civilians in Kandahar. Sgt. Robert Bales snuck out of his barracks in the middle of the night, unseen, and fatally shot several people in one nearby village before he quietly returned to his camp for an hour, only to leave for another village and shoot more civilians, 16 in all. Finally, James Eagan Holmes and his shooting spree in a Denver multiplex during the opening scenes of *The Dark Night Rises*, disguised as the Joker, follows and will be linked to Adam Lanza's mass murder at a Connecticut elementary school in December 2012 (these two specifically for the way they inspire conspiracy theories explored in Chapter 5). They are all linked to each other and trace back to Columbine and to Harris's opening salvo, "We want to kick start a revolution, a revolution of the dispossessed" (Transcripts of *The Basement Tapes*, March 1999). Some are aware, some are not, of what they are doing: all are revealing important insights into the inner workings of a control society at war with itself.

Every single one of them glided under the radar of those around them; Holmes was as "anonymous as a glass of water" (Healy & Kovaleski 2012), Lanza was a shy, quiet boy who did not like to be touched (but we find out he took several trips outside his home to malls alone to scout for equipment for his spree), and in the cases of the Finnish and German school shooters, they were all described as "quiet," often "generous and nice." Or later, bystanders wondered why no one had ever tried to do anything to help them, as was the case with Cho, Breivik, Holmes and Hasan, all of them shuffled through psychiatric institutions, formal reviews, academic institutions and so on while they continued to "pass" unnoticed. Finally, Jahar Tsarnaev's friends have provided evidence, and "what emerges is a portrait of a boy who glided through life, showing virtually no signs of anger, let alone radical political ideology or any kind of deeply felt religious beliefs" (Reitman 2013).

If our shooters are "canaries in the coal mine," then we must stop scrutinizing the canaries and begin to map how the coal mine operates in order to obscure our vision of what's motivating the canaries to commit murder or suicide or psychotically break; that is, how they decide that reality is not really worth the trouble any longer. As I will argue, they plan these acts methodically (and still usually fail to enact most of their plans), so their acts fall somewhere between those of the impulsive patriarchal identified wife abuser (who takes his whole family with him to spare them the shame, or selfishly not allow them to live without him) and the calculating psychopath so adored by the FBI who has a really difficult time ending a cold, calculated and selfish life. They are produced by their environment, take on many of its aspects and plan to die in an infamous way. They need publicity; they do fetishize guns and bombs; they identify with hatred in its most popular (and available forms); they have to prepare to commit the acts (in most cases it's not natural or enjoyable to them: Breivik took Testosterone before his attack, Lanza studied gory images of children, etc.); they are mentally ill (in an as of yet undefined way); and they are suicidal. If we take all of these factors and put them up against previous "youth movements," we can say that they lack a counterculture. If there was a space outside (an "outside") they might still crave publicity but would be able to get it symbolically; they may resort to violence but only against an oppressive agent, like the state or bourgeois norms; they would probably use feelings of disgust and even hatred against the state as a source of agency or to formulate a strategy of civil disobedience; and they could act out this disobedience with a relatively clear conscience. With every available source of discontent explained away as an individual's failure (the solution to which is available in the modular agencies) and shunted into another failed mediation, they realize there is no exit (not even an outside from which to complain).

Unfortunately, nearly every reading of school violence is on the side of the *control society*, because this is the only way one's ideas can be allowed representation, especially in mass media. As Kiilakoski and Oksanen contend, riffing off of Newman et al.'s framework of the "cultural script of the school shooting," which is a perfect example of theorizing from the side of social control as they reduce the overall analysis to the shooter's intentions, they offer by contrast, "The cultural script, however, is the wider social background which makes school shootings appear as a meaningful act. It is the prescription for behavior. To use Wittgensteinian terms, the cultural script is meaningful in a life that views violence as a solution, combines manly behavior with violent acts and views school shootings as a way to reverse intra-generational power relations in schools" (Kiilakoski & Oksanen 2011, 250). While they add the important element of the "cultural products and discourses that affect a script" such as music, films and stylizations shared by shooters to an analysis of the script, this addition *transforms the level of analysis* significantly, making it possible to see in such mass attacks not just the result of a "failure to join" a school environment, but to reach beyond it to the society that informs such an environment, as well as providing responses to it. The school and the society are always connected; schools are not "black boxes" that we must penetrate to unearth their hidden workings, rather, schools are a reflection of the social dynamics within the society in which they are housed. Newman et al.'s analysis makes it possible to discuss all the obvious advancements made by Harris and Klebold over previous shootings, most importantly, "to conduct a school shooting and gain notoriety by using a precise media strategy" (ibid., 250), only to stop short of calling it a "movement," that is, to deny that its social impact could resonate beyond the walls of Columbine High School or Eric Harris and Dylan Klebold's warped minds. The question remains, in spite of the horrors inflicted and the tragedies that ensued, what if they actually had something to say? As Kiilakoski and Oksanen argue, such shootings work on both interpersonal and intrapsychic levels while referencing previously available scripts, such as Columbine, which I would argue is the *pilot* for the second generation school shootings that follow. As they write, "The different levels of the script (cultural, interpersonal, intrapersonal) both form the background of the act— they deal with masculinity, revenge, acquiring power in public space—and give detailed guidelines on how to act in given situations" (ibid., 251). In the Jokela, Finland shooting in 2008, they offer, "the events of Columbine were emulated in an attempt to claim a large number of victims in trying to create destruction to the school building (pipe bombs in Columbine, trying to burn down the building with gasoline in Jokela) and to reach the public and *describe the event as a political act*" (ibid., 251).

While Muschert worries that school violence research suffers from a multidisciplinary approach that has obscured any "unified" approach or understanding of this social problem, I would argue that there is an important claim to be made that these are not only *social problems* (certainly they affect the local communities in which they occur more than any other actors in the event: the media, the public at large, e.g., the media viewer) but that they can be read as *political statements* of a new kind, which will be discussed in Chapter 4.[11] This became clear with Columbine. The analytic separation between what have been called the "first wave" of school shooting sprees, occurring between 1996 and 1999, and the "second wave" is that the first school shootings are figured as social problems, i.e., they are committed by shooters emphasizing the script's intrapsychic and interpersonal elements only. Thus, for Barry Loukaitis, it was an identification with *Natural Born Killers* and other forms of media, as he brandished the sawed off shotgun and trench coat; for Carneal it was largely intraspychic, with an over-identification with the scene from *The Basketball Diaries*; or for Kinkel it is an intense episode of psychosis laden with interpersonal tropes that switch between the school and the family dynamic, guns and popular culture and for Johnson and Golden (both set free from juvenile detention in 2001) it was both, a chance to get back at "girls" through a dramatic form of revenge for romantic refusal and the lure of copying the rifle sniper script (they set up a rifle with a scope and pulled the fire alarm to get the students to leave the building). These events share similar traits and differ from the post-Columbine wave in fundamental ways. First, these early events may have all, as Dewey Cornell has argued, been preoccupied with getting the attention of peers by leaking information about the shooting beforehand, giving clues which were not connected to the shooters' intentions. "All of these behaviors reflected the strong developmental need of adolescents for peer acknowledgment. Similarly, the decision to carry out an attack in the open, public setting of a school reflected the adolescent's need to make a compelling statement to an audience of peers" (Cornell 2011, 45). This first wave is at school because the shooters are angry with some aspect of the school environment, but they do not intend to gain a media audience. These are also not suicides; the shooters may be suicidal (i.e., they idealize it), but they either cannot carry it out or refuse to (Golden and Johnson, 11- and 13-years-old, respectively, planned a "getaway"). This latter distinction is important because Harris and Klebold made sure they were able to commit suicide at the end of their rampage. Interested parties wonder what they were doing for 30 minutes between killing and suiciding themselves; they were making sure the time was right. Harris and Klebold were not interested in sticking around to find out if they "make a compelling statement to an audience of peers"; they enlisted a third party to do that for them, the media. This is where the politics happens, at what Galloway calls in video games the "moment of gamic death," which is "the moment the controller stops accepting the user's gameplay and essentially turns off"; further on "this moment usually coincides with the death of the player's character inside the game environment" (ibid., 28). By emphasizing the spectacular nature of the event, complete with bombs (that failed) and diaries, videotaped interviews, even their clothing revealed the final message: "natural selection" and "wrath." The key difference between the first wave and the second is that in the former the rage is unfocused, and the rampage and suicide largely fails in that both are interrupted; in the latter rage, rampage and suicide are harmonized—the gamic algorithm of school violence is established.

The Many Tropes
of Columbine

The reporting problem gets camouflaged by repeated layers of "scholarship." One scholar bases a paper on faulty reporting, which gets cited by another scholar, then another—until a book like this appears with a bibliography full of academic citations. Academic weight increases as the research grows farther from the source, which is rotten at the core.

—Dave Cullen in a review of Jessie Klein's The Bully Society

The Pilot

The script changes in Columbine. As Sumiala and Tikka maintain, it becomes "iconic," and prefigures the advanced ritualized forms of sacred, heterogeneous communities that would later be built around it in 2005, after the debut of YouTube and the triumph of this form of communication through remediation (Sumiala & Tikka 2011, 150). But I want to add something to this idea of a heterogeneous social (indebted to Bataille in his reflections on Durkheim and Mauss), and that is that each new shooting that achieves mediated status adds to or improves upon the script created at Columbine; this is what I earlier referred to as their methectic quality, with each episode adding something new, a substitution, or bricolage[1] (whether it be using gas instead of bombs, emailing or posting the media package directly to social media rather than relying on the professional mass media to air it). These are serial events. Columbine is the pilot for the next wave (which does not take off again until 2005)[2] of shootings that are much different from those that preceded it. In fact, Harris and Klebold make reference to previous shootings, but not to admire them, rather to make fun of them:

> They both wanted to commit the deadliest school massacre ever, and belittled shooters who only killed or maimed a few. And they did in fact ramp up the concept of the school massacre, adding bombs to the mix and reaching for the moment, unprecedented levels of planning and death. But they were followers even in Columbine, using the script of the other school shooters who showed them the art of the possible. (Kass 2009, 183)

How did Harris and Klebold euphemize their intended act? They called it NBK, or *Natural Born Killers* (a nod to Barry Loukaitis?).[3] This heterogeneous social does not exist together in time or space; they fetishize the acts of the dead. They do intend to transgress the laws of the sacred, and they do follow (roughly speaking) Bataille's notion of fascism. However, the extermination they carry out has no meaning *for them*. Following Balibar and a few other thinkers, my intention is to describe these events in a way that contributes to understanding the phenomenology of this extreme violence that flows out of a certain kind of *cruelty*. It is also literally self-sabotage, as in most cases they are suicides or end in psychotic breaks. Philosophically speaking, cruelty has a history. For Nietzsche it is produced from below—it is democratic. However, most of the analysis thus far has been concentrated in sociology and criminal justice, two disciplines that often take the society of control as a given. Larkin (2007) begins this process and for this reason stands out as an exception because, as one reviewer put it, he "sets it into a context" that encompasses: "the culture of celebrity in post-modern America," the "growth and popular enthusiasm for para-military culture in the mid-west," "the deeply intolerant and self-satisfied evangelical Protestantism in the area and the school itself," and finally, "the ethos of the school, in which elite male athletes were encouraged to behave like pampered white sons of plantation owners in the pre-civil war South visiting the slave quarters, and the leading crowd were left free to bully and harass everyone else in the school" (Delamont 2008, 166–167). Kass will corroborate most of this through his journalistic project. However, the first important step has been taken to remove the focus from the perpetrators and give some emphasis to the environment in which they operated. This means suspending the media's fixation on psychological explanations that reside in the individual, and sociology's explanations (at least many so far) which take the disciplinary society as a given and assume we function in a normalized civil society; it is assumed that it is only these few individuals who cannot adapt. Second, however, we must explain why there are no relevant cases until 2005,[4] and still no more media-generating ones until Virginia Tech in 2007. Some scholars have made the connection between the availability of such scripts via YouTube, the likes of which first appears in functional form in 2006.

Columbine: Hyperreality

> Yet the ability to grasp subtleties and provide historical context was not evident for many reporters and book reviewers going over Columbine. As they attempted to rewrite the Columbine story on the ten-year anniversary, the subtext was, "We blindly put our faith in the early news reports. Now we are told they were wrong. We are now blindly putting our faith in the latest story we are hearing."
>
> —Kass (2010b)

In the summer of 2009 the only celebrated book of critical journalism covering the Columbine shootings was published by Dave Cullen, a decade after the event itself. This book, entitled *Columbine*, received many accolades and praise for being the definitive account of the Columbine shootings, an accurate portrait of the shooters, undertaken by a local journalist at the *Denver Post*, with a national outlet online at *Salon.com*. *Columbine* disputed all the media's mistaken reporting: the Trench Coat Mafia, the idea and importance of "cliques" at Columbine, the bullying that Harris and Klebold experienced, their role in the Columbine pecking order as being grossly misinterpreted, the "unlikely martyrdom of Cassie Bernall" (which I had detailed in my own book 6 years before [Webber 2003a, 104], as had Watson in 2002), even Misty Bernal admits this in her book *She Said Yes*, which came out in 2000, and this is where I sourced the claim for my own argument. However, when I read the book, I couldn't help but think that Cullen's success and all the attention he was drawing were not based on how well his arguments matched the investigative facts he produced in the book through his connection to several key investigators in the case. Rather, Cullen's arguments were not questioned, it seemed to me, for two main reasons. First, he was seen as "local"; therefore, because of his proximity to the case any doubt that unfamiliar readers may have had put toward his narrative were eradicated. After all, this was a national journalist who spent ten years studying this horrible tragedy, speaking to victims and family members, interviewing law enforcement, and hanging out with the FBI. It was as if being near Columbine made any claims one made about it more authentic. The problem was there was only this one account or, so most people thought (and still do). The problem is that even critical journalism now works like conventional media: shutting out alternative voices to the exclusion of one popular story.

Second, Cullen's narrative exonerates the homogeneous social; that is, it defends Columbine, the school. Bataille's depiction of how social homogeneity neutralizes "unruly elements" or "disruptions" like Columbine is apt:

> As a rule, social *homogeneity* is a precarious form, at the mercy of violence and even of internal dissent. It forms spontaneously in the play of productive organization but must constantly be protected from the various unruly elements that do not benefit from production, or not enough to suit them, or, simply that cannot tolerate the checks that *homogeneity* imposes on unrest. In such conditions, the protection of homogeneity lies in its recourse to imperative elements which are capable of obliterating the various unruly forces or bringing them under the control of order. (Bataille 1979, 66)

Cullen's book is a symptom of our own fetishistic disavowal of the cruelty that is pervasive in public schools and elsewhere in declining capitalist societies. What is unique now about the production of heterogeneity, which Bataille describes as a "split off" part of homogeneity, is that it is nearly impossible for it be relatively autonomous to the homogeneous social. In fact, as Žižek has argued that capitalism "detotalizes meaning," we can now see the true force of the acronym TINA (There Is No Alternative) to the capitalist forms of social organization that follow from it. That is, there is no alternative to the homogeneous social. Market forces and apologists of all stripes for them (and for their apologists) find ways to capitalize on strategies for bringing heterogeneous elements back under the sway of "productive organization." Furthermore, it does not matter if these strategies "work" as they have no objective other than keeping the subject within the modular framework; in this they are consumerist because they ask the subject to submit himself to their regimes in order to be pronounced "well" interminably. For Harris and Klebold, "diversion" was such a program. We will investigate this toward the end of the chapter. First, it is important to outline the productive function of Cullen's text; it is his mastery of "bringing unruly forces" under the "control of order" that makes his text so popular.

I have already mentioned the confusion between proximity and knowledge. My first queasy feeling came with Cullen's too close for comfort relationship with FBI investigator Dwayne Fuselier, a psychologist (Cullen erroneously calls him a psychiatrist, a not insignificant form of misdirection), on whom he relies for most of his portrait of Eric Harris. I was familiar with the tactic being deployed in this discussion as with two person episodes (as in Jonesboro, Arkansas, in 1997) there is a societal bias in favor of making one the "instigator" and the other a follower or flunkie (Webber 2003a, 51–53). The media exploit this bias whenever they insert the claim into a news analysis of a shooting that "police are looking for a second shooter." In some ways, the police *are* doing this, but only because the shooters themselves plan their attacks very carefully to create illusions about the number and nature of the perpetrators in the opening scenes of their mass shooting scripts: for example, Klebold and Harris wore trench coats at the beginning and took them off (at different times), hence, competing eye witness accounts would indicate more than two shooters. Cho staged a domestic violence shooting at Ambler Johnston to allay fears of the campus police and community and avert necessary warnings, and so on. In Cullen's case he labels Eric Harris a psychopath and Dylan Klebold his suicidal friend (and easily suggestible). This comes from the FBI, and we should be wary of this interpretation. Further scrutiny shows that the portrait of Eric Harris that Cullen provides is patchy at best. There is a great amount of dramatic effect presented when we hear "Eric's" voice. Even reviewers pointed this out about Cullen's book, but did not come to the conclusion that they should question its claims. Consider Jennifer Senior's review of Cullen for the *New York Times Book Review*:

> "Columbine" is weakest when Cullen tries to channel the voice of Eric Harris. ("Five or six hundred dismemberments ought to be enough for one awesome afternoon of TV" is one such example.) As the author himself makes clear, Harris's mind isn't a particularly interesting place to inhabit—just sneering and young and unfathomably angry. But his nuanced dissection of the differences between Harris and Klebold is first-rate, leaving readers in the strange (and challenging) position of feeling pity, almost, for Klebold. Cullen walks us carefully through the definition of psychopathy, and how it differs from insanity, noting how perfectly Harris met the profile—particularly in his egomania, outsize contempt for humanity and talent for manipulation. (Just months before the attack, a teacher wrote on one of his essays, "I would trust you in a heartbeat.") Whereas Klebold, for most of the book, seems forlorn, awkward and miserable. "The anger and the loathing," Cullen explains, "traveled inward." (Senior 2009)

Cullen's distinction between insanity and psychopathology offers little in the way of clarity, unless we are only looking at it through a juridical framework. As Margaret Price has argued, following Allen and Nairn's work on media depictions of mental illness, omissions or poorly constructed texts "through a strategy of juxtaposition and omission" (precisely the way Cullen does with Harris and Klebold), "does not merely invite the reader to draw certain conclusions; it also implicates the reader in those conclusions, so that the reader becomes a cocreator of the association between violence and mental illness" (Price 2011, 147). This also happens when pieces of information are juxtaposed next to each other in a story and usually draws a timeline from one dramatic act to the next, as when Kazmierczak was in a story that she argues presented this actual content to the reader, "Kazmierczak, 27, Killer of 5 Students, Studied Mental Health Issues, Worked at Prison" (ibid.). The media is already framing how we view this problem of "Kazmierczak" from its own point of view. Anyone interested in understanding how this violence proceeds would need to abandon media as a source for information. If Cullen is weak when describing Harris, shouldn't we worry that his analysis of the relationship between him and Klebold was more complicated than the one he presents? Cullen admits he had unequal access to both shooters' parents; the Klebolds have always been more forthcoming, while the Harrises have all but disappeared.[5] Just like in the prisoner's dilemma, one gets the blame when the other snitches, only this time, Cullen's journalism is superimposing this semblance of a confession onto Klebold. Reading this "nuanced dissection of the differences" between the two that leaves us "in the strange (and challenging) position of feeling pity, almost, for Klebold" is not unlike reading the media interpretation of what happened at Westboro Middle School between the "Hunter and the Choir Boy" (Labi 1998). Another book that debuted around the same time as Cullen's, also called *Columbine* and also by a Denver native following the events very closely, was largely overlooked by popular media, even though it dispelled most of the ideas presented by Cullen. Jeff Kass's book suggests (to me, anyway) that how we view Harris is more socially and politically important to us, as viewers and onlookers, than to the truth of things. Cullen saves us the difficult task of having to confront the more obscene aspects of American society that most are happy to ignore. Kass suggests that Harris and Klebold were in fact low on the pecking order at Columbine, but the problem was the threshold American culture places on achieving the status of "bullied" is rather too high. Furthermore, Kass presents an interesting thesis that it doesn't matter "objectively" whether people liked or hated Harris and Klebold: they *felt* like outcasts; self-perception is important.[6] Cullen also presents evidence that because Klebold went to the prom, he was popular and because, he claims, Eric Harris was successful with the ladies, he wasn't an outcast. When I read these passages in Cullen's book in 2009, I said aloud, "This is beside the point" because what Cullen seemed to be presenting to his readers affirmed their own bias as Americans: if you are bullied or feel downtrodden, you cannot have any trace of enjoyment at all in your life. If you do have evidence of enjoyment, then any claim to marginalization is discounted. As it turns out, Klebold's prom date was a friend and the one who bought the three guns used in Columbine, and as Kass recounts a last scene of Klebold in *The Basement Tapes*[7] for us, says he didn't want to go to the prom but his parents are paying for it, "Since I'm going to be dying," he adds, "I thought I might do something cool" (Kass 2009, 139). Eric Harris's sex life was probably nonexistent.

As Kass said in an interview shortly after his book debuted to little media attention, "I feel they were outcasts. I feel they were among the most unpopular kids in the school—and my evidence is their diaries. Pick up almost any page and all they talk about is how much they are outcasts, how they don't feel part of the school or any community." And on the connection between Harris and Klebold that seemingly exonerates Dylan in Cullen's book, "Dylan's writings show him to be pretty entranced by the plan. And their code word for the shootings—NBK, which stood for *Natural Born Killers,* one of their favorite movies—came from him. He was the first to mention doing an NBK, going NBK. That says to me that he wasn't such a secondary participant" (Kass 2009). Kass also explores the backgrounds of both Harris and Klebold (going back to their grandparents) and gives a context for their class and socioeconomic background. Klebold's family was wealthy enough to have a guest house, and Harris moved from town to town as his father worked as a transport pilot in the military.

Though Kass draws no conclusions for the reader, he offers the evidence and allows them to decide; he states his opinion but in a way that the reader can feel independent of it. Klebold was going to college, and Harris had just been rejected by the Marines. Klebold was, in Kass's depiction, "passive aggressive" and depressed, whereas Harris might have been a malevolent psychopath. We fret at the words "psychopath" because that's what the FBI would like us to do, but we blink at passive aggressive. By contrast, Kass notes that Dylan shared more features with more of the school shooters than Harris; "shy," "wants to be part of the group but cannot" as he says of him. "Dylan was the deceiver in chief" (180). As a passive aggressive he "undermines or sabotages helpful acts at one level with passive aggressive behavior on another level," and "it seems like when Dylan helps a person he's hurting a person" (181). The observations come from examining Dylan's apology letter to the diversion program officer (which both Cullen and Kass agree set them off), written in a bothersome, hard to read font, defacing someone's locker who has offended him (rather than having a confrontation) and insulting people while appearing to praise them. Kass observes that it is ironic that Dylan shares more features with the other shooters (shy, unnoticed, etc.), yet, as he says, "he is the one to watch for" (180). What is very interesting about most of these cases is how the coverage always looks for evidence of any kind of overt violent past or behavior when in reality someone probably should have looked at someone like Klebold (or Cho, or Lanza or any of them) and said, "how is this person taking all this in without reacting?"

Larkin, by contrast, contextualizes the entire school and societal environment in Jefferson County in this way: "It was a fairly common fantasy, especially among outcast students for whom attendance at Columbine seemed to be an invitation to harassment, humiliation, and abuse. Given that nobody had ever bombed their high school before, such talk was dismissed as fantasy" (Larkin 2007, 130). More importantly, if we can accept that such acts are seductive for their possible infamy and a reinforcement of the shooter's masculinity, then why do we assume they would reveal all the humiliations they experienced in their diaries for us to read? Isn't it an anathema to hegemonic masculinity to reveal one's vulnerabilities? Wouldn't that ruin the effect of the infamous act itself? School shooters leave behind what they want the audience to read and destroy the rest, even creating "media packages" that can be cited in subsequent school shooting scripts. Larkin further complicates the single-minded focus on Eric Harris as a psychopath that has been produced by the media through Cullen's book: "In my view, the evidence for Eric's psychopathology is, at best, mixed" (Larkin 2007, 150), and further, "Clearly, Eric did not display empathy on April 20, 1999. But in talking with people who knew Eric, a quite different picture emerged: Eric had a pet dog that he loved and cared for. He was described as a good friend who could give emotional support to people he liked; he empathized with those like himself who were victimized by the jocks. I doubt whether the profilers talked to any of his friends" (Larkin 2007, 151). As he concludes, "Environmental influences give direction to psychopathology," meaning that any motive that can be attributed to any shooter in these cases is not determined by the label "psychopath"; even psychopaths' intentions are provided by the environment. While the form of the psychopath largely remains the same (cold, detached, lacking empathy), the content is variable (who or what do they feel cold, detached and lack empathy *for*?). Kass will give another outside expert's opinion who adds the qualifier "malevolent" to psychopath. In such cases, he argues, they have "cold-blooded ruthlessness, an intense desire to gain revenge for the real or imagined mistreatment to which they were subjected in childhood" (qtd. in Kass 2009, 177).

Cullen's book, at least when it characterizes Harris and Klebold (the lump sum of the problem of *Columbine*), gives truth to the lie of American culture as identified by Slavoj Žižek in his analysis of the "obscene underside" of American forms of belonging. Žižek argues that it is ritual forms of humiliation that accompany our acts of community building or "joining." More important is the way that we protect these ritual forms from criticism by failing to point out that they produce and sustain our most celebrated categories of citizenship: democracy, freedom and civility. As an example, Žižek discusses the way he encountered the Abu Ghraib photos; initially he thought they were performance art from the West Village. As he says, the difference in Abu Ghraib is not that the soldiers were terrorizing the Muslim captives but that they were initiating them into American forms of belonging, e.g., degrading sexual acts and torture. Žižek does not mention this, but one could add that all the protests against the soldiers that took the form of cultural relativism (you can't treat Muslims like that, they have religious convictions about sexuality and women, etc.) were really saying: we Americans don't have any convictions when it comes to our rituals of initiation other than that the victim remain silent about it in exchange for his membership in our "community." This is the obscene underside that accompanies nearly every personal case of school shooters but must be ignored because it might disturb our collective protection of such practices as our "way of life." As Žižek writes,

> Abu Ghraib was not simply a case of American arrogance towards a Third World people: in being submitted to humiliating tortures, the Iraqi prisoners were effectively initiated into American culture. They were given a taste of its obscene underside, which forms a necessary supplement to the public values of personal dignity, democracy, and freedom. Bush was thus wrong: what we are getting when we see the photos of the humiliated Iraqi prisoners on our screens and front pages is precisely a direct insight into the core of the obscene enjoyment that sustains the American way of life. (Žižek 2008b, 176)

And when Žižek considers Christopher Hitchens's weird suggestion that since the soldiers were not acting under direct orders, they were the acts of "mutineers, deserters or traitors in the field and they should be taken out and shot," Žižek replies that "they were legitimized by a specific version of the obscene Code Red" that Americans consistently disavow. To return to Cullen's portrait of Harris, what if this obsession with producing him as a "deserter" to the human race (a "psychopath") ignores the obscene practices at Columbine High School that might disturb our collective belief in education and democratic socialization as the institution that produces (and reproduces) the very "civility" we value? Furthermore, why does Klebold evoke "pity" when he participated in the mass killings as joyously as Harris did? The acceptance of such schizo-affected presentations of Columbine should tell us something about what the public is hiding from itself and from the world. As I said, in all these cases, we can only speculate as to the humiliation each perpetrator experienced. We do know from Kass, Larkin and others that they were pushed, shoved, called "faggot" repeatedly, forced to bus other kids' trays during lunch, had tampons saturated with ketchup thrown at them, etc. Cullen, relying exclusively on interviews with survivors and the FBI and school authorities, comes to the conclusion (again, from the review of Klein's book):

> Worse, Klein positions the 1999 Columbine massacre as her prime example. She regurgitates botched reporting that was debunked years ago, exhuming resilient myths about jock-targeting and the Trench Coat Mafia. The shooters, Eric Harris and Dylan Klebold, left journals and videos to explain themselves, in which they complain about every petty topic imaginable, from slow drivers to the WB network, but not once, mysteriously, about bullies. The closest Harris comes is complaining about feeling left out, in a brief passage contradicting nearly everything else he wrote. Yet Klein cherry-picks to present the boys as bullied outcasts hunting jocks. (Cullen 2012)

To reiterate, why would they write about being bullied? If Harris and Klebold wrote about these experiences and any others that may even be more gruesome, would they inspire the fear that most adults felt after Columbine? No. Furthermore, explaining the humiliation only serves to further underscore and legitimate it, especially in American culture, where blame is always shunted back onto the victim: Why can't you just get over it? Did you do something to provoke the humiliation? Why are you so weird anyway? That is, in a culture where passive aggressive behavior is not only overlooked, it is rewarded (what else is there in the control society, where all decisions about social relations and politics have been decided in advance by the market and its morals?). Finally, another important point is that no one is ever going to admit that they bullied these school violence perpetrators. So when investigators like Cullen find that there is no bullying, it's because he's asked the correct people the wrong question.[8] Who in their right mind would admit to the FBI or a journalist that they bullied the two most famous school shooters in the history of school violence, inadvertently producing the deaths of 17 people and harming many others? No one in their right mind would, and what is interesting is that we keep telling ourselves and letting Dave Cullen tell us that if it were true, there would be evidence! Besides any level of humiliation was never going to match up with the damage Harris and Klebold inflicted on Columbine, and that was the point: they did want to be seen as more powerful, more sovereign at the end than any of the victims they created. As Balibar maintains, "the essence of extreme violence lies not so much, perhaps, in destroying peace or making it impossible, but in annihilating the conflict itself, imposing on it a disproportionality that deprives it of any history and any uncertainty" (Balibar 2009, 28).

> There is blood on the walls, blood on the chairs. I've never seen anything like this. It's like something in the United States.
>
> —first responder to the elementary school where Wellington Oliveria committed a mass shooting in 2011 (Esposti 2011)

A Culture of Honor?

Many of the school violence observers in the United States have argued that there is a definite pattern to the rage. Since most of the shootings (they argue) take place in the South or West or rural areas, then it must be something peculiar to these areas that produce the mass school attack response to humiliation and rejection. Kass, in particular, is drawn to this thesis. There are several problems with it. First, there have been many shootings outside the South and West, and even the outside the U.S., that fit this pattern. Second, when political scientists discuss how authority works in regions in the United States, they tend to use a formula described by Daniel Elazar. There are three regions: traditional, moral and individualistic. What matters is how people view politics in these cultures. In traditional political culture, "government is primarily understood to maintain the status quo," that is, it is managed by elite culture. The south is mostly traditional. Colorado, however, is "dominated" by moralistic political culture where "Serving the community is the core of the political relationship even at the expense of individual loyalties and political friendships. In practice this often results in more amateur participation in politics than in the other political cultures. Upper New England, the Upper Middle West and portions of the west are the central areas for this culture type." In a moralistic political culture, politics (and therefore authority and leadership) is derived from a moral framework, not from the status quo, not from the honor of elites, especially if it violates the community's standards. What is acceptable is to legislate as if one's views should dominate all others because they are morally correct (Elazar 1970, 1972). I do not see Columbine, or any shooting that comes after it, as a case of wounded "honor." If there was an honor culture in Littleton, Colorado, and that is what was violated in Harris and Klebold's symbolic universes, then wouldn't they have used one of the acceptable (established) means of restoring one's honor in that context? School shootings are not bar fights writ large. They are not corporate battles. We tend to think of dueling as an obscene (outmoded) practice when it in fact served a rational, ethical purpose in aristocratic cultures (LaVaque-Manty 2006).

School violence perpetrators want to annihilate the conflict altogether; if they do not accept the terms of the culture in which they live, why then would they act it out? Why do we make the curious slippage between dueling (based on trial combat) and bombing to kill an entire contained population? Elazar's mapping is much better because it syncs better with Larkin's observations about the culture of Columbine being overtaken by "Deep Christian" students (1/3), a force in American society, but especially in Colorado (where many evangelicals and others made their homes in the past decade), as it is where Focus on the Family is headquartered (70 miles away in Colorado Springs), as well as other new age spiritual groups. They worked in tandem with what he identifies as the celebrity jock culture who acted with impunity and established a kind of normality surrounding football; that is, as we shall see, it is only normal (read: moral) if you are a fan of football or a player. Kass says that areas like Columbine are unlike the "sober Puritans, Quakers and Dutch farmer-artisans" from the Northeast; in Colorado they promote a "culture of self-defense" where "everyone is a newcomer." "Public spaces are few and far between. Where there are sidewalks they are desolate. Where people do live together it is a kingdom of private residences, tract home next to tract home, with cars as fiefdoms on wheels" (Kass 2009, 186). I really agree with Kass on many points, but I would like to finally welcome him to the United States, indeed the globalized world of the twenty-first century. For many interpreters, it is as if these places are untouched by globalization; it's the same for Newman et al. It may be a sociology problem. One review I read of Larkin's book was particularly revealing for the way that people fantasize about the south and the West:

> Larkin's book is interesting, and he has succeeded in tracing many survivors and getting them to talk about the school and its culture. His location of the issue in "postmodern America" seems odd. Larkin (179) suggests that the American Hinterlands have produced a backlash against postmodern culture from those who are "rural, unhip and unsophisticated." It is surely not a backlash? Those sectors of American society have never embraced the Enlightenment project and have never accepted science, rationality, or evidence. That is, they have never been *modern*, and certainly have no intellectual basis upon which to be *postmodern*. This sector of American society has been opposed to the elite culture of the East Coast for two hundred years, rejecting its values when it was committed to the Enlightenment project. (Delamont 2008, 168)

Wow, eh? Focus on the Family and evangelical movements arrived in Colorado in 1984, just in time to usher in Reagan's second inauguration. They entered politics in the late 1970s to defeat Carter. They are a product of what Hofstadter has called "the paranoid style" of American politics that has existed since the country's founding, but they are not exclusive to these areas as they have existed in the fetishized Northeast as well (Lyman Beecher worried about the soul of the West, but he stayed in New York). Those who cling to the stereotypes about the West (but also the South) have to bracket the impact of the past decade of economic restructuring.[9] What I cannot understand are the arguments that add to

Kimmel's notion that the South and West are cultures of "honor" and therefore bullying in these places tends to produce school shooters because they cannot take it, it doesn't match up with their self-assessment as "proud." Are, then, the Midwest and Northeast not cultures of honor? Do they have no honor? How do young men in De Kalb, Illinois (65 miles from the center of Chicago), like Steven Kazmierzcak, deal with humiliation? Do they just reassure themselves that they are "still a man" when people call them "Strange Steve"? When Douglas Kellner writes about "multiplying forms of domestic terrorism" he is clear to distinguish it from ideological forms like Al-Qaeda inspired acts and compares them as the "dark side of the spectacle" in the British riots of 2011 and the Norway spree killings committed by Breivik, can we be satisfied with the determination only that they are "common crises of masculinity and male rage exploding into acts of violence that create a media spectacle in which the individual agents, through acts of societal violence that give them an illusion of power and hypermale macho tough guy identity," allow them to "become part of a greater story than their often failed lives" (Kellner 2012, 24)? To be sure, he admits that all these acts are "overdetermined" and need close sociological analysis in each case, but how can they all feed from hegemonic masculinity? And if they do, how does their overdetermination then allow anything to be said of masculinity that is useful? I believe we need to stop analyzing these cases from the perspective of masculine domination. These are not dominant males and they do not (often) seek to witness the aftermath of their rage (as dominant men do). Instead, they judge an environment, often one that spans beyond the school, but they also want to impress each other: the other members of the heterogeneous social produced by the ever increasing homogeneity of our societies. There is a critical distinction to be made between the leaders of what Sumiala and Tikka identify as the "homogeneous" culture of the sacred and the production, mediation and ongoing serial drama that is the heterogeneous culture of school shooters.

As to Harris and Klebold's "enjoyment" during their last year of life (after they decided to attack the school, nearly 8 months before), it is curious that Cullen assumes that spending so much time disproving the media's fascination with their unhappiness should change a critical observer's view. Most people are happy (or at least relieved) when they decide to commit suicide. In fact, this happiness often acts to deceive those around them (e.g., the parents of Klebold and Harris), usually making their attempt successful. I am not surprised they that they may have tried very hard to get laid, or go to prom or get along with those around them by going to bowling class (Michael Moore). Kass's depiction of Harris disputes all of this enjoyment and suspects they were both virgins (a close analysis of one's own high school experience and male bravado that attended it, might prove Kass correct). Details about the shooter's forays into Adultfriendfinder.com or Match.com to seek "shenanigans" (Holmes) or to call a prostitute to a hotel in the last days (Cho) or to watch sadomasochistic pornography (Steinhäuser), or to be unsure whether one ticks male or female on their community college application (Lanza) or to seek out illicit bisexual encounters (Kazmierzcak) do not tell us anything other than that they all knew it was coming to an end and wanted to enjoy sex, the way most people imagine they would at the announcement of the end of the world, that is, of their existence.

Cullen's book is evidence of an ideological move because it protects American cruelty, the obscene underside of its "civility" from criticism; it is a journalistic form of inoculation, where deeper questions about the nature of social relations within schools and other American institutions will remain buried under the surface. And all this happens, sadly, under the mantle of "critical journalism." It allows the audience to "sleep." Cullen's portrait is the half-time show for the control society, leaving the established order within schools unquestioned, even, to some extent, leaving the impression that Columbine really only suffered at the hands of the "lone wolf terrorist" that was Eric Harris. That's the kind of interpretation one gets from taking so much stock in an analysis from the Federal Bureau of Investigation and their fetish for "profiling" potential school shooters. As Geert Lovink argues:

> To me, the link between gamers and the military is a myth. They may be the perfect techno-warriors, but, who knows, they may as well have an entirely different set of values, incompatible with NATO and the Pentagon. Perfectly skilled, yet unusable. The dominant techno-liberation mentality does not always go well with authoritarian agendas that often reintroduce state regulation (and ultimately state terrorism). (Galloway, Lovink and Thacker 2008, 103)

This quote adds some sense to the contemporary discussion around gaming. By the end of this chapter, we will review Galloway's interpretation of gaming and how it relates to social realism, that is, for gaming to translate into reality, the meaning of the actions performed in it must assume some "fidelity of context." As the quote surmises, there's not much in the way of similarities between the mindsets of gamers, particularly those like Harris and Klebold, and the military. And yet, these kinds of arguments make a gruesome kind of sense to many thinkers. Cullen's book would provide a template for any theoretical interpretation to "fill in" the blanks of the Columbine thesis around their preferred variables (be they games, violent music, guns or even bombs). This is because Cullen's book pronounces Harris's problem to be that he was a psychopath, and therefore, any and all means of reinforcing his already cold-calculating tendencies could now be normalized as explanations for how the act was passed into reality. In Chapter 3, we will explore these episodes of violence as *passages à l'acte* where the executor connects directly with the real and bypasses the symbolic. For now, we must attend to the readings of Columbine that still (by tiny strings) cling to the notion that elements of popular culture play a stimulating role, even if combined with mental instability. Cullen became popular, indeed widely cited, not only because he was handsomely placed within the corporate media structure to promote his book widely, but because the way he structures his argument (and ventriloquizes Harris in particular) allows researchers to breathe new life into all the old Columbine theses and present them as if they are something new. Cullen's text neutralizes arguments that focus on bullying and systemic violence at the school site. As Price has argued, it takes the "social" out of "psychosocial" and further on in such representations, "madness is generally assumed to be the *cause* of the shooters' actions," when, upon close reading one finds, "madness operates in the representations as a *mechanism* through which the shooters are placed in a space of unrecoverable deviance" (Price 2011, 144–5).

The inoculation that Cullen's book performs on Columbine will color the way that subsequent shootings would be interpreted (even retrospectively, for Virginia Tech and Northern Illinois, as the book did not come out until 2009). But, in a more insidious fashion it derails the political interpretations of important academic work. Seen as the "definitive" account of the Columbine event, rather than the "only" one, it has become something of a reflex action for critical readings of school violence to offer their thanks and reliance upon Cullen's "excellent reporting," even as his readings skew their own (Protevi 2009, 141). I give as a primary example, John Protevi's case study of Columbine in his widely acclaimed book *Political Affect: Connecting the Social and the Somatic*. While I cannot do justice to Protevi's entire argument concerning "political affect" here, I will focus on the sources he uses to make major theoretical claims. It's not that the theory is bad, but perhaps misapplied. There are many contradictions to expose in Protevi's analysis. Before getting into those, I would like to offer some critiques of the foundations of his knowledge of the case. My problem is with the sources that Protevi's relies for his reading of both Columbine and "thresholds." One, is of course Cullen's book. It relies specifically on the portrait of Eric Harris as a "psychopath" in order to read the "how" that allowed Harris (and Klebold) to commit his act through another problematic text, Lt. Col. Dave Grossman's *On Killing*, and his subsequent and unsubstantiated claims that videogames made the Jonesboro, Arkansas shooters do it. In my last book I looked at Grossman's work, which may be relevant for understanding military *combat* violence, where there is *fidelity of context*, but is wholly inadequate for understanding episodes of mass violence by young people in schools and other spaces of civility within contemporary societies. Grossman was regularly featured as an expert on the Columbine Thesis concerning video games. He argued that their degree of realism made them primary precipitant in school violence because they erode the subject's natural aversion to killing. This is the standard thesis outlined by Galloway as unconvincing: "games plus gore equals psychotic behavior, and around and around" (Galloway 2006a, 71).

Protevi claims that the interesting question about Columbine is not "why?" but "how?" I share his concern, but would note that they cannot be separated no matter how intensely an analytic approach is applied because the sources we must rely upon for our content, our "data" are largely focused on the why question. Furthermore, feigning to bracket the "why" is a depoliticizing move. By the time we get to the story, as academics, journalism has so thoroughly polluted the facts with its own will to power that we cannot do anything except read sources against one another in an effort to expose contradictions. It is very difficult, especially in light of the fact that there were so many errors and so much data withheld from the public, to have a clear indication of what happened, how they could and did do it, and so on. Most of it relies on videos but also on eye witness accounts which have been notoriously contradictory. Cullen's book emerged from this disaster scenario as the most promoted, therefore it became in the public's eye the most reliable. So, this leads Protevi to ignore several problems with the research and journalism that he is drawing upon to build his case study of Columbine. The first problem is Grossman's research which may be appropriate for understanding military violence but is wholly inadequate for understanding mass school shootings, or even other mass shootings that happen at concentrated areas in liberal societies. Grossman begins with the assumption of a chain of command, a hierarchy. This chain is respected because a soldier takes on and embraces the military code of conduct. Among other things, Grossman's preferences for a law and order society, really a standard Hobbesian reading of society, is a stand in for the military hierarchy he so longs to see present when he looks at school violence in particular. This is problematic because it is this very Hobbesian focus that allows Grossman to make his claims about operant conditioning: if the soldier is not held in check by his code, he is held in check by an implicit hierarchy in society. But we live in a liberal, market-based society. What authority could video games be undermining that wasn't already secondary to marketing, developmental educational programs (our Rousseauian school system), the script pad, mental health experts, the Internet, etc. Video games might undermine some forms of military hierarchy; excessive violence undermines the authority of those above us or provides more colorful contexts in which to engage the "enemy." But, as Galloway points out, where is the fidelity of context between a military themed video game and an American teenager? More specifically, for Grossman, video games undermine parental authority. But one could argue so do social services, free birth control, organized religion, a laissez-faire attitude about sex, government-funded abstinence programs, and commercialism. Grossman is a parents' rights fan, which, in American culture means a social conservative. Grossman's politics generate his answers to school violence, not the other way around. The assumption of hierarchical authority does not hold in the control society. As Protevi, a scholar of Deleuze himself, offers, "Affect is inherently political" (Protevi 2009, 50). That is, there is more give and take among populations than a hierarchical analysis of society is willing to allow. Then, Protevi brackets two kinds of power: "pouvoir" and "puissance".

> we can say that *pouvoir* is transcendent power: it comes from above. It is hylomorphic, imposing form on the chaotic or passive material of the mob. In its most extreme manifestation it is fascistic: it is expressed not simply as the desire to rule, but more insidiously as the longing for the strong leader to rescue us from the chaos into which our bodies politic have descended. *Puissance*, on the other hand, is immanent self-organization. It is the power of direct democracy, of people working together to generate the structures of their social life." (Protevi 2009, 50)

In spite of the fact that folks like James Der Derian and others have been describing the "infotainment of war" for over a decade, most scholars have tended to ignore the effect of this blurring on the military itself, which has become "flexible," so the authority of the command structure in the battlefield has waned as well in favor of "lateral zones of flexibility" (Fountain 2001). The contemporary military does not rely on the traditional authority both Protevi and Grossman assume is necessary in military cultures (at least not in combat); rather it relies on the same flexibility that is promoted in our schools, on the "protocol" that Galloway theorizes follows on the heels of the control society.

Protevi even says that there has been "seepage" from the military into common life through video games and violent music (here's where he drops his hat). He tries to regroup and claims the relationship is not a matter of linear causality but rather how these aspects of popular culture become distributed throughout a "population." Meaning, some people constituted in a certain way will use these technologies to increase the "threshold" of intensity at which the act of killing becomes permissible. As a deliberate strategy, they know they need to overcome their "protoempathetic identification" with others, humans, which is "'emotional contagion,' or shared affective state: you feel what another person is feeling" (Steuber 2006; Protevi 2009, 29). Protevi discusses the role of the "gut" in luring us away from the act of killing, and using Grossman's work on military studies about non-firing rates in the military and the techniques used their to overcome the soldier's natural inhibitions to interspecies killing (Grossman compares military techniques to video games which train the soldier to overcome this protoempathetic resistance to killing in the precise work they do on the nervous system; it is not cognitive but neurochemical). In these cases, the subject (of reason, of agency) drops out of the equation. Protevi must explain how it is that Harris and Klebold were able to interact with their victims, to taunt them, and to belittle them rather than "drop" out. Therefore, unlike "berserker" rages or "blind" rages where the subject drops out of the killing agent, in Columbine, Protevi sees Harris and Klebold "complementing" each other to produce an agent capable of raising the threshold at which killing becomes possible. He writes, "That their killing machine finally broke down, that the bodies of Klebold and Harris could not sustain the intensity, indicates that they weren't really cold-blooded, but hyperintense: they did not lower the intensity of the act of killing; rather they increased the threshold at which a nonsubjective rage agent would have kicked in" (161). It's not cognitive. It's not that Harris convinced Klebold to do it (the implication left by Cullen's analysis, who says that had Klebold been convinced otherwise or interrupted he might have lived a relatively normal life) but that the combination of their affects ("cold-blooded" Eric and "rage-filled depressive" Dylan) produced a killing machine that based itself on "superiority" over fellow humans at school. Borrowing from the control society analysis, Protevi gives some weight to the thesis that they might have felt judged and then turned that judgment around to all the students they taunted during the act: this is, he says, modular, not molar, based on a feeling of superiority rather than a reaction to established political and social identities (for example, race or gender). However, he also urges the reader "to remember high school" defaulting to a common stereotype, universal and unchanging, as if the disciplinary high school is like the control society one.

Therefore, it is not the schools or social environment that has shifted (since he went to high school) but that Harris and Klebold (messed up affectively) combined together (first order body politic focused on mass murder), using "guns and bombs" and videogames and violent music to lower the threshold at which killing would be (not merely unthinkable but undoable) possible. Again, like Newman and Cullen, Protevi reifies the school site and the larger milieu of the society. I would argue, in light of our earlier analysis of Deleuze, that the schools are still operating according to the logic of some combination of the disciplinary society (hierarchies of social groupings; punishments for official infractions, etc.) with control aspects superimposed on top of the old architecture. That is why they are widely perceived to be a failure. Politicians and citizens would like them to function more like a purely control oriented culture, promoting flexibility while producing profit.

To sum up, the analysis of a predator/prey relationship based on combat violence is inappropriate to understand a rampage shooting. Protevi focuses on this by making Harris and Klebold into a killing machine (much like a Deleuzian desiring machine), a first order "bodies politic" that is motivated by thanatography, which, like pornography, needs ever increasing images and levels of violence (thresholds that must be crossed) to maintain excitation. He defines it in this way: "representations of violence provoking physiological changes, analogous to the provocation of physiological change with pornography". The analysis of thanatography needs to be differential and population based: there are no simple linear functions here: rather, there are patterns, thresholds, and triggers distributed in a population" (159). We could just say along with Balibar that they "idealized hatred" and turned to commonly recognized "paranoid styles of American politics" (Hofstadter 2008) like Waco and Oklahoma City to express their angst, and this led them to what we will later describe as an offshoot of violence, cruelty. But Protevi must get the video games in there. He is content to ignore the fact that there is no evidence for the "thanatography thesis," since "details of their own training are lost in the morass of fantasy writings they left behind" (141). It's pretty clear that most shooters have to get themselves whipped into a certain kind of state in order to carry out these acts: as mentioned earlier, Breivik took testosterone, Lanza gazed at pictures, and the rest get written off as "crazy" as if mental illness is somehow an understandable trigger for homicide. As Wayne LaPierre said in the wake of the Newtown shootings, "Isn't fantasizing about killing people as a way to get your kicks really the filthiest form of pornography?" This was in relation to a host of ten-year-old video games that he listed as being primarily responsible for the violence epidemic in American society. As the *Atlantic* noted, "Okay, that's one opinion, from one of the most powerful lobbyists in America" (Abad-Santos 2012). And, as game defenders like to point out, violent crime is at an all-time low and has been falling steadily for nearly two decades. What stands out are these violent, shocking episodes. Explaining them will necessarily demand not a population based approach (looking at numbers and influence) but a detailed, biographic phenomenological reading of these violent events.

A second problem is that Protevi categorizes the Columbine shootings as "mass murders" and parenthetically defines this as "when the motives are private," and this is defined through a binary logic where he opposes it to terrorism, which is killing "for political motivation"; however, it is not yet clear how this is not for political motivation; look at the shooters they've influenced over the past decade who admired their work. But this is just the tip of the iceberg: he then makes a move two pages later to say that Harris and Klebold form a "bodies politic," after he had made the claim these (bodies politic) are personal (that he does not follow up anywhere in the chapter). Furthermore, beyond standard American juridical ways of determining responsibility (i.e., based on age and maturity), Protevi has violated one of his axioms from the second chapter, where he outlines the difference between adults and children:

> Finally, and most important, we should note that the synchronic form of mutual presupposition of first- and second- order bodies politic appears only with adults who are set in their ways; this mutual presupposition or synchronic emergence is produced by diachronic processes of acculturation of infants and children, and it is reinforced or mutates according to the relations of repetitive and experimental practices present in the group. (Protevi 2009, 42)

Are these children or adults he's analyzing in Columbine? He never says. Does this make a difference? The Supreme Court has said that it does. In the case of Columbine, Protevi's reading is misleading because it too provides a semblance of truth for all the lies produced by the media during that event: that violent video games and music, guns, are all to blame for "why" Harris and Klebold did it when he says he is looking at the more important "how" of the event. Yet, such an ahistorical and apolitical construction of "how" is largely unhelpful and only serves to make Cullen's and Grossman's irresponsible forays into mass media consumption look more legitimate, even while study after study demonstrates that violent video games do not cause violent behavior, at least not in such a direct, causal manner and not in a uniform fashion across populations (i.e., some people who are already weakened emotionally may be influenced).[10] The chances of *both* Harris and Klebold being influenced in this way is impossible; all commentators agree they are different people whose emotional pathways differed significantly; however, the target of their rage is uniform and documented: Columbine High School. While Protevi is clear that he is not making the causality argument Dave Grossman, whose work he refers to as "fine," *is* making, the causality argument is about an under-theorized yet highly cathexible term to the American public: psychopathology.

Protevi characterizes the pair as "an emergent killing machine (Klebold-plus-Harris-plus-bombs-plus-guns) and distributed nonsubjective reflexes, rage agents, or awareness threshold decisions" (Protevi 2009, 159). As to the question was it "cold-bloodedness" or "raising the threshold of intensity," Protevi opts for the latter, following with: "Cullen (2004) cites the conclusion of a psychiatrist and the FBI agent in charge of the Columbine case that Harris was a psychopath (hence, low-intensity, cold-blooded, stimulus hungry) and Klebold a rage-filled depressive" (158). Thus, begins our foray into the Pied-piper narrative that so often follows these conspiracy shootings around. In point of fact, the psychiatrist on the case only read the case file, and if one takes the time to read the case files of these events, they are always poorly constructed FBI narratives filled with claims about a shooter that lack evidence and are of more of a qualitative nature.[11] We have already heard from Kass that NBK was Dylan's idea. Furthermore, Kass recounts another theory about psychopaths: they tend not to be suicidal nor seek fame (177). Strike One. Also, they do tend to lie for enjoyment or "duper's delight," as Kass cites evidence from Eric's journal where he recounts having to lie to "save his own ass," and he does not appear to find it particularly enjoyable. Protevi's chain of events is also curious. He notes that Cullen pulled a "Gotcha!" on the guns charge when he (or rather the FBI) revealed that they intended to bomb the school and then shoot people as they fled the building (Johnson and Golden, fire alarm, anyone?). If this is the case, then how can they have been using thanatography (video games and violent music) to prepare for the rampage part (Grossman's work is not about bombing, it is about hand-to-hand combat, and he is very specific about this as these techniques were developed to aid in Vietnam in guerilla warfare)[12] when they were hoping the bombs would do most of the awful (rationally planned, predetermined) work they put into them? I would venture to say that they used target practice at the gun range for the event they originally planned (that's what the home videos show, them at a gun range—long range), not in front of *DOOM*. Most of the shell casings were found outside the building (they entered shooting along the sidewalk after the bombs did not go off inside the cafeteria). One presumes they had guns to shoot at survivors from the bombs' explosions as they fled the building. This would mean the "rampage" was never planned as such, unlike our earlier cases in the nineties when no bombs were set. Also, we recall that Harris let Brooks Brown go home, in fact, told him to go home. In a few instances Harris and Klebold spared their friends during the act. "Subjects they were," he writes, "but trained subjects working in tandem with technological extensions," whose "training" induced "reflexes in them" (158). They are even truer subjects than Protevi is willing to allow. He argues that they stopped shooting after only 19 minutes when there were still targets left in the building. Has Protevi seen Columbine? Has he been there? It would not be that easy (except in the library and the cafeteria, where most of the carnage took place) to have open targets; it is the same reason why Cho locked the doors to Norris Hall or why several of the shooters chose schools with security guards (they are lulled into a sense of internal security within the building). They exchanged fire and killed a security officer at the beginning (e.g., Weise and Oliveria). They saw the police outside the building and made claims they were going to "Go and kill some cops," according to eyewitnesses. Finally, Protevi ponders the 40 minutes it took for them to kill themselves and what they might have been doing during that time. According to Kass, it wasn't 40 minutes; it looked more like at most 15 during which they took shots through windows of the library at police and paramedics and set off a Molotov cocktail. As he writes, "A tiny blaze triggers a library fire alarm above their bodies at 12:08 p.m. Harris and Klebold are already dead" (Kass 2009, 18). The spree began outside at 11:19. According to Kass's timeline, at one point Harris asks Klebold, "Dude, you still with me? We still doing this?" This is not the wearing off of an affective state nor the onset of a depression too great to bear, nor the awareness that one would no longer like to live without these thresholds of intensity. This is called sticking to the plan, even after the bombs did not go off. They left suicide videos, explaining to their parents why they did it and whom to blame. As Joan Tronto put it in her review of *Political Affect*, "To some extent, the way that Protevi has framed these cases leads to the outcomes that he reaches. But could we not have arrived at some of these same insights without going through his arduous method? Conversely, might not a less skilled interpreter have produced less interesting results?" (Tronto 2011, 798). Cullen certainly did.

And yet there is one last problem here, but it is significant, and Protevi's research on Columbine will help us later when we look at military assaults in Chapter 5 where it can be helpful to contrast with the episodes that we are looking at here and so far have labeled "school-related," following Muschert. First, the main issue with Protevi's analysis is that in looking for a correlation between violence and technologies like guns, bombs and video games, he focuses only on the violence in them as objects. In constructing the Columbine killing machine, Protevi focuses on two main aspects: Harris and Klebold's affective cocktail and technological extensions like guns and video games (thanatography). He labels this combination "machinic." However, one sentence in particular stuck out at me: "Subjects they were, but trained subjects working in tandem with technological extensions" (ibid., 158). Protevi separates Harris and Klebold from technology, whereas it would be more helpful to see them as completely merged. To be clear: I mean that Harris and Klebold were merged with the technology through their vision, that is gamic vision, and yes, it is "machinic." It is not the violence in these extensions (there are certainly nonviolent video games, as well as films, etc. that use the same action-based techniques, such as point of view, hereafter, POV) that they mimic. It is rather that shooter games "have expanded the definitional bounds of the subjective shot" (Galloway 2006a, 63). What this means is that certainly Harris and Klebold have a fetish for violence, but it does not come from the game, the gun or the bombs, it comes from the school and their interactions in it, its seeming injustices, their relative inadequacy to dominant groups within it, and their inability to see a future for themselves in such a society. So, Protevi adds "school" to the end of the emergent killing machine he names, but it is an afterthought, nowhere examined in the discussion. They use the gamic vision supplied by certain FPS (first-person shooter) video games to stylize the experience of their violence. As Galloway argues, in order for something like a "violent video games cause violent behavior thesis" to work, there would have to be a "fidelity of context" between the happenings in the game (in this case *DOOM* or *Quake*, early FPS games that Harris and Klebold obviously played) and Columbine High School. Even though Harris tried to reprogram his game in certain trivial ways, as Larkin pointed out, it could not come near to the true experience they craved: a video game, an unfolding three-dimensional space in front of them that resembled Columbine High School. Make no mistake, there is no "cultural lag" here behind our technologies and the people we suppose should use them. As Galloway argues, we are all already hooked into our "machinic" vision when we turn on a desktop and look into cyberspace. Another important element about video games, or more specifically, FPS games, is that they use a subjective shot that eliminates the need for montage, a feature of the cinema that in American films often collapses space and time to show the evolution of a character or set of characters into a new form. To give an example, the most popular one has been the athletic montage, as showcased in *Rocky* to demonstrate as he trains for the big fight, often accompanied by popular soft rock music. When Eric Harris said—reportedly—in *The Basement Tapes* that the massacre was going to be like *DOOM* and a host of other events, including Oklahoma City, the L.A. riots, and so on, and he kissed his shotgun saying, "that fucking shotgun" (he kisses his gun) "straight out of *DOOM*. Go ahead and change gun laws—how do you think we got ours?" (2005, 4–20). If we recall Galloway's arguments about FPS games being an extended version of the subjective shot in film, basically, that FPS games rely on a three-dimensional, unfolding universe that relieves us (in film, viewers, in the game, players; note the difference) of the need for montage. We can now see that the violence isn't the attraction of the games (they already have that down), it's the unfolding action that Galloway outlines as attractive. The emotional release provided by montage, literally catharsis, was important in film because it allowed the audience to identify with the character's quest (in spite of the fact that it's a device that allows filmmakers to keep the story moving along quickly). The active seeing in FPS video games does the same thing only better and in a more realistic way. But while Galloway cautions that such games not only "require the player to avoid violence as much as confront it," such violence is common in other non-FPS games (Galloway 2006a, 69). In fact, in Galloway's reading the games do not have "violent vision." As he writes, "Unlike film before it, in gaming there is no simple connection to be made between the first person perspective and violent vision." What was predatory in cinema is now simply "active" vision. It is "the affective, active, mobile quality of the first-person perspective that is key for gaming, not its violence" (ibid., 69). Ultimately, what video games privilege is "action."

What about training, then? There's also the assumption, made implicitly by Protevi but also ubiquitous in the media, that these FPS games "train" civilians to be military grade soldiers. For this, we might have to get a bit morbid. First, I would say that if we look at (and will later detail) the number of rounds fired versus the number of actual hits, most of these perpetrators are not trained very well. In fact, once the shells were recovered from Columbine, there was a difference in firing rates between both shooters, as well as whether they were inside or outside the school. Harris seems to have fired the most inaccurate shots outside. Inside at close range, they were more accurate, yet still far below the bar they had set for themselves. Remember they had originally planned for the bombs to complete most of the violent (indirect) murder for them. As we see going forward in other cases, the very same problem presents itself. Finally, what does characterize the shootings beyond Columbine is that they add diversions or subtle changes to the script that allow them to increase their numbers, not through skill, but through close up interaction. This was certainly the case with Virginia Tech as well as in Norway. While most of them go to target practice before the event, they don't have the years of training and experience that it would take to reach the levels they set for themselves, and they take into account the emotional factor of their own biological doubt at the time. As Protevi says, the "gut" does become a factor at some point, no matter how they pump themselves up for the event, and subsequent shooters would become aware of this and take it into account. Finally, there's the very real consideration that we've mentioned from the start, "fidelity of context." Where is the violence located that Harris and Klebold identify with and find meaningful? Is it, as one defender of *DOOM* said following Columbine:

> We'd have to really be either extremely stubborn, in deep denial, or lying to say that the violence in our games doesn't affect people," mused Mike Gummelt, a programmer at Raven Software. "But I don't think it's *DOOM* that's the problem, it's the *free proliferation and general acceptance of violence in our society.* In movies, on TV and (to a lesser degree due to limits of realism) in games. That kind of widespread violence and cruelty in media definitely takes the shock out of violence and gore." (Brown 1999)

What does it mean to say "free proliferation and general acceptance of violence?" Is it the kind that goes on without remark? Is it because of our "imaginary relationship to our ideological existence" that we do not notice it? Is it a problem of civility?

Civility: Columbine II

> The stoic serenity of McVeigh's last days certainly qualified him as a Henley-style hero. He did not complain about his fate; took responsibility for what he was thought to have done; did not beg for mercy as our always sadistic Media require. Meanwhile, conflicting details about him accumulate—a bewildering mosaic, in fact—and he seems more and more to have stumbled into the wrong American era. Plainly, *he needed a self-consuming cause to define him.* The abolition of slavery or the preservation of the Union would have been more worthy of his life than anger at the excesses of our corrupt secret police. But he was stuck where he was and so he declared war on a government that he felt had declared war on its own people.
>
> —Gore Vidal, *The Meaning of Timothy McVeigh* (2001)

Balibar might agree. What emerges later on in years after Columbine is that they did not choose Hitler's birthday. They chose the anniversary of the end of a government raid of the Branch Davidian compound at Waco, Texas (known as "Waco"), which occurred on April 19, 1993. The raid resulted in the deaths of 76 men, women and children (including David Koresh, their designated leader) after the FBI stormed the building and it caught fire. This was after a 51-day standoff. Timothy McVeigh was put to death for planting the bomb that blew up the Alfred P. Murrah Federal Building in Oklahoma City, Oklahoma, on April 19, 1995, in retaliation for Waco. Apparently, Harris chose the 19th of April, but one of the ingredients they needed for the event was delayed by one day, so they were unable to carry out the attack on the 19th and settled for the 20th. The Columbine shooters were not led by Hitler to commit this act. Harris and Klebold were mad about being enrolled in the diversion program in Jefferson County.

In reading the detailed accounts of Larkin, as well as the evidence provided by Kass from interviews and other archived material, it is clear that both Harris and Klebold felt they were being singled out by the justice system at Columbine, as well as the one in Jefferson County. They had been caught breaking into a van and had stolen equipment out of it. I can't help but recall here Galtung's curious footnote in the famous structural violence essay where he notes that violence against things is seen as a kind of "foreboding," and that in particular, "This is a recurrent theme in much of the analysis in the U.S. violence against property is seen as training, the first window-pane crushed to pieces is also a blow against the bourgeois in oneself, a liberation of former constraints, an act of communication signaling to either camp a new belongingness and above all a tacit rejection of the rules of the game. 'If they can do that to property, what can they do to persons'" (Galtung 1969, 170; 187, respectively). The van break-in was treated very seriously by everyone involved. They were charged with felonies but allowed to enter a diversion program, which offers that if they are able to follow the program guidelines of community service and constant monitoring (including urinalysis, grades and other training programs; mainly designed for the criminal justice system's idea of the poorly socialized and unhygenic individual, in other words, the poor), that the charge would eventually be expunged. The probationary period was not less than two years in this case, and they entered the program in March of 1998, and they were of the 15 ever discharged early (out of 500 up to that point) in February 1999. Yet, they had begun planning a month or so after entering the diversion program. As we shall see in Chapter 3, following Stanley Aronowitz, one way to interpret their "exit" from middle-class life is to see it as an indictment of what stands in for civil society.

While both were willing participants (except for Klebold's passive aggressive fonts, lateness and lying), they seethed to each other and in their diaries about this indignity. In contemporary masculinity studies, these two might be called "marginalized" except for the fact that they meet none of the formal criteria: they are not disabled, gay or working class (Coston & Kimmel 2012). They are white, middle-class (possibly upper class in American cultural terms), and straight (well, Larkin gestures at Klebold's latent homosexuality as a reason for his going along with Eric's plan, as well as the romantic notion of it all, 2007, 146–149) young men. Larkin does not address them as "marginalized" within the literature of masculinity studies. Instead, he puts them in the category of "fringe masculinity" that develops in response to what Hofstadter defined as the "paranoid style" of

American politics: "The paranoid style is an old and recurrent phenomenon in our public life which has been frequently linked with movements of suspicious discontent" (77). Hofstadter cites Lyman Beecher's worries over the settlement of the West, anti-Mason conspiracy theories, and the long-time suspicion with the Catholic Church, etc. Larkin sees a new phase of this beginning with the rise of the Reaganite movement and the corresponding movement of the evangelicals into politics following the election of Carter. From this, *Rambo* came, with his obsession with the "good" Vietnam and the lost veterans, as well as the rise of the Neo-Nazi movement and Timothy McVeigh. However, what these subjects *like* about these paranoid styles is not their intention (as Galloway reminded me, which is to negate knowing reality as symbolically mediated) but "The paranoiac perceives the unknown in every miniscule detail of life. Every little thing is a clue into an intricate conspiracy against the paranoid individual" (Galloway 2006b, 4). Harris and Klebold at least find these episodes interesting for their *effect*, not the interpretation of the world they filter through the eyes of the paranoid conspiracy theorist. It is the effect of the bomb at Oklahoma City, not the narrative of revenge that sutures it to McVeigh, Nichols or any other militant fringe masculinity. They did not obsess that everyone was out to get them; they clearly felt marginalized, like nothing. If one reads the passages cited by Kass from Klebold's diaries, he felt like he made nary an impression on anyone, same for Harris, who regretted having to start over at each new school. Larkin puts Harris and Klebold into a genealogy that begins by noting that American culture doesn't readily mark as *political* the acts of students and youth. In a familiar leftist move, we begin our narrative at lunch counters in North Carolina and end it with "the revolt of the angry white male, 1992–1996." While I confess to finding this historical trajectory compelling in terms of civil rights and the influence of the political right to untie those important developments over the last three decades, I cannot make the passage from there to "angry white teenagers" (Larkin 2007, 167). Larkin mentions video games and makes a different kind of fidelity of context argument, that in video games like *DOOM* and *Quake*, combat is glorified but there is no "military discipline," and this makes them more like paramilitary cultures which are "based upon revenge for past wrongs," the "mythos of the warrior, who is not subject to military discipline," and the "hypermasculine," hence, the revenge is for the humiliation by dominant males, and finally, the fundamental ethic of paramilitary culture is "death before dishonor," combined with "dying in a blaze of glory" (Larkin 2009, 171). At least Larkin is sensitive to the idea that video games must be communicating something that is meaningful to the players (high praise for that), but I can't quite get behind this paramilitary argument for several reasons: I believe that many of the stylizations in these events are stagings, in the sense that Harris and Klebold want the audience to think it's about the Trench Coat Mafia (so they wear trench coats; this is not paramilitary, by the way, this is *Basketball Diaries*, a citation), and they wear baseball caps, etc. Besides the paramilitary culture argument has now been readily accepted by the media and law enforcement: it is the "Lone Wolf terrorist" we will visit in Chapter 3. There are now plenty of video games that feature this character and allow any number of angry white teenagers to imagine themselves in his stead.

There is also the problem of the internal dynamics at Columbine High school. Matching his own interviews against the report commissioned by the governor of Colorado, the 2009 Heurter Report, Larkin gives a description of the Predators and concludes that they bullied with the tacit agreement of administration (Larkin 2007, 85). The two main sport teams making up the Predators were the football and wrestling teams. One student, a stalker whose name repeatedly came up in various interviews with Columbine students, achieved an untouchable status. Known as "RH" in Larkin's interviews, this particular football player was well-known and harassed most students. He also had a restraining order against him by a fellow (female) student, which he routinely violated at school, and the administration refused to enforce (they suggested the family pay someone to follow their daughter around school). This student missed school on the day of the shooting because of harassment, and RH followed her to her home that day. He later spread rumors about her when she did not return to the new school after the shootings (Larkin 2007, 109). As he writes:

> The dominant view about bullying and harassment was that it occurred, but it was relatively rare. The administration was aware of The Predators, but figured that they had the situation under control. However, Principal DeAngelis claimed, rightly, that students are not going to harass and intimidate their peers in front of adult authorities. Therefore, the vast majority of harassment and intimidation occurred outside the purview of faculty, staff and administration. Because of this, many school officials radically underestimated the amount of violence that occurred in their school. (Larkin 2007, 95)

Connected to the sporting teams were the "Deep Christians" who became well-known after Columbine as they took over most of the memorializing of the event in the press and on television. Together these groups formed the dominant social formation of the homogeneous social at Columbine. What is jarring is how both groups (whose members often had dual allegiances, the coach was also the "Young Life" director at the school) evinced a kind of "moral elitism" that was known to be fake: "several young women who were former Columbine students complained about members of Young Life claiming piety, but who were heavy partiers, drinkers, dope-smokers and sexual players. The fact that the worst predators on campus also identified themselves as deep Christians, who were also abetted by the coach who was the sponsor of Young Life, tended to make many Columbine students cynical about the religious commitment of their peers" (Larkin 2007, 105).

Some of the "outcasts" later formed what came to be known as the Trench Coat Mafia, which was originally a term used by the moral elites against outcast students. Adopting the moniker and turning its meaning around, some outcast students began to think of it as a way to protect each other by staying in groups. It was when they were separated or outside school or in unowned spaces that they were most likely to be attacked. Furthermore, having had a conflict with one of the moral elites adjudicated by the administration meant that the outcast could look forward to daily taunting, humiliation and cruelty until graduation. As the Huerter Report identified:

> I spoke with some … Trench Coat Mafia [members]. They talked about not being picked on as a group, but about individuals being picked on when they were separated. Specifically, females remembered being called 'sluts' and 'Nazi lesbians' by jocks. Other times there were accounts of members being shoved, through into walls, pushed and on at least one occasion having a bag of ice water thrown onto a Trench coat Mafia member by a table of "jocks." On this particular occasion the jocks and the TM were in the cafeteria, the bag was thrown, words were exchanged, and both groups got up to go outside and fight. "Sid," a security person, intervened and escorted those in the TM to administration. The TM members were suspended for 3 days while none of the jocks were taken to administration nor received any apparent disciplinary action (3–4). (qtd. in Larkin 108–9)

When discussing Huerter's analysis of the findings that "student culture was rife with stories about the special treatment of the jocks, especially those who were members of The Predators," Larkin makes an important intervention by noting that Huerter then backtracks on these finds when she doesn't find evidence in the school newspaper that the Jocks are celebrated to the exclusion of all others, noting that "all types of successes were noted." I am certain that people reading this report nodded their heads in agreement. Anything that will neutralize the bullying interpretation is readily accepted as evidence. Larkin rightly concludes that Huerter rejects her own data in order to come to this conclusion. As he rightly argues, "school peer culture" is not found in "posters on the wall or official school bulletins," but in informal interviews with the students themselves (113).

Larkin also discusses how responsibility for managing conflict (bullying) at the school was shirked in a number of ways including: the teachers assuming it was the administration's job (so letting it go), the coaches who were teachers encouraging it as an "atta boy" mentality, and the administrators acting like it wasn't something they knew about. When you're trying very hard not to look it's easy not to see. The differential treatment was particularly striking, as one jock was allowed to park his $100,000 Hummer in a 15-minute parking spot every single day, as well as a coach who became concerned at the low attendance of students at football games, encouraging his players to "treat everyone with respect in order to increase attendance" because they were faced with having to switch stadiums due to students boycotting games over bullying (qtd. in Huerter 2000, 112). So, respect is utilitarian; you only extend it in order to get something you need.

As Larkin further argues, "any student complaining about their treatment by the jocks could not depend upon protection by the administration would open themselves up to retribution. It was common knowledge at Columbine that "jocks ruled"—it was even written on the bathroom walls—and victims appeared powerless to do anything about it" (201).

Given that, as Larkin reports, Harris and Klebold no doubt witnessed first-hand the disparate impact of "justice" at Columbine, and even in the larger Jefferson County community between jocks and outcasts, they had perhaps some reason to accept the bullying itself, but the knowledge that if the authorities became aware of conflict between the two groups or in isolation, in either case, the outcasts would be punished (often severely in detention, expulsion or felony charges) while the jocks would be left alone. This must have chafed in a way that previous generations of students bullied in American schools did not experience. They could have at least, as Balibar notes, thought about leaving, or of surviving in another space free of these dynamics. Harris and Klebold knew something about the control society, whether it was cognitive or not makes no difference; they knew that when there was friction the weaker, non-celebrated subject position would be punished, while the other would be celebrated. So, in Aronowitz's terms, we are not just talking about a middle-class social contract breaking down where "having one's day in court and feeling heard" would nudge one back into the norms of civil society; no, we are talking about a situation where there is no society, only the endless modulations of the control society that function too often to produce forms of inferiority that do not challenge the status of dominant groups. Larkin's term *moral elitism* is apt and he links it to celebrity culture. However, it seems like his linkage to celebrity culture is focused on Harris and Klebold and the "fame" they hoped to gain from committing the atrocities at Columbine, but what about the celebrity culture so detailed by him throughout the book, the Predators. One reason they were able to get away with their crimes was that they were the elites; they provided a service for the control society: they gave every parent and teacher a reason to stand on the sidelines on Friday nights, reliving their own glory days or making a fantasmatic one for others. This I call the "subjectivity on the sidelines" and we will return to it in Chapter 4. For now, however it is important to note that Harris and Klebold saw it clearly. In a video tape prior to shootings they said: "I know we're gonna have followers because we're so fucking godlike. We're not exactly human—we have human bodies but we've evolved into one step above you fucking shit. We have self-awareness" (Zoba 2000, 131–32, qtd. in Larkin 60). As Larkin notes, "in an ironic twist, the moral elitism evidenced by the evangelicals was incorporated by Klebold and Harris into a justification for their murderous rage" (61).

Klebold confessed in a chat room to admiring the Oklahoma City bombing, and from the diaries we know that they hoped Oliver Stone would make a film about Columbine, but these are just stylizations or fetishes. As Balibar says, "do they take the place of ideals?" It was at this time ("days" after the arrest, Kass says) that Klebold mentioned NBK in his writings. They were both overmediated by the adults around them. Harris's father begans to make journal entries (later used against the Harris's and subpoenaed in a civil case attempting to prove they knew something was wrong with him and were worried, but did not take sufficient action) about getting him a therapist. He was enrolled in therapy (Klebold was not, in spite of the fact that he was a depressive, and his parents admit he had problems with both loneliness and authority) and begans a regime of Prozac (which didn't work and made him tired and agitated), and then he was switched to Luvox (by the time we got to the Columbine event, Harris was taking upwards of 200 mg per day; later toxicology results show it was in his system). Kass shows Klebold to be getting in trouble shortly after the van break-in. He attempted to scratch something onto a student's locker who angered him (with a paper clip) and was given a three day suspension (which even his father thought was overdoing it). Horvath, the dean in charge at the time, met with both of them and recounted to Kass that he saw them both as very intelligent and Dylan especially aware of the politics of the school. Dylan, he said, "understands the politics of how like a school system works. He was smart around that. And he was angry at the system; not angry at me, but angry at the system; that the system would be established, that it would allow for what he did to be a suspendable offense, if that makes any sense to you. He was mad at the world because he was being suspended, but he was mad at the system because the system that was designed was allowing him to be suspended" (Kass 2009, 91–2). Furthermore, Klebold "swore" in front of him (Horvath) about the injustice, and he was "very upset with the school system and the way CHS handled people, to include the people that picked on him and others" (Kass citing from a police report, 2009, 91). They are angry, but they are not paranoid, which is the *seduction* of paramilitary culture (at least as it exists in fringe groups in the U.S.). Rather, these are the acts of overmediated individuals who cannot see any other means of exiting the system, so they decide to make it into a kind of cruel art. If Klebold thought the same injustice inside Columbine was connected to or similar to any injustice he may experience once he left it, he truly did not see a light at the end of this tunnel. Indeed, we might even speculate with Balibar that the kind of violence at Columbine may not have been overt or physically debilitating, but maybe as he says,

> to say that the extremity of violence annihilates the possibilities of resistance, in whatever form, is to say that it does not contribute to any dialectic, not even that which Hegel had in mind. In his famous discourse regarding "independence and dependence of self-consciousness" (more commonly known as the "master-slave dialectic"), Hegel described the possibility of an "exchange" between submission and life, making it the origin of cultural development. To negate that possibility is to annihilate a certain complementarity of life and death that is itself at the foundation of the linkage of generations and the formation of communities." (Balibar 2009, 13–14)

If there is no longer an exchange between submission and life, if the violence serves no purpose and leaves no room for a future, if it "annihilates" even the "possibilities of resistance," then we are past the point of revenge fantasies, of scenes, we are in the ever-unfolding real.

3

Passage à l'acte

New Thoughts on Civility

"When NATO drops bombs on Libya or other locations they calculate less than 10% civilian casualties … that was my aim too."

—Breivik qtd. in Siddique (2013)

It is as though America as a whole had espoused this sect-like destiny: the immediate concretization of all perspectives of salvation. If America were to lose this moral perspective on itself, it would collapse. This is not perhaps evident to Europeans, for whom America is a cynical power and its morality a hypocritical ideology. We remain unconvinced by the moral visions Americans have of themselves, but in this we are wrong. When they ask with seriousness why other peoples detest them, we would be wrong to smile, for it is this same self-examination which makes possible both the various 'Watergates" and the unrelenting exposure of corruption and their own society's faults in the cinema and the media, a freedom we might envy them, we who are the truly hypocritical societies, keeping our individual and public affairs concealed beneath the bourgeois affectations of secrecy and respectability.

—Baudrillard (1988, 91)

In spring 2003, while researching this book, I read a cover exposé in the *New York Times* on international "behavior modification" schools where U.S. parents can send their teens to learn about "compliance" to authority structures, parental supervision and family values. Loaded terms, especially in the U.S., but one of the major motivational factors in sending troubled teens away is to keep the "family together"; indeed most teens interviewed said they are actively trying to divide their parents and families to siphon off some of the family power for themselves.[1] The article stressed that the parents who had sent their teens to these "international" schools where *traditional authority* was school policy were "relieved" in spite of the fact that they hadn't conducted any background checks on the schools' policies, philosophies of education or psychological approaches to dealing with "troubled teens." In fact, the schools' catchy advertisements on the Web indicated that they had fair success rates and could bypass many (to their minds) cumbersome laws surrounding the humane treatment of students in schools. These schools could respond to the paranormal behavior of the troubled teens with the discipline they so desperately needed; at least this is what the ad indicated. I use this term to underscore that teens in the U.S. do live in a paranormal state, even though their behavior is categorized as "pathological" or "disorderly." Paranormal works because teens live in a virtual world: during the space between adolescence and adulthood (legally, monetarily and emotionally), teens have not yet made crucial decisions about the world they will inherit; they are waiting, and in the case of school violence and in the United States, swathed a virtual and real culture of violence, they are not waiting very patiently. Their parents are not patient either; as the article made clear, one parent simply jumped on the Internet, "I sent him (her son) there sight unseen," and "I went searching around on the internet and found the Wwasp program. I contacted them and made the arrangements, and that's pretty much it. It didn't take me any time at all" (*New York Times* 5/9/03, A-10). It seems that what postcolonial states have to offer the world market, in addition to cheap labor and natural resources, is a model of authority not available in the United States. In this, a new "comparative advantage" emerges for the postcolony: remote discipline for American teens. As was outlined in the quotation by Baudrillard from *America,* U.S. citizens could retain their self-perception as morally righteous even while allowing others to commit injustices against their own children in their absence. And Baudrillard is correct, this is not hypocrisy because Americans do not have the "bourgeois affectations" of secrecy and respectability: they thoroughly believe that their values are consistent with their practices, in spite of evidence they are not (Webber 2003a, 2005). The United States lacks a feudal past, or rather it lacks a belief in a feudal past. As Žižek argues, there is always the tension or anxiety surrounding meaning in the United States because we believe there is no shared past. In Europe there was a feudal past, a monarchy, and hierarchical social class relations that still retain a sense of meaning and provide a basis for all kinds of unworkable universalisms: French republicanism, British social class, German "post-holocaust" civility," etc. As he writes,

> In Europe, the ground floor in a building is counted as 0, so that the floor above it is the first floor, while in the U.S. the first floor is at the street level. In short, Americans start

to count with 1, while Europeans already know that 1 is a stand in for 0. Or to put it in more historical terms, Europeans are aware that prior to beginning to count, there has to be a ground of tradition which is always already given and, as such, cannot be counted, while the U.S. a land with no premodern historical tradition proper, lacks such a ground. Things begin there with self-legislated freedom. The past is erased or transposed onto Europe. (Žižek 2008b, 164)

The conceit of self-legislated freedom is what makes Americans so easily reject self-reflection. The ideological tradition that makes this possible in the United States is pragmatism, which is a blend of technocratic certitude and faith with little interest in revealing or acknowledging social class differences. It also makes possible the relative indifference to international standards of justice and law, such as the Geneva and Hague Conventions that would be circumvented to fight the war on terror in remote locations like Abu Ghraib and Guantanomo Bay, Cuba. Even Michael Ignatieff noted prior to the invasion of Iraq in 2003 that Americans did not have reverence for international rules of conduct (Ignatieff 2000, 182). While we may not have this classical tradition, or we transpose it onto Europe, I would argue that our lack of certainty or meaning is made up for by corporations: they represent our contemporary premodern form of tradition (in fact, they found it). The outsourcing of authority is as natural and unremarkable to the United States as any other form of labor (domestic, serving staff, laboring, etc.). Like Arendt's reflection in the last chapter, we rely on curriculum standards and methods to stand in for authority in school and other institutions (for example, talk therapy is viewed with suspicion, and medications provided by corporations are the primary means to deal with mental illness or social anxiety). We never look to the break down or complete lack of civil society as the contributing factor.

In the last two chapters, we put to rest a number of "Columbine theses" and put forward our own: that Columbine is a pilot that launches the game of mass extermination, of depriving random people (usually one's peers, fellow citizens, or innocents who represent those who wronged us in the past) of their own (*natural*) end through a form of violence relatively under-theorized in the phenomenological sense. That is, how does this violence work? How does it function? Can it having meaning? Where does it fit into our symbolic universe? We begin by noting that many school violence episodes after Columbine occurred from 2005 onward. Thus, once school violence went "viral" and evidence for it was available on the Web, the number of occurrences increased (only of this unique type, not of school violence generally, which like crime rates in general, have been steadily declining in the U.S. for over two decades). What defines this kind of act is that it is focused on extermination, on a grand scale, and in a relatively dramatic form that cites from previous acts (whether through clothing, weapon choice, site or style of killing, mode of reaching social media). Most of the time it does not offer a narrative explanation (i.e., there is no note or commentary and it is non-diegetic). In each case, the perpetrator (so far they've all been single individuals following Columbine) does not interact with his victims (they are mostly asubjective acts, we speculate). Nearly each one has been bullied, passed through several modulations in the control society, planned the attacks for great lengths of time, cruised under the radar to those around him, then suicides. Usually there is a discrete failure just prior to the act: Harris not getting into the Marines, Holmes flunking an oral exam, Cho's psych hold, Weise's expulsion, and in the case of both German shooters, more school failure. In Finland we have already mentioned Sumiala and Tikka's work using Bataille, specifically his notion of the heterogeneous social and its relationship to the sacred and fascism. However, we need to situate this analysis in a more contemporary setting. Bataille was looking at fascists who took the state, the psychological structure of which was intent on imposing a unique kind of sovereignty on the socially anxious and politically deprived and usually working classes. Today, in the societies that produce school violence episodes like the ones under scrutiny here, capitalist production looks rather different, and the state is no longer the exclusive site of sovereign power. In Bataille's time, capitalism had a worthy adversary in the form of socialism or communism. As most speculate, especially Žižek, German fascism, which is to say, Nazism, was primarily organized around fighting off communism to the benefit of wealthy capitalist patrons (which Bataille discusses, the confusion of aims between Hitler and the capitalists and Mussolini and his). As we shall see, since capitalism detotalizes, meaning it becomes impossible for people to find their political place in a world without reliable opposition, who would these shooters idolize? What cause would they find worthy of their lives instead of capitalism or the homogeneous social? There isn't one. John Walker Lindh was punished severely for joining the Taliban, and we can also see evidence of this in the disproportionate sentences passed on to Internet hackers who threaten the system at its level of control. So why do these young men (usually) commit suicide or pass into full blown psychosis?

Something Else

Étienne Balibar confronts this problem of youth violence in a different way. In a series of lectures from the 1990s, he looks at the problem of youth violence in

Western and Eastern Europe. The proximity to the wars in the former Yugoslavia made European intellectuals more sensitive to the types of violence emerging in those areas that differed from the national violence witnessed during the World Wars and colonial independence movements. Balibar calls this violence, often committed by youth, "ultra-subjective" in that it bears no relationship to any kind of *rational* national identification on the part of its subjects. It is a kind violence that proceeds from a *fetishism of cruelty* (Balibar 2002, 34), is *inconvertible* (which means it is not guided by a larger spirit of national or other kind of unity to produce new forms of social administration and belonging, or in our American-school violence speak, it is "senseless") and "wears a Medusa face" (Balibar 2002, 143). Starting from Hegel's point of view, Balibar reminds the reader that the forging of civility apropos the subject is a violent process, one that works on the axis of identification: "Hegel's idea is that primary identities and senses of belonging have to be virtually destroyed in order to be not purely and simply eliminated, but reconstructed as particular expressions and mediations of collective political identity, or a belonging to the state" (Balibar 2002, 31). Thus, we are born into families but our initial identification with that unit is dismembered, to use Bataille's term, so that it can be reconstructed for the purposes of the state, to ensure national unity and state allegiance. The institutions that accomplished this task in recent times were schools, which as Althusser reminded us, "reproduced the relations of production," that is, they make us good capitalist subjects but also make us *civil* to each other and our leaders in the process. Schools, from a political and economic vantage point, reproduce both efficiency and civility. Further on, Balibar explains:

> Let us say that there is a simultaneous double movement of *disidentification* and *identification*, but this is controlled in advance by the state or the 'higher' community, so that the result is *guaranteed*, since it has been prepared well in advance by the ethical formations of civil society. This movement clearly has universalistic implications, and indeed it produces an effect of intensive universalization, because it takes the individual out of 'natural' confinements within a single community (the model for which is the family) by opening up a space of free play for him in which—at times simultaneously and at others successively—he will assume several roles and personalities. All in all, it allows each subject to move from 'membership' to 'joining', which always presupposes the relative possibility of a choice, albeit a choice within an existing framework. (Balibar 2002, 31)

Balibar calls the successive state of identification after the family, a "civility" which may or may not be institutionalized by the state within which the subject resides. But he notes that Hegel was either "unaware" or did not "acknowledge" some problems with this process: first, it is extremely violent; second, he does not acknowledge the possibility of a "fictive ethnicity," which is "an identification of disidentification" and is "the mediation necessary for propelling barbarism outside one's borders, for attributing it to 'others,'" and also and it is formed out of "family, linguistic or religious bonds, and vested in sites of historical memory" (32). We might now call this "ethnic cleansing" or racism. Finally, third and most important to Balibar's framework, Hegel did not see how this state would eventually be subsumed by the economic processes of capitalism, namely, abstract labor, which leads him to ask of his contemporary European scene: "we have to ask not whether the state never plays any role in the constitution of a civility, but under what conditions and within what limits it may do so" (33). One could see the beginning of this civil conundrum when the social chaos produced by Columbine provoked a *reluctant* state to address it as its own problem through a series of White House Task Forces charged with "investigating" the role of Hollywood, video games and psychiatric drugs in contributing to civic breakdown. Obviously, there was no determination made or causal mechanism identified. The end result was then to default to "zero tolerance" policies combined with peer reporting and increasing security at schools throughout the country. The result was that corporatism would decide how to deal with Columbine in a way that ensured its profits. Much like aggrieved parents shipped their kids off to disciplinary camps "site unseen."

But then Balibar reverses his focus, taking the onus off the state and its presumed sovereign control and asks what it means that throughout the twentieth century for citizens to have taken it upon themselves to "force the state to recognize their dignity" through education, work reform, civil rights and so on. Subjects have been *willing agents* in forming civility. But they are also limited by their participation in a "globalized space" where "borders are both hystericized and vacillating in which the transnational machinery of communications, surveillance and credit reaches into individual's own homes," and "there is no equivalent to the state and its *Sittlichkeit*, no "civilizing heights" (Balibar 2002, 32). Here he has described slightly differently what sociologists of education have called the paradox of reproduction and resistance in education (and work). That is, subjects are reproduced according to the designs of the capitalist class (by the schools, at their direction) to know and accept their place within classes and learn the norms and skills necessary to perform work in efficient and nonviolent (i.e., civil) ways. However, such subjects also "resist" their place within this structure of efficiency through intentional "failures" (work shut downs, vandalism) that lead up to the "incivility" they present to the state in the form of civil disobedience, strikes, work refusal, and so on. It is only clear how to be in(civil) when there is a representative of the *Sittlichkeit* to confront. The méconnaissance between conservatives like Alan Bloom or Mortimer Adler and radicals like Henry Giroux or Michael Apple is that one group sees the state (and its authority) as universal whereas the other sees the state as a reflection of the interests of a third party, namely corporations. Neither of them realizes the state cannot respond and won't respond to these issues. But Balibar invokes a third way of understanding civility, namely, through *ressentiment*: how do we *know* that such "bottom up" civility is not slave morality? How do we know that what liberals and radicals call "progress" (here I would define it as coming from the masses and not the state) is not a chimera or another form of managing liberation, of presenting one's self to the state as "free" in order to ensure further enslavement, as Foucault once said? For Balibar then, who has hope that such a reversal of civility is possible (indeed necessary) to not only move forward in history but also to thwart the contemporary problem faced by youth who "have no ideals," a universal political movement that disidentifies with global capital (and its "civilizing heights" which tend to depoliticize social and economic contradictions through substitutions: for poverty, charity and microcredit; lack of employment, training) while resisting the urge to cast aspersions on the "other" is the challenge of today.

In a later lecture, Balibar zeroes in on youth and their relationship to violence in Europe. He writes, "The excluded youth of today, objects of potential manipulation of neo-fascism or, rather, *potential objects of self-manipulation* … are not fundamentally in search of cultures; they are looking for ideals—and they naturally seek these in symbols, which may at times take the form of fetish—objects" (Balibar 2002, 51, emphasis mine). Here, we can think of Weise's identification with the National Socialist Green Party or Breivik's more detailed defense and celebration of Aryan identity, or even Harris and Klebold's identification with McVeigh and the militia movement so entranced by the *Turner Diaries* and provoked by the events at Waco, Texas. We can think of Vidal's portrait of McVeigh, even as a Henley-like hero born in the wrong time. What Balibar means by fetish objects is that the attraction of such violent and exclusionary ideologies for young men is that they act as a support structure (in the absence of attractive ideals) by providing a necessary fantasy. This structure inevitably fails to hold and is possibly replaced with the more specific symbolic identification with other shooters online and through social media. As an example, Sumiala and Tikka have studied the relationship between four of the shootings through the circulation of online materials. They argue that through the remediation and sharing of violent images from previous shooters (including their own online videos, suicide notes, etc.) viewers form and embrace a "heterogeneous social, the world of dark desires and instincts that are hidden from daylight—in this case, they lie beneath what is covered in mainstream news media" (Sumiala & Tikka 2011, 153). Using Bataille's notion of the heterogeneous (the elements expelled from the homogeneous social, our social and consumer conformity discussed in Chapter 1), they argue that YouTube's debut in 2005 marked a turning point in the school shooting series since, to use Balibar's term, those who identify with such forms of violence, were able to easily (and somewhat confidentially) "gaze" at these images. As they argue:

> In these communities, people scattered around the world come together through a visual discourse of violence, hatred, and destruction; in the spirit of Bataille we may consider these ephemeral encounters of stranger sociability *sacred communities of destruction*. These are virtual communities held together by a social imaginary constructed around the visualization of texts and death and violence that emanate from specific nations (in this case, the U.S.A. and Finland), but almost instantly transcend the national level. These communities, fostered by the dark side of the social, cancel the distance between the 'real' and the 'virtual' and cohere around endless circulation, remediation, and sharing of visual discourses of hate and destruction. (ibid., 153)

The heterogeneous social would be the niche spaces of marginality discussed by Murray Forman in our introduction. To be sure, this is what happens. As we know from reports out of the Newtown press, Adam Lanza kept a long list of past school shootings (the officer who leaked the information described it as a "dissertation" that must have taken "years" to construct (Lupica 2013), this is one of the few reports that has not been refuted by police in this case). Further leaks provide us with the idea that Lanza admired three shootings in particular: the Norway shooting, the shooting in Brazil and the attack on the Amish school in Pennsylvania. Since he smashed his hard drive, authorities believe they cannot find any of his possible connections to other shootings. The hard drive now becomes the "brain" where knowledge about a shooter's intentions is housed. Even more leaks inform that Lanza had taken instruction in some indirect way from Breivik on how to prepare to undertake the rampage (Haq 2013). Some reports also suggested a similar awareness to the one Breivik undertook in "gazing" at pictures of bloody bodies to desensitize one's self to the sight. Later we find out from an email communication between Lanza's mother and a friend that she found two "gruesome" photos in Adam's belongings that fit this description (Lysiak & Hutchison 2013). So whether or not they actually socialize with one another, students and former students who are attracted to this form of violence, to fetishizing it, as Balibar contends, are able to find symbolic support in these forums (it is incorrect to call them communities in the traditional sense) for their eventual means of exit. We could also possibly see Lanza's gazing as an attempt to "increase the threshold" at which violence becomes prohibited, following Protevi, only this suggests that violent FPS games are not the desensitizing agents but that the shooter purposefully exposes himself to what might seem otherwise gruesome images. They are not hooked on "thanatography"; they are mad as hell and need a strategy to pull them through the event.[2] Yet, this doesn't tell us *why* shooters are attracted to the sacred community of destruction that flows directly out of the Columbine (and later, Virginia Tech) script. It only tells us *how*.

At this point, we must distinguish between two types of users on these forums: those who gaze for its "implication in transgressing the sacred" or, as Nathalie Paton calls them, "fans" who "constantly remain on the lookout for upcoming shootings, commenting on the time elapsed since the last one and the probability of another," who "Once a shooting takes place, they exchange information and compare it to the precedent and give their assessement" (Paton 2012, 221). These users should be distinguished from those who have already decided they will transgress it in actuality. What is implied in this is that they are a kind of community of infamy: "School shooters explicitly name or represent one another. Oliveira refers to Cho as a brother in arms; Castillo points out that his cultural tastes are like those of 'Eric and Dylan'; Auvinen uses images from the Columbine shootings surveillance camera and devotes several videos to the Columbine killers. This aspect underlines the fact that the boys actively take part in associating themselves to a group. Such statements act as signs of recognition that work toward creating a group rationale" (Paton 2012, 217). And further on Paton confirms Larkin's claim that these are political acts, "Through their videos, the issue becomes one of confirming, via imitation, to this signification system in which shooters find their place, thereby substantiating the notion of a political act (Larkin 2009). However, they are thereby entwined in a paradox whose outlines they have woven, caught between their need to be singled out and the necessity of adopting a pre-existing model" (ibid., 217). Several things need to be sorted here. First, it is not quite a "group rationale" as these individuals do not correspond to each other in real time; in fact, they are memorializing each other since the one who comes prior is already dead. It is, as we argued, following methexis, a form of "group sharing" that occurs via telepresence (more on this in Chapters 4 and 5). Second, the "confirmation via imitation" is also not clear: it seems more like memorializing through methexis, rather than simple mimicry (what the media calls "copycatting"). As was noted in the introduction, methexis is "group sharing" when members of "the audience participates, creates and improvises the action of the ritual." This is Greek tragedy in action, not membership in an ideological or institutional cause. There is a key distinction here: an institution or ideological cause has rules, explanations, policies, and goals.

At a broader level, this isolates another commonly found problem with most analyses of school shootings: there is an almost doctrinaire conviction that these episodes are primarily motivated around regaining a dignity that is insured by violent masculinity (or what we define in the Western tradition as "revenge") without any proof that this is the case. Kellner, Kimmel and many others reify our knowledge about school violence and reduce it to a knowable, endlessly repeated—static script about violent masculinity. While I do not disagree this is an important concept for understanding many kinds of violences, most specifically gang rapes and subsequent image sharing of those acts (e.g., Steubenville), violent masculinity must be hegemonic (that is, of the predators [Larkin's findings about the jocks at Columbine]). We need a new analysis and a new language to discuss school violence that specifically distinguishes it from hegemonic masculinity. So far, this kind of analysis has done nothing but contribute to the bullying problem even more: now we must be on the lookout for bullied kids to pull out of school, medicate them and share confidential records so that *they* don't go crazy and shoot up a school. We will forever be silently exonerating bullies if we continue to discuss school violence in this way, or as Žižek says, protecting the "obscene underside" of American (and perhaps others, I leave it those experts to decide and describe it) rituals of belonging. The idea that school shooters are caught in a "paradox" is *imposed* on the discourse about school violence *by theorists* who are wedded to the notion of violent hegemonic masculinity and its applicability to these subjects. How do we know perpetrators see it as a paradox, especially if they willingly refer to each other and share credit with the group? Finally, suicide is not in the violent masculinity playbook, unless it is part of a failed romantic plot. While many experts have tried to make the connection between many of these shooters and a "girl" or stalking or revenge, for the second generation we are focused on here, that doesn't seem to be the case. Kazmierzcak sent his girlfriend an engagement ring (she had no idea he was going to attack NIU) and thought they were still in a relationship, while Cho had no relationships with women, so to speak of a failed romance is nonsensical. Lanza seems asexual, as do Breveik and Holmes. We must confront the cruelty and humiliation they undergo in the bullying itself (and possibly how they see this bullying and the stigma it produces as forever separating them from the possibility of a romantic plot, failed or otherwise), and we must look more closely at the kind of language many shooters use when they discuss humanity: they all subscribe to a kind of pseudo Nietzschean social Darwinism. Furthermore, if they are so interested in infamy, why don't they decide to wait it out and have their revenge the way that Trey Parker advised: by growing up and using the ultimate fetish, money, to buy away their deficiencies and poke fun at their enemies? This is the unsaid assumption of every claim of violent masculinity made against school shooters, and yet, if they were following the script of hegemonic masculinity they would *know*, as R.W. Connell once said, maintaining silence about bullying and harassment by boys is "a short term cost of maintaining a long-term privilege" (Connell 2001, 167). In other words, men commit all kinds of violence against one another in contemporary societies (always have, even in feudal ones), but as long as there is the realistic promise of "long-term privilege" not only is it tolerated, it is celebrated and protected as tradition, at one point even ornamental and gamed in chivalry, as manly love, as brotherhood, as "taking one for the team," as what we properly term homoeroticism in gender studies. *This* kind of violence is different and it may not necessarily be confined to men, perhaps it is just that they have a harder time tolerating it. There is something wrong with this kind of masculinity, but it is not centered on violence and power, but on cruelty and humiliation that are not recuperated or subsumed into an otherwise meaningful existence. This is a Hegelian problem.

Passage à l'acte

The original use of *passage à l'acte* comes from Jacques Lacan who used it to explain the actions of Antigone. Since Antigone (Oedipus's daughter with Jocasta) could not bury her brother inside the city nor mourn him on pain of death (since he had gone to war with his brother over control of Thebes and been labeled a traitor by the new king Creon), Antigone declares a "higher" law than that of men from the Gods and breaks the law, burying her brother and mourning him. It should be noted that her other brother who went to war with Polynices is given a traditional burial and mourned. Once found out, she is walled up and hangs herself. This is the version as told by Sophocles. Antigone's actions are said to be "senseless" because they defy the laws of men. Furthermore, she is "walled up" from humanity and can no longer communicate with anybody. When Lacan described the *passage à l'acte* he was describing the movement from sanity to break, when a subject that can no longer tolerate the unjustness of the laws of the symbolic universe and passes over into the Real. It is important to stress here that no one in Thebes but Antigone could see the meaning of her act. She is alone. As Linda Belau has written about the *passage à l'acte*, it is a different kind of ethic, no longer situated in relation to the "good," or in our case here the "elite," it is "entirely devoid of pathological content; one passes to the act not for symbolic recognition or return, but for some other reason that takes one beyond such concerns" (Belau

2003, 2). But there is more. The psychotic, which is what the subject who passes from "intention to act," is not situated within the larger symbolic universe since he has not been barred by the Name of the Father. Basically this means that he has not been socialized properly to not only understand but believe in the norms governing the society in which he lives. He has been disrupted from a normal ritual of socialization, the entry into language by being barred from unmediated access to the mother; that is, he doesn't know he can't have desire for his mother. He remains outside the symbolic universe and supports himself through whatever imaginary he has concocted along his sloppy developmental path. This is the clinical version of this story, focused on an individual. Yet, it has some resonance for our understanding of civil society related to mass murders because it zeroes in on acts that cannot be understood by society and because its etiology is the application of a kind of unfairness perceived only by this particular subject to be so intolerable that he cannot bear it. The term can also be used loosely to describe events that might be deemed political, but it is always contentious to make this claim, and the state or King Creon never wants it uttered aloud.

Both Balibar and Žižek make mention of "senseless" or "explosive" forms of violence as *passages à l'acte*, the Lacanian term for acts that instantiate a break between the subject and reality, a psychotic break. Žižek adds the qualifier "impotent" to his use of the term and specifically addresses it to the outbreaks of violence in Paris in 2005, as well as terrorist suicide bombings. In each, he makes slight qualifications to address their meanings in the political sense. Both are failed, that is impotent, in the sense that they fail to achieve anything political or impose a sovereignty onto the symbolic field. In other words, we do not understand what they are supposed to mean to us as observers. This makes sense since we've been looking specifically at episodes of violence that unfold in fairly similar fashion over the past two decades, so roughly within the same generational framework, yet we still have no idea what they mean, and they are "senseless" unless we can find some direct causality between these acts and a precipitant like guns, films, video games, or masculinity. What if, however, some of these items work their way into these scripts as fetishes, like Balibar says, props that support the fantasy structure that is keeping them from doing harm by sublimating it, and others become a full-fledged way of telling the story of the individual? There is an intermediate level of meaning here that needs fleshing out. Let's go further into Balibar and Žižek and see where we come out.

For Balibar, a *passage à l'acte* can take on the second type of cruelty he discusses in the important chapter, "Violence, Ideality and Cruelty." "Ultra-subjective" violence most accurately reflects this kind. Both are concerned with forms of violence after the Holocaust, and with the widespread notion that after the Holocaust nothing will be compared to it, and its significance marked historically in order to prevent more violence. Both thinkers question the idea of a post-ideological era that is often invoked to deter analysis of violence in order to understand its genesis. Rather, the term *post-ideological* performs a specific function in that it claims that only *action* can deal with violence (containment, zero tolerance, force) for Žižek (we will return to Bailbar's warning about this later). Hence, Žižek's ethical claim at both the beginning and end of his book *On Violence* to "do nothing" but think about violence. Balibar is similarly hesitant in that he thinks we should question the idealism behind the motive to eliminate violence. As we shall see below, he even suggests it may *cause* cruelty or *create conditions for it to thrive*. Žižek says very specifically "if" the idea of a post-ideological era "makes any sense" it is when discussing the "series" of *passages à l'acte* that run from terrorism to the Parisian riots. My interpretation of why he qualifies the term *post-ideological era* is this: to say that we are in a post-ideological era is to proceed from an understanding that all utopian visions have been (or will be) realized by global capital and its democratic machinery. Recall Galloway's claim that Althusser's formulation should now be that we are subjects with "imaginary relations to our ideological conditions." Furthermore, what this means is that agitated individuals who do not see themselves as included in this utopian vision have neither the symbolic mandate nor skills to communicate their exclusion and make concrete demands. Instead, he argues that the Parisian riots assume a "phatic function" in that the protesters actually wreck their own neighborhoods and that "there was only an insistence on recognition, based on a vague, unarticulated *ressentiment*" (Žižek 2008b, 75). Žižek as much as confirms this symbolic failure later when he writes that "capitalism is worldless" in that it "detotalises meaning," and just prior to that he writes that its main danger is in its "depriving the large majority of people of any meaningful cognitive mapping" (Žižek 2008b, 79). A reference to Jameson's conceptual phrase, "cognitive mapping" is a term that Galloway will also use repeatedly to discuss gaming, and it is an aesthetic developed "to enable a situational representation on the part of the individual subject to that vaster and properly unrepresentable totality which is the ensemble of society's structures as a whole," and its understanding of the ideology that obscures this relationship is governed by Althusser's formula for ideology where "ideology represents the subjects imaginary relationship to his or her real conditions of existence" (Althusser 1972, qtd. in Jameson 1991, 51). What does this mean? It does not mean that people suffer from false consciousness; that is, in the old Marxian framework they are alienated from the true/real core of their existence by capital and will (in ideal conditions) realize this multidimensional separation and take action: seize the state, corporations and redistribute wealth and democratize labor. It means that the discourses of capital (or what we have been calling, after Delueze, corporatism) continuously subvert our "relations" to our ideological conditions of existence. As Galloway reflects on the idea that "Today's culture is not questioning capitalism," he writes, "The economic industrialization of the nineteenth and twentieth centuries provoked a strong immune response in the human form, first rejecting the foreign tissue of capital, then healing, scarring, and deforming in response to it. But today we have a new healthfulness around capital, an economic modality of disaster and ruin that nevertheless coexist on the very terrain of health, with a new, secure social body" (Galloway, Lovak & Thacker 2008, 107). Hence, there is no outside. So, to return to our question about the "post-ideological era" above, in Žižek's argument we see that he is being ironic because it is only so due to the subject's incapacity to symbolically communicate, to read his own desire into the social field. For Balibar, it is similarly post-historical because of a particular condition that that subject finds himself in: after the dismantling of the welfare state and social security, he continues to be unemployed. That is, unemployment is no longer a "cyclical phenomenon, a provisional stage used by capital to lower the wage level in the course of continuous expansion," instead we have a situation where "millions of disposable human beings are at the same time excluded from labor—that is, economic activity—and kept within the boundaries of the market, since the market is absolute; it has no external limits. The Market is the World. When it excludes you, you cannot leave it, search for another America, settle there and start again.…" (Balibar 2002, 142). Again, there is no outside. Caught within an idealist system (because you must love it because you cannot leave it, it seems like capitalism is the ultimate form of violent, hegemonic masculinity!) with no way to make proper sense out of the real frustration felt by being excluded from the valuable part, yet caught within. At this point, it becomes clear that both thinkers agree about the *what* and the *where*, but what results is slightly different. Žižek sees frustrated groups and individuals who have no way to ask the right questions about how to end their frustrations, endlessly trying to "join" the very structures that exclude them and pathetically acting out in ways that the symbolic structure can reject as out of hand (e.g., Sarkozy calling the rioters "scum" and basically getting away with it), or as Žižek puts it in his introduction, the very same liberal communists (such as Bill Gates or George Soros are indirectly responsible for the economic shocks that cause people to be systematically disenfranchised from the capitalist system, and then turn around to "rescue" them as the humanitarians we all celebrate!). Attempting to act within a structure while accepting its limits as valid, perhaps even ideal, makes achieving reform/democracy impossible. This is why they are impotent.

Balibar sees cruelty as a product of this totalizing system of ideality in that the violence no longer serves a purpose but becomes a function of enjoyment itself: "The forms of cruelty have a relationship with materiality that is *not mediated* (especially not symbolically mediated), although in this immediate relationship with materiality some terrible idealities return, so to speak, or become displayed and exhibited as *fetishes* and *emblems*" (Balibar 2002, 137). Further up, he argues, like Sumiala and Tikka, that cruelty does bear a relationship to the heterogeneous social. However, he takes it further to describe that it must have a different, unmediated relationship to ideality. Sumiala and Tikka speculate that it will eventually dissipate as the idea of "transgression" in the Bataillean sense begins to "lose its social function." This occurs because "The Bataillean community ceases to exist as soon as no affectual stimulus remains. In order to flourish again, it needs new videos of torture, killing and abuse. The social dynamics in the mediated orgy both enforce the cruelty and banalise it" (Sumiala & Tikka 2011, 154). Yet, as we have seen, the methectic quality of these events provides much affective stimuli (for both potential actors as well as onlookers). There is always in transgression the notion of "threshold," and in this case we may speculate about, not a threshold of violence, but of cruelty as a central aspect of the series. If we return to Balibar's outline, then we must see this cruelty as "ultra-subjective" in the sense that the individual here identifies with the sacred ritual, but put aside the idea that these are "communities" in any traditional sense. They do not occur in the same spatial or temporal dimension. For Balibar, they not only mark the individual's wish to separate from the homogeneous social, but from humanity altogether. This is their suicidal dimension; Bataille's notion of the heterogeneous does not allow for self-sacrifice, whether in ending one's own biological life or symbolic life. Furthermore, Balibar sees these forms of cruelty as arising not from simply a failure of "integration and compatibility," which was the goal of the nation-state (and left indeed an unincorporated "residue" however minor and relatively unthreatening) (Sumiala & Tikka 2011, 148). This heterogeneous social was on the outside. Instead they are the "result of a blind political preference for 'consensus' and 'peace' not to speak of the implementation of law and order on a global scale" (Balibar 2001, 15). In this scenario the heterogeneous has no "cover" and must be forcibly mediated back into the homogeneous social, whether through therapy, peace education, anti-bullying programs, indeed, all components of our *privatized* "justice" systems.

Ultra-subjective forms of violence are "those inversions of the will to power into a will to 'de-corporation', to forced disaffiliation from the other and from oneself—not just from belonging to the community and to the political unit, but from the human condition" (Balibar 2002, 25). He goes on to describe examples from mainly the Bosnian War, horrific acts of cruelty against peers in any context, teachers with pupils, neighbors, etc. Other examples given are wartime rape in Yugoslavia and public forms of rape in India (Balibar wrote this in 1993 and reedited it for publication in 2002), but we have seen the expansion of these public rapes in India and Brazil in the past few years in brutal kidnapping and gang rapes of women and girls by groups of men unaffiliated with military campaigns or nationalist causes. Furthermore, these acts correspond with what he sees as an "idealization of hatred" that exists within any and all cultures of Europe. Youth in Europe are singled out in his chapter entitled "European Racism" as being particularly prone to ultra-subjective forms of violence because such forms, in Neo-Nazi or Neo-fascist formulation, idealize hatred of the other. Youth are particularly prone to them because, as he says, they are "looking for ideals" as a function of their age. More importantly, these kinds of violences cannot be remedied by education (in Europe this has primarily been an education in multicultural tolerance, the 'vanishing mediator' of European liberalism) because they are not based on 'fear' of the other but on desire for the other to be, ontologically speaking, the source of their own failures and thwarted dreams. You cannot educate away such desires; they are, in Žižek's terms, properly fetishistic: "a kind of symptom in reverse." That is to say, the symptom is the exception which disturbs the surface of the false appearance, the point at which the other scene erupts. While the fetish is the embodiment of the Lie which enables us to sustain the unbearable truth" (Žižek 2009, 296). You can however, be educated to desire in a particular —possibly pathological—way, and in my last book, *Failure to Hold*, I asserted that the American ideology of liberalism did indeed educate school shooters, and their acts put into relief a hidden belief system at the heart of American racial and sexual politics (I was wrong, Protevi is right here that this is a modular hatred not a molar one). There I called it, after a well-known formulation in critical pedagogy, the "hidden curriculum" of schooling. I quoted Michael Apple: "The hidden curriculum of schools serves to reinforce basic rules surrounding the nature of conflict and its uses. It posits a network of assumptions that, when internalized by students, establishes the boundaries of legitimacy" (Apple qtd. in Webber 2003a, 3). If we recall Larkin's book on Columbine, in particular his findings about the school administration overlooking the bullying that went on there, we see it's not exactly hidden but dismissed as being seen as a problem, indeed, more of this dismissiveness is seen as *the* solution. But, let's back track for a minute and return to Balibar's quote and take that apart carefully. Balibar's claim that such forms of violence force disaffiliation "from the human condition" is an important statement in two respects. First, it corresponds to what we've explained is the communicative function of the *passage à l'acte* (or lack thereof) in that rather than communicating to the symbolic, it connects with the real (that which cannot be symbolized, but if we can use this term inelegantly, it represents a "traumatic kernel of enjoyment" (Žižek 2003). As García and Aguilar Sánchez paraphrase Žižek's argument nicely:

> Beyond the specificity of a given economic and social formation, the constitution of social reality presupposes the primordial repression of an antagonism that sets out the process of symbolization. The last foundation in the critique of ideology is the 'real' ([Žižek] 2003: 36). Žižek exemplifies this aspect with the class case study of the symbolization of space in the tribes studied by Levi-Strauss: whereas the dominant sub-group perceives its village as circular, the subordinate/subaltern group perceives it as two spaces separated by an invisible border (Levi-Strauss, 1976: 119–146). The Real does not reside in any of the two perspectives, nor does it in the 'objective' disposition of the village houses. The Real resides instead in the traumatic kernel that those inhabitants could not symbolize, a fundamental imbalance in the social relations of their village. (García & Aguilar 2008, no pages)

Second, Balibar sees these "excessive" forms of violence as having a counterpart: "The counterpart to the experience of cruelty is always some sort of particularly demanding thirst for ideality—either in the sense of nonviolent ideals, or in the sense of ideals of justice" (Balibar 2002, 144). He further argues that there is no such position as one of "nonviolence," and seems to be arguing that the split off parts that social movements take as their ideal goal, nonviolence may in fact produce not simply more violence but the conditions for cruelty, for ultra-subjective and ultra-objective forms of it to thrive. As he writes, "the ultra-subjectivity of violence is written into any subjection of individuals to the rule of a spiritual authority which is sufficiently ferocious and incomprehensible to demand 'more than death.'" (Balibar 2002, 27). Balibar's universalism here is similar to Galtung's "structural violence" in that he sees cruelty as the second generation of forms of violence that Galtung theorized were the results of a structure indifferent to the imbalances it caused at both the structural and personal levels in terms of "human potential."

This insight, if correct, has enormous consequences for the way we might view our cases of school-related (or civil society) violence. These subjects already find an outlet in public through the media. However, what if they are produced by the very forms of justice (in public education, crime control, immigration reform, multicultural tolerance, etc.) that act as the "spiritual authority" over them? All of these forms of justice produce a surplus population that cannot be included, or they unfairly describe the forms of violence they aim to ameliorate. Some people have called this domestic neoliberalism in that these forms of justice jettison true reconciliation of parties in favor of market based or efficiency based solutions.

> "Life as it is today is the most miserable thing the world has to offer."
> —Bastion Bosse, Emsdetten, Germany school shooter, 2006 (Steinberg 2006)

> "What is government, if words have no meaning?"
> —Jared Loughner to Rep. Gabrielle Giffords (D-AZ), 2007 (qtd. in Baumann 2011)

The Turner Diary Effect: Overdetermination

Let's return to fetishes. Many of the shooters we have mentioned thus far have entered into the series with a history of Neo-Nazi identification or some version of what in the United States would be labeled a "Turner Diary complex," or in Europe with Neo-Nazi ideologies that are routinely expressed in minority political party views. Larkin specifically places Harris in the vein of a "righteous paramilitary fighter" after reading his school papers (Larkin 2009, 173). Klebold and Harris both made a fetish of the Oklahoma City bombings in *The Basement Tapes*. In fact, the bombs they set in their own parked cars in the Columbine High School parking lot were set to go off as soon as the police arrived to forestall their entry into the school. As well, they placed pipe bombs inside the cafeteria (that did not detonate) that were supposed to kill every person in the room that day by the time it had reached full capacity (220) at 11:15 a.m. (Kass 2009, 163). Bloggers who claimed to know Steven Kazmierzcak responded to an online investigation into his Internet activity and noted that he would have been pleased (retroactively) to know that the first responders to Cole Hall made quite a fuss over the duffle bag he glued shut and carried with him onto the stage. In Jokela, Finland, Pekka Auvinen sprayed a mixture of gasoline and oil around the school and attempted to set it on fire. James Eagan Holmes, in possibly the most elaborate bomb rigging to date, set up a trip wire linked to explosives in his apartment. Between 11:30 p.m. and 1 a.m. his neighbor heard loud techno music coming from inside (a rare occurrence, she noted) and went to investigate. Finding the door unlocked, she decided not to open it, and as luck would have it, investigators believe the door was rigged to create an explosion and divert authorities from the rampage shooting that Holmes would be undertaking at the midnight screening of *The Dark Knight Rises* at the Century movie theater. At Virginia Tech, an NBC report later stated, "The shootings, which came just four days before the eighth anniversary of the Columbine

High School bloodbath, in which two students killed 13 people and themselves near Littleton, Colo., created panic and confusion at the university, which was already on edge after two weeks of bomb threats" ("Worst U.S. Shooting Ever Kills 33 on Va. Campus," 2007). The Virginia Tech Report says that Cho tacked a bomb threat onto one of the chained doors of Norris Hall on April 16 warning that opening them would set off a bomb. However, a faculty member found it and took it to the Dean's office upstairs, instead of calling the police, as is policy (*Mass Shootings at Virginia Tech* 2009, 89). Though there have been no reports of bombs in the Red Lake, Minnesota shooting, Jeff Weise was identified as having posted on a Neo-Nazi website, "Over a five-month period between March and August 2004, someone identifying himself as Weise posted numerous messages on a talk board hosted by Nazi.org, the website of the Libertarian National Socialist Green Party. The party promotes a Nazi philosophy of racial purity" (Guardian 2005). His screen name: NativeNazi. While many thoughtful analyses of school shootings have underscored the role of masculine identification in the stylization of the acts, they always seem to forget about the important role of the bombs and the planning that goes into these acts. Kalish and Kimmel, for example, in their contribution to understanding second generation shootings or "Columbine Goes to College," have accomplished two important ideas: one, it makes no difference whether, as Cullen argues, the shooters are mentally ill; a sociological analysis is still necessary (something the FBI, with its emphasis on profiling, is prevented from doing). Second, the role of humiliation is key to understanding what they call "suicide by mass murder," and the gendered understanding of masculinity makes it acceptable to carry out violent acts before committing suicide (something men tend to do in larger percentages, they tolerate toxic environments less than women do). However, Kalish and Kimmel make a curious claim, "These young men were all socialized to see violence as a way to prove their manhood. Additionally, they were socialized in an environment that provided access to firearms. The access to guns proved a crucial element of the trajectories, since without such availability, it is unlikely that these young men would have made the same decisions. They may have wanted to end their lives, but without access to guns, their suicides would likely not have been preceded by mass murder" (Kalish and Kimmel 2010, 462). Really? What about the bombs, and the diversions, and the media packages, and all the planning? What about the shooters who killed their parents before they got to the scene of the event? Larkin makes this point very clearly when he outlines the differences between first- and second-generation rampages in Chapter 7 of his book, focusing on the bombing and planning that separate Columbine from these other acts; for nearly six years there were no repeats of Columbine. We need to examine the motivations for these attacks that go beyond simple analysis of "aggrieved entitlement" which we assume to be linked to masculinity in American culture. Not because this aggrieved entitlement does not exist; indeed it does, but usually only for the jocks and Wall Street traders of this world, which lately have been getting their way without much interference (see James 2012).

Without resorting to some kind of reductivist interpretation (i.e., it's the guns, video games, and violent movies), we also cannot include these other shootings in Finland, Norway, Germany, Brazil and Canada (among others) that we know are linked through social media in the realm of the "idea" and some kind of kindred spiritualism in the material existence of these shooters. Even if they do not communicate as a group, there is some isomorphism to their experiences that we can say gives rise to their shared hatred of what they see as "common" people. I agree with Balibar that this works like a kind of fetishism, supporting the potential school violence subject for a time, allowing him to delay (but also plan) the violent event. We will discuss this more in Chapter 4 when we look at the effect of bullying and stigma on the shooters' mental health.

In the American mind, there is a close connection between areas said to "lag" culturally. These areas are the recently de-industrialized areas of the Midwest and the chronically lagging areas of the American South that have the closest connection to a kind of American feudalism with their history of slavery and plantation ancestry. It is almost commonplace to agree that of course these are places that lack modernization and culture. This notion of cultural lag then gets grafted on to ideas about the masculine subjectivities in these spaces. It is often believed that the appeal of the *Turner Diaries* is most often found in these spaces. However, as we noted in the last chapter, to do this we now must include virtually every area of the country with the exception of metropolitan areas. We also cannot further contain this phenomenon to the South and West (as Kass does) and a culture of "honor" since it happens outside these regions as well.[3] Even though Virginia Tech is in the heart of the old South and contains Jefferson Davis's grave (where fresh flowers are arranged daily), Cho and most of the students there hail from Metropolitan D.C., a place often more ruthless than Wall Street in its social competition. Yet another way of containing it is to describe it as a mindset that emerges historically in displaced white men. This mindset develops following the U.S. war in Vietnam; it can be identified as the so-called Rambo effect of a decline in *universal* masculine privilege and heroism. This discourse, powerfully used against returning Vietnam veterans upon their return to the United States, existed not only in the anti-war movements (as is often the only place noted) but also in the VFW (Veterans of Foreign Wars) halls, in the discourse and judgment of the successful war heroes from World War II (Boose 1993). This discourse continues on in the responsible "violent" epics surrounding World War II, the "good ones" that can only recuperate the (white, straight) American male. The honor bestowed on the good war implies a humiliation that is attached to the failures. Someone might also argue that this mindset was cultivated by republican strategists or right-wing parties in Europe in order to have an elusive enemy (the government) after the end of the Cold War to support paranoid or delusional fantasies of these men who perceived themselves to be displaced, and also whose votes could be gained by it (after all, with help from the Supreme Court, it is probably what got Bush narrowly elected in 2000). What is more interesting, however, is understanding the disavowal at the heart of all of these structuring fantasies: if it is dueling or Southern culture, then we (the spectators) do not have to confront the deeper questions about bullying culture or what Balibar calls, in a categorical spin-off from violence, cruelty. To be sure, these acts are cruel: but do they only come from mimicry? From idealizing hatred? Could their source be the first instance of cruelty that produces the new subject, tearing him away from his original identity and forcing him to replace it with abject humiliation? For Žižek, in the U.S. these are rituals (rather than mediations) that we disavow take place, and when they are revealed, we act as if they were free choices, to be excluded or to join (provided we undergo the humiliation) exactly the way that Newman has described them.

Žižek places these rituals of humiliation that are the United States' "obscene underside" at a very important center of American identity, and that which must always be disavowed or ignored so that this identity may continue to function at the core of our collective being. The best analysis so far of the environment at Columbine High School has been provided by Larkin, whose book, as we have seen, actually investigates the "toxic" environment at the school where jocks are celebrated by the administration and teachers (and pretty much allowed to act as predators without any check on their behavior; in fact, Larkin calls them "the Predators") and the evangelical students who were identified by one student as "deep Christians" (see Larkin 2007, Chapter 3, 105–106).

Balibar also points to "soft" violence and cruelty in the statist system. He refers to Bourdieu's work on the children of academically successful parents who experience a separate kind of violence in that they overidentify with the institution and its violence and are unable to overcome, disidentify or walk away from it the way that other differently situated students might who come from working or middle-class backgrounds and can fall back on another way of life (Balibar 2002, 140–141). Lanza had stopped communicating with his father and brother in 2010 who were both working in the same field. His father, a vice president and tax director for General Electric Financial Services division, is now the subject of conspiracy theories that began after it was revealed that James Eagan Holmes's father was a fraud analyst in 2009. Holmes's father has a graduate degree, and Holmes himself was shockingly described as the best student to graduate from the University of California Riverside.[4] Eric Harris and (especially) Dylan Klebold were seen as two of the brightest students at Columbine who blew their potential (reading self-chosen books in class instead of doing the graded work). Teachers describe meeting Tom Klebold and deciding Dylan was brilliant just like him and his intellect was a bit "intimidating." Cho's sister had recently received a graduate degree and was working successfully on the East Coast. Numerous reports discuss how Cho's parents worked 7 days a week to provide a new life for him and his sister. Kazmierzcak was overidentified with academic institutions because he had no others left to fall back on (the tragic separation from his mother and his father's revelation that "she had not changed her mind about him" upon her death, plus the termination of his graduate program at NIU). While he was enrolled in a new program at the University of Illinois, it was not his primary interest, and he began a steady decline, stopped taking his medication and did in fact work (briefly) in a prison. Anders Bering Breivik is an interesting case since he seems to have been viewed as a success in school, someone who helped the bullied and even engaged in his own online (illegal) business selling diplomas in 2003. This business allowed him to move into his own apartment and begin to support himself. By 2006, however, the prosecutor in the case noted that he descended into the video game *World of Warcraft* and spent an entire year playing it. After that, without the funds to live separately, he moved in with his mother and began searching online for the 28 items that would later make up his "uniform" during the attacks. To this case, and his spectacularly cruel *passage à l'acte*, we now turn.

Eurabia

When Žižek echoes Hardt and Negri's claim that the walls that have been erected by liberal capitalism to keep the multitudes out of privileged zones of economic exchange and social inclusion, he is framing the social field in which Breivik directed his attack in Western Europe. This is a regime of discourses, products, commodities and rationalizations that serve to protect certain groups and individuals from contact with the other, while proclaiming multicultural tolerance. Žižek says that commodities are the only object allowed to circulate freely under global capitalism and that people are excluded. Breivik's racist manifesto attempted to justify this limited circulation but laid the blame at the feet of the supposed multicultural relativism of Western societies. Unable to identify with Norwegian Muslims as an already disenfranchised and excluded group living at the margins of European societies in zones of exclusion and bare servitude (they make up only 8% of Norway's population), Breivik mistakes their mere presence in Norway and the empty calls for tolerance made by political leaders with them having achieved a privileged status. Adopting a "settler" mentality, Breviek accuses Muslim immigration of being a threat to the Norwegian welfare state. This is not unlike the confusion in the United States experienced by people who rail against the welfare state while their very economic status is subsidized by it through unnamed sources of welfare in the tax code.

Breivik adopted Fallaci's term for this condition, "Eurabia," but he also took his cues from Samuel Huntington and Patrick Buchanan. It is widely understood that he wrote *2083: A Declaration of European Independence* online using a variety of (often plagiarized) sources. As Feldman argues, it was his "first act of terrorism" as Breivik intended for this manifesto to function as a "terrorist do-it-yourself kit," followed second by the nail bomb at the capital and third by the rampage shooting on Utøya. Feldman calls it "broadband terrorism" in that it inspires those who act "alone," or what will later be called "Lone Wolf terrorists" (Feldman 2012, 193).

Andreas Malm considers the fate of Islamaphobia in Europe, describing it as a "scapegoat fetish." As he says, "As a rule, a fetish is adored and admired, but the Islam and Muslims of Islamophabia are targets of hatred. A fetish is attractive; Muslims are seen to be loathesome." So Malm goes to the origin of scapegoat in Leviticus, where a goat carries off all the sins of the Israelites to a remote place. As he says, "In Islamophobia all the sins of society—be they gender discrimination, job loss, alienation, crime, hollow democracy—are put on the head of the Muslim minority and, discursively to begin with, expelled to a 'remote place.'" As he says, "It answered a profound social need: hemmed-in political energies were channeled in a direction harmless for capital, whose power now blocked other routes leading through social reality. Islam was, in other words, constituted as a negative fetish, reified, personified in the Muslim minority, and ritually abhorred" (Malm 2012, 198).

Vincent W.J. van Gerven Oei argues that Breivik's acts differ from school shooters in three main ways. First, his act does not express an "existential dilemma" to which the main question is "How to perform an act which is fully my own?" and they conclude that such an act would be self-annihilating. I agree except this doesn't make them any different from regular suicides, and these are also exterminations, as I've already argued in Chapter 1. As the quote at the heading of the chapter indicates, Breivik insisted on a logic to his killing that followed that of NATO in its own bombing raids across Eastern Europe and other spaces. Apparently, Breivik also paused his shooting on Utøya to call the police several times and confess. When they did not answer, he resumed his rampage until they arrived, at which time he threw his guns aside and put his hands over his head (Andersson 2012a). As he said later, *"Since they hadn't called me back*, I thought they didn't intend to let me surrender, so I might as well continue until I am killed" (Kissane 2012). Althusser anyone?

Kissane then affirms that Breivik did not commit suicide. Indeed, he was more than happy to greet the police at the island, surrendering with a smile on his face, and his grandstanding at this trial was widely noted in the international press, including his pleasure at hearing his screen name uttered by the prosecutor. Yet, Breivik is reported to have made several references to his impending death in the years and weeks before the attacks, including saving up for a high-class prostitute. When asked in court about suicide, he said that he had considered it at Utøya but decided to stay alive "for my cause" (Kissane 2012). "It was a suicide attack. I did not expect to survive the day," he also stated after justifying the attacks as protection for "his" people whom he labeled "indigenous" (Syson 2012). Later in the trial he called for the death penalty, reiterating his original plan to die. It seems more like he hoped to die from "suicide by state," which would have really turned Norway's self-conception on its head. He did not succeed.

Third, van Gerven Oei claims Breivik doesn't see his act as "an authentic singular act" and instead is very clear, as we noted above, that the publication of *2083* is the first act of terrorism, where he "considers his act only to be the beginning of a pan-European resistance movement against Islam" (van Gerven Oei 2011, 216). On this latter claim, I would argue that Breivik could still see this as an authentic singular act, or he could see it as the next act, giving ideological content to what had only been a formalized ritual to that point. How then, shall we explain the fact that Breivik does not attempt suicide? *Passage à l'acte.* While Breivik was clearly not communicating with the symbolic for a good period of time prior to his acts, he was luxuriating in the fantasy structure provided by the theorists of Eurabia. Islam was a convenient scapegoat for his own personal failures. As van Gerven Oei recounts, Breivik spent a lot of time fretting about his "strength" and "morale" using synthetic Testosterone to bolster it. He also rewarded himself with *World of Warcraft* marathons and expensive champagne to "toast" his impending act (years running, it is alleged that he planned it for nine). His character or "Mag" was female ("Justicar Andersnordic"). As most players and fans of *WoW* can attest, the game is far from militant, and more like a fantasy role-playing game with feudal themes and wizards and dragons. This did not stop Breivik from rewarding himself for his future "martyrdom" with one full year of game play, between 2006 and 2007 when he moved into his mother's Oslo flat. Perhaps Breivik knew he might die and planned for it to be by the police. When they did not shoot him, it was be more evidence of the weakened state of multicultural, "open" Norway in his mind; no doubt, this was a "win-win" proposition. This did not stop Mr. Holden, the prosecutor, from making a connection between the video game and the event. As one news outlet reported:

> Mr Holden portrayed Breivik's progress from this point almost as an extension of his role-playing, starting in 2009, when he bought 36 separate items from eight countries to make his 'Knights Templar' uniform, including an arm-patch brought from a UK supplier, sporting the words "Marxist hunter England", which Breivik altered to read "Marxist hunter Norway". (Orange 2012)

There are Tea Party references in *2083,* as well as other influential sources. Most readers suspect that Breivik was trying to straddle both European and American audiences to make a bridge between them in terms of disaffection. As one commentator put it, though Norway is technically an open society, several experts on right-wing terrorism in the courtroom "iterated that there may be thousands of people in Norway harboring the same ideological position as ABB, albeit not necessarily supportive of his terrorist deeds" (Eide 2012, 280). Furthermore, this is a place where we can begin to flesh out the intermediate stage mentioned earlier: is it the scapegoat fetish that supplies the fantasy structure holding the subject in place until he moves from "intention to act"?

In a remarkable turn of phrase, one theorist said, "If Breivik is now declared mad, the rest of Norwegian society is by definition declared sane" (Walton 2012, 10). In the end, Breivik was declared sane. An initial report released in November 2011 concluded that he was paranoid schizophrenic and under Norwegian law was entitled to psychiatric treatment, not incarceration. However, after harsh criticism, the court appointed two new psychiatrists who pronounced him sane (Andersson 2012, 425). Interestingly, the neologisms that Breivik deployed in his original psychiatric evaluation were seen as evidence of a disorganized mental state, making it characteristic of paranoid schizophrenia. However, as these reports came to light, it was found that these were words commonly used among the far-right groups in Norway (Måseide 2012). Apparently, the psychiatrists were unfamiliar with them. One wonders if Anders Breivik's rhetoric itself is the functional analog of the "obscene underside" of Norwegian culture. Andersson notes that there has been very little critical discussion of structural racism in Norway until the mid-2000s.

Indeed, the dominant national image is that of "innocence," according to Andersson, because of Norway's past colonization by Denmark and then Sweden until its independence in 1905 and memory of Norway's earlier colonial status and the German occupation during the Second World War. These are central aspects of the national imaginary in which Norway tends to be seen as an exception to the Orientalism and racism that marked other colonies and/or occupied nations in Europe during the nineteenth and twentieth centuries. Although Norway's involvement in the transatlantic slave trade is now well-documented (Kjerland and Rio 2009; qtd. in Andersson 2012), research on the discursive constructions of national identity among contemporary Norwegian development works reveals an ongoing construction of Norwegian innocence with regard to historical and contemporary justification (Fretheim 2009, qtd. in Andersson 2012, 419).

By Norwegian law, Breivik was sentenced to 21 years in prison (the strictest term available in that country) which raised more questions outside of Norway than within. As we will see at his trial in the near future, the status of James Eagan Holmes is very similar. His attorneys fought to have him declared insane, even subjecting him to an unorthodox psychological test, and the trial judge finally issued a "not guilty" verdict for him. Later, Holmes's attorneys made a formal request to change his plea to "not guilty by reason of insanity." The problem here is that in a jury trial (which Holmes got in Denver) his peers largely decide his sanity based on the testimony of experts brought by each side, and the definition is very narrow: "*at the time of the crime*, the person did not appreciate the nature or quality or wrongfulness of the acts." And this defense can always be negated by foregrounding the main issue in the cases that inevitably come under scrutiny: planning. For Breivik it seems clearer how this initial diagnosis was allowed under Norwegian law, especially in light of the "culturally inappropriate" label here: "Persistent delusions that are culturally inappropriate or implausible are one of the possible symptoms of paranoid schizophrenia. A person with this diagnosis is considered to have psychosis under Norwegian law. Cognitive abilities may remain intact, which might explain the fact that Breivik was able to successfully plan and complete his horrific attacks" (Måseide 2012). Once the validity of far-right discourse was entered into the social field, Breivik could be labeled sane. One thing is for sure in these cases, a new kind of massacre has entered into the methectic script: lone attackers, largely stylizing and reasoning in similar fashion to second-generation school violence like Columbine, Red Lake, Jokela, Rio de Janeiro, Quebec, Virginia Tech and Northern Illinois have become detached from the "school" referent and now circulate around more recognizably political sites: a labor camp, parliament buildings, military bases, the Boston Marathon, and the office Christmas party. We cannot review all these cases here, and I'll save them for another time, but it is important to note that the media and other scholars tend to separate these acts into different groups. Paton in particular, in following fans on the Internet has found that those with "premeditated" videos and writings achieve a certain status that allows them to be viewed as within the purview of the Columbine event, while others get excluded: "for every Auvinen we get one Kazimierczak" (Paton 2012, 18). I would not let the social meaning of the acts get obscured by either fans or the media, who often have their own agendas to settle in picking and choosing among shooters for inclusion in what might be called a "subculture." Part of the problem is with trying to recognize how these acts may or may not be political, as the Larkin quote attests. To see these acts as political implies they represent the views of a group that is excluded in some way from the formal political sphere of representation. Yet, as we noted in the first chapter, in a control society there is only one way to be: amenable. Any kind of political action taken against the established order is either immediately co-opted by global capital as a new fad to sell, or seen as an expression of terrorism, depending on the subject's religion or ethnicity. As we move further along the spectrum of this violence, some will be labeled "crazy" or seen as the victim's elaborate conspiracies, (Lanza and Holmes) and still others will be called "lone wolf terrorists" even if they have no salient affiliations with actual terror networks but can still be framed as "other." Deleuze has now been repurposed to explain any violent act that either cannot be contained by the social order or media or institutionalized. We now have violent actors who are detached from any violent referent, and we must fight them, but how?

The Post-Ideological Era: The "Lone Wolf Terrorist"

When the bombings first occurred in Oslo, it was made manifest in the media and elsewhere that the common belief was that the perpetrator was most likely of the Islamic faith and a terrorist at the same time. First, most of these "lone wolf terrorists" plan to commit suicide by the end (the only ones who did not were Holmes in Colorado [we can only speculate here] and the Tsarnaev brothers in Boston), so they either literally take the exit option from human life, or, as Johann Galtung has suggested with Breivik, they instantiate a break with the present reality of the human condition through their identification with a historical past: in Breivik's case the date of 22 July is the date of the onset of the Crusades in 1099 when Christian militants stormed Jerusalem, as well as the date of the explosion of the King David hotel by the Jewish terrorist group the Irgun Gang in Jerusalem in 1946. As Galtung also says of Brcivik, he's neither Norwegian nor right-wing (in the sense of the ideology of right-wing parties in Europe):

> I see him as living in the past. The questions he gets in court are too much geared towards the present. You see, he lives at the time of the crusades. He's made his terrible deed, his deed on the 22nd of July. The 22nd of July 1099 the Crusaders conquered Jerusalem. The Knights Templar, he associates with them. But that doesn't mean that he has a group today called the Knights Templar, you see, he thinks, if I should use the word, the Norwegian police are suffering from presentism, too much focusing on the present. (Galtung 2012)

This presentism is interesting. No doubt, as Galtung says elsewhere in his talk with Amy Goodman on *Democracy Now*, Breivik's thoughts do represent some group thinking in Norway that is formalized in political parties elsewhere on the continent; however, Breivik's discursive worldview is neo-fascist in that he wants Muslims to return to wherever they may have immigrated from (even though they are integrated, long integrated, into Norwegian society, and many lost family members in his spree). You can, as Galtung says, substitute "multiculturalism" for "miscegenation" in his discourse and it follows the same logic. Moreover, he points out that Breivik aimed at the "center of decision-making" in bombing the parliament building. He also confessed the decision to go to Utøya came after the fatalities were not as high as he would have liked (he even expressed remorse at the death of those he deemed "innocents") and originally planned to decapitate the former prime minister but could not do it for logistical reasons (Siddique 2013). We can quibble with Galtung over which past Breivik is stuck in, but it's not very useful. He's stuck in a past he never experienced but being there is better than being here in the present. There are groups like this the world over, from fundamentalist Christians in Colorado, to evangelicals in many patches of Central and South America. Apparently, they are also hiding out in that most cherished space of progressives: the Nordic countries! But no one is surprised by Germany, right?

There are a growing number of people who believe in the past over the present apropos of Balibar's "fictive identifications," and this is an effect of trying to arrest it for corporatist goals. The less people are allowed to think outside their modulations, the more they retreat to a past that explains why the present is so bad. We could return to the comments in Chapter 2 here about Littleton, Colorado, being a place that the Enlightenment never touched or Balibar's comments about idealizing hatred. Again, we could mention Žižek's (I think) competitive claim that there can still be a political act that would register in this new global network of media, and then filter down to the people in a way that would incite them to go back to simply an "imaginary relationship to their real conditions of existence," since as Žižek knows, there cannot be a *real* relationship, at least not for long and not without some kind of coherent symbolic mediation. As we have seen with Breivik, right-wing discourses were allowed symbolic expression in his trial because he needed to be tried as sane. Breivik was even awarded a victory recently when he renounced his inheritance from his mother's estate, forever withholding that money from his victims and their families. In a related case, Hasan was allowed to represent himself in the Ft. Hood shooting and entered a defense of "protection of others," meaning he claims he shot his fellow soldiers because they were going to go to Afghanistan and kill Muslims (whom he believes should be protected).[5] Interestingly, the Obama administration allowed this case to be classified as a "workplace" shooting and not an act of terrorism (even though Hasan taunted them in this direction), which made it problematic for the Obama administration vis-à-vis other similar cases.

Going forward we can see that many of these acts are artificially separated from their connections to each other by the media. Usually they use the age of the perpetrator or the target of the attack as a way of distinguishing them. Yet, if we focus on the violence and cruelty itself, we can see that they are profoundly related. In the next chapter, I will make these connections clearer by looking at a cluster of events that happens around 2007–8 that many analysts group together because they refer to each other and seemingly share a semiotic space. However, while I do think they are connected, they are not isolated from attempted attacks prior to them, or seemingly different ones that come after. If we focus on the methectic quality of the acts (that they are each new iterations of the original act, adding their own twist or interpretation) while zeroing in on the ideological conditions of the contemporary control society, mostly found in modular institutions, we will see that they are very, very similar.

4

The Failure of the Middle-Class Social Contract

Everything happens as if attention detached itself from life.

—Henri Bergson, *Matter and Memory*

I am gorging on my entire rage, and one of these days I'm going to let it out and get revenge on all the assholes who made my life miserable. … For those of you who haven't gotten it yet: yes, I'm going to go on a rampage! I don't know what's the matter with me, I don't know what to do, please help me.

—Sebastian Bosse qtd. in Robertz (2007, 58)

Wherever shame is publicly present and mobilized by groups or peers, there is rage. Rage is allowed to float freely as an element in contemporary control societies. It is never acknowledged openly as something connected to an event or the outcome of a punitive gesture, but is usually heaped onto the individual as another index of problematic behavior, such as a failure to comply with society's ever changing standards for ethical conduct. The inherent mobility of shame and rage to elude any collective attempt to map the linearity of cause and effect is what Baudrillard has named the "transparency of evil." Whether we are seeing Serbs committing outright atrocities in front of television screens or American soldiers mistreating Iraqi prisoners or Harris and Klebold aping for the cameras inside the library of Columbine High School, we are seeing the reality effect of the transparency of evil, that is, the radical failure of ethical narratives and fables of responsibility (Keenan 2004) linked to social contracts between subjects and forms of governmentality;

that is, the failure of civil society we discussed in Chapter 2 apropos of Balibar's insights about civility. The kind of cruelty these ultra-subjective forms of violence result from is more like hostage taking in the sense that Baudrillard described it as "dissuasive terrorism" where it "experimentally stages an impossible exchange or the historical loss of the scene of exchange … and the social contract" (Baudrillard qtd in Rubenstein 2010, 225). Ritualized mass killing in civil spaces is transpolitical in that it stages the obscenity of our mass culture. In this sense, Larkin may have been only partially correct that these were political acts; we may more properly call them "transpolitical," which has a slightly different meaning in that it acknowledges that the context has changed; there are no longer *any* properly political acts, contrary to Žižek's emphatic claim that some sovereign acts can still be effected through some form of divine violence.

As we saw in the last chapter, both Žižek and Balibar get "lost" in the politics of meaning. For ultra-subjective violence to "make sense" requires *political work* in an era where both those terms are unsettled and confounded. Both "politics" and "work" have transcended their original (or last and still most deployed) meaning. Aronowitz recognized this about work over two decades ago in *Post-Work*. The problem with the "post" prefix is that it makes work a problem of the past, rather than focusing on how the future has been co-opted by our continuous present. Unable to project a future and stuck in an interminable present that presents itself as utopia, our subjects choose to exit this system but not before engaging in violence against others in it. It is only in looking at these forms of violence (indeed they are cruel in their specificity) as the staging of a lack or absence of politics, of civil society, and of civility, that we can see how and why they follow the particular paths they do. They "stylize," meaning they seek to conform to a particular style that leads us away from the realist depiction of a story, of representation. Each of our perpetrators seeks to conform more closely to the original script, adding their own details: trench coats, baseball caps, evocative phrasing on the body or clothing, hand guns, automatic weapons, groin shields, etc. Furthermore, each of these stylizations trope off of a particular frame that will interpellate sectors of the public into believing it is a question of some kind of cultural difference or schism produced by social dislocation: gaming, guns, bombs, violent film and television, military garb, Nietzschean discourses of superiority. The question this chapter addresses is: Where is the failure "to hold" found in public narratives and critical theory, and where is it grafted onto proposals for understanding rage and violence in contemporary society? In my earlier work, I found this failure in contemporary society to occur when young people slipped through a generational crack that was formed during the progressive era of the United States's civil rights movement ideologies and their subsequent policy manifestations in shorthand rules and diagnostic tools formulated by experts. This is what the study group designated by President Bush to analyze the information breakdown at Virginia Tech has called "information silos."[1] In other words, the unsaid consensus between the public and authorities is that they do not want to understand these violent events, they only want to predict them. Thus, they have the same reaction to terrorism, which is to provide more information to governments and other authorities. The most popular preventive tool, "leaks" of information by a potential perpetrator to peers and elsewhere, is certainly a valuable short-term solution; however, this tends to be where thinking about this topic *stops*.

In this chapter, I will examine several commentators' readings and proposals from a number of different popular culture arenas: sociology of education, the film industry, the culture industry, humanitarian relief agencies and finally, the therapeutic industry as they read Kosovo and/or Columbine as coterminus events in media and public life. Each of these theses proposes their own kind of "cultural lag" as explanation for the violent and cruel events. I argue that cultural lag, a sociological thesis that enjoys attention during times of social dislocation and crisis, particularly of the technological sort, provides the "primary framework" for the media's analysis of traumatic events (Goffman 1986). The social dislocation is not led by the technology; rather, technology (or software, one and the same) mediates the *compromise formations* that produce the social dislocation in the first place. We act *as if* these interactions replace civil society.

While these cruel events are indeed a reaction to extreme deprivation and often bullying, they are not epiphenomenal; that is, they are not the byproduct of technological advances (even and especially in social media) that our human culture lags behind. Take under consideration the common question posed to a school violence theorist in the late 1990s: I was bullied. I hated my life. I fantasized about revenge on my bullies. Why did I not shoot everyone at school the way that these kids do? Out of this line of inquiry comes the inevitable conclusion that it must be new advances in society that youth get hold of and that motivates them to become violent. However, if the entire nature of our social being has shifted dramatically over the past 15 (or in some cases, 40) years, doesn't it make sense to see that the context has changed and made new forms of violence possible that arise out of new forms of cruelty and their disavowal? The difference, I am suggesting, is not in the technological advances, it is in our disavowal of them. *We are in it; we simply find ways to disavow it.* This is embedded in all the arguments about violent video games, automatic weapons, YouTube, and masculinity. What they presume, in Hegelian fashion, is that we are always already stuck inside some iteration of the *aufhebung*, waiting for the dialectical process to work out the kinks and show us how this present had gifts to offer (this is their most progressive form), or they assume that these are objects that introduce sin and vice into the world and must be abolished to recover a more innocent past (a more theological form). Ingar Solty has deconstructed the boundaries between these two, collapsing them into a modern day interpretation of "sin": "Pathologizations and culturalizations are hardly modernized versions of medieval witch hunts. Saying someone is simply 'crazy' or video games made him crazy, i.e., took over his will, is saying someone is 'possessed by the devil' in more modern terms. And it is no coincidence that the word 'evil' is commonly used by commentators and politicians to denounce violence that is not state violence" (Solty 2012, 2). In this our violent school shooters become framed as unwitting and confused, led astray by technology they are obviously too young to understand (innocent, in some sense), or they are using the technology to adopt poses that are far too mature (and inappropriate) for them to understand yet they identify with their content, and this usually said to display aspects of violent masculinity. Yet, as we've seen violent masculinity is perhaps in many cases tautological; there is no "good" masculinity, at least not one that is popularly known and held up as ideal.

As we have seen the way the masculinity argument is made in many thoughtful analyses is the result of a kind of default to commonly understood tropes, coupled with the vague notion that most of these new technological advances are viewed as exclusive expressions of masculine subjectivity. In this, one often overlooks the number of young women who play violent video games, or perhaps just imagines they're not playing them because of the mass media saturation surrounding violence, video games and masculinity. We are bombarded with arguments and implicit generalizations about violence in the media, in masculinity and in video games, but the connection is never satisfactorily made. We can see why it is so popular though, because a cursory look at film and video games, and even the larger political arena, demonstrates a serious rollback on any kind of gender equality, with male superiority as the sign of the times. However, this is probably not the objective driving it, though it may be a happy fringe benefit for those in power (women are a cheap source of the flexible labor that is now a large part of advanced economies). The problem is with representation itself. We do not need a "civility" in the sense that Hegel understood it as the state providing meaning to the violence (rationalizing it). In this, these episodes are framed retrospectively to have occurred so we could progress as a culture and society and find newer and better forms of civilized organizational living. So, for example, in one version, the violent film version, the interpretation of bullying and the dynamic that allows it to thrive is that it seduces the subject to act out what director Derek Cianfrance has called a "ballet of violence," which he attributes to the contemporary *cinematic* fetishization of violence:

> I feel like oftentimes recently, I've been seeing violence which is just fetishized and violence that is just cool. If I have to see another slow-motion bullet come out of a gun and hit someone in the cheek and spray their brain, paint their brains on the walls, I'm gonna throw up because I don't think it's beautiful. I don't think it's art. I don't think it's cool, it's aesthetic, a fetish, you know? To me, violence—I wanted to deal with violence in this movie not in a viscous way, not in a "How realistic can I paint the brains?" [way]. Not, "How can I make the sound of the skull crack?" I wanted to deal with violence in a narrative way. I wanted you as you're watching this movie to experience the story of violence, to experience all these choices and adrenaline and decisions that lead to a violent moment with a gun. A gun is so fast—so fast, if you've ever shot a gun. It's so fucking fast. The speed at which there's no going back from. It happens in real time, and so there's no sanctity of flashback. There's no going back, and there's a sense when you're watching this film [*The Place Beyond the Pines*] that it's like, "no, no." There's a transcendent moment of denial that happens in the audience. (Cianfrance qtd. in D'Addario 2013)

True enough. But this is still on the terrain of images and representation, which is not where political violence is figured. Cianfrance is describing gratuitous violence, which means it does *not* enhance or change the meaning of the story being told. As Galloway says, it makes for affective responses, but no authentic action. This works alongside Galloway's depiction of cinema as the "snuff film." In *Gaming*, he contrasts film with gaming in terms of representation; as he says "the subjective shot [in cinema] is a close cousin of the snuff film, connected as they are through the coupling of predatory vision and the impotence of the gaze" (Galloway 2006, 53). The important point that he makes in this chapter, and that is helpful for us in understanding how we view our cases of violence, is that the first person shooter game (which mobilizes the POV, point of view screen shot) originates in cinema. Filmic representation of the POV is simply a more rudimentary version of the same gaze deployed in FPS (first person shooter) games which can now use digital enhancement to invite the viewer into a world; montage "wanes," but the three-dimensional unfolding of worlds increases. What FPS games allow the user to do is to be active rather than passive; as he says, games are "sadistic" but film is "masochistic: in film, the subjective perspective is marginalized and used primarily to effect a sense of alienation, detachment, fear or violence, while in games the subjective perspective is quite commonly used to achieve an intuitive sense of motion and action in game play" (Galloway 2006a, 40). Hence, violent video games (or any video games for that matter) do not cause cognitively able individuals to become violent; neither do films, except maybe out of frustration. However, the control allegories that they mobilize and that these particular individuals use and draw upon to construct their ritual is "gamic," but in a way no different from games that have been played for centuries. What is different is that they are played on computers, which, as Galloway says are "ethical" in the sense that games display "a broad set of principles for practice within some normative framework" (ibid., 57). And for Galloway, at least with *World of Warcraft (WoW)*, that normative framework is given by the information economy, a "new socioeconomic landscape, one in which flexibility, play, creativity, and immaterial labor—call it ludic capitalism—have taken over from the old concepts of discipline, hierarchy, bureaucracy and muscle" (ibid., 27). What might be common to all of our cases here is an *identification* with past acts (the original being Columbine) and the rhythms established for them is featured in something we are generically calling game play. He cites Huizinga:

> The rite, or 'ritual act' represents a cosmic happening, an event in the natural process. The words 'represents' however, does not cover the exact meaning of the act, at least not in its looser, modern connotation; for here 'representation' is really *identification*, the mystic repetition or re-presentation of the event. The rite produces the effect which is then not so much shown figuratively as actually reproduced in the action. The function of the rite, therefore, is far from being merely imitative; it causes the worshippers to participate in the sacred happening itself. (qtd. in Galloway 2006a, 22)

This is how ideology functions in the present moment, not according to representation within some fixed field of meaning. Instead networking can take random data and produce conformist results, and yet the social field is in flux, largely determined by market forces (destabilized ones at that) not democratic or even cultural norms, as Balibar says, "Gewalt." Ideology also does not gesture at a failed political project since what do shooters leverage in suicide since there are no martyrs for capitalism? (We will discuss martyrdom in the next chapter). Finally, it is not even the result of a structure (as in Althusser and in Balibar's most recent universalism). Workplaces, schools and public spaces are now "blended" as they have been cracked open by corporate interests. Institutions of former democratic arrangements are now forced to respond to each new market demand (standards, efficiency, profit motives, etc.). Instead, it is "better understood as a problematic, that is to say a conceptual interface in which theoretical problems arise and are generated and sustained precisely as problems in themselves" (Galloway 2012b, 58). Galloway suggests, following Wendy Chun, that we view software as ideology, and the interface between software and technology as the "unworkable" one that agitates. What this means is that "the interface effect is also a kind of segregation effect whereby data is relegated to the realm of ideas and machines to the realm of technology" (ibid., 59). Hence our identical "unworkable" need to look at the *content* of the computer's hard drive, to see what sites or games the perpetrator might have been playing and then translate this back (awkwardly) into a narrative we understand, usually by referencing the violence or obscenity of the content. Again, a kind of automatic reflex to link up with representation. Instead, we should view the connection between the user, the computer/software and our society as one. We are all networked; it is only the illusion that we stand outside this relationship that allows us to disavow what we've already mentioned, following Galloway, are the algorithms that structure our everyday life. As one reviewer put it, "mastering a game means mastering its underlying algorithm, a process that he [Galloway] suggests enables a player to recognize real world algorithms of elite control" (William 2007, 75). Galloway, following Chun again, emphasizes that the focus on sight in thinking about representation, while not always flawed, may be in this case: "the separation between the visual and the machinic in software is important because it is an allegory of the social" (Galloway 2012b, 63). We will return to this in the conclusion. For now it is important to understand that what is ideological about video games is not the images, but the logic embedded in software generally. We are all mediated by it, whether we surf the net, pin stuff in a fetishistic frenzy on Pinterest, amass "friends" on Facebook, stream instant content or trade stock. Video games hold out the promise of agency through their elimination of the barriers imposed by the symbolic, yet they also impose a ruthless social in the form of other players' attempts to thwart a player's aims.

For the perpetrators who play video games, the games' emphasis on action is probably the most appealing aspect about them, allowing them to vent what most commentators rightly argue are their feelings of "impotent rage" at the complex power dynamics they cannot confront. Recall how Harris reconfigured his game to more closely resemble some of the social dynamics at Columbine. Moving outside Columbine, it has been most closely demonstrated between the acts occurring in 2007 and 2008 between Virginia Tech and Finland where the shooters mimic one another's media poses. Indeed from 2007, basically starting at Virginia Tech, which we've already mentioned stages a second spectacular incarnation of the Columbine script, the shooters in Finland and Germany begin to use the "pose" manifesto that they distribute immediately prior to engaging in their acts, online. Unlike Cho, they do not mail their packet to the media (and allow them to decide what to air) but bypass it altogether and post online. Their poses are eerily similar. Finnish police later established the YouTube connection and some online contact between Pekka-Eric Auvinen (Jokela, November 2007) and Maati Saari (Kauhajoki, September 2008) (Allen 2007). Paton (2012) and van Gerven Oei and Staal reproduce them in their publications, showing the still shots of them pointing guns at their heads and the camera, reminiscent of Cho, but also of what viewers of *The Columbine Tapes* reveal (which were only shown to media and other select representatives). Kazmierczack admired Cho but did not make a media packet, and no hard drive was found, so perhaps this is why he is downgraded by "fans." At first sight, what is in these poses is none other than a kind of juvenile mimicry, so we default to the copycatting thesis. And perhaps there is some truth in this, but the perpetrators do stage these events and seem think critically about timing them to coalesce with media openness (i.e., not during the early years of the war on terror). Are these media packages and web manifestos a parody of representation? Also, note that none of the subsequent shootings in the U.S. feature these media packets, perhaps because the brand is so well-known it doesn't need images to frame it for viewer consumption. It is already understood what is happening. Yet, to return to Cho since he had the most elaborate of the packages and his message has been summarily dismissed as "meaningless" by most media, is there some kind of message that transcends politics as usual?

As E. J. Carvalho has said of Cho, he "transfers the value of self to a poetics that will outlive him" in his acts and through his (media selected) political manifesto (Carvalho 2010, 416). For van Gerven Oei and Staal, these perpetrators act from a position of depression which is the only (and last) form of resistance against the "digital mediacracy" where mass media come to structure all of our understandings and experiences outside of real time and space (2009, 5). This is evident in the way that mass media creates a set of uniform narratives to explain the actions of these perpetrators:

> Having media sources pick and create an organizing principle necessarily leads to the exclusion of other practices, reactions, sentiments, and conditions. Similarly, creating a narrative for Cho—one of mental illness—is a parallel construction to organizing September 11th around the narrative of "trauma." (Kolenic 2009, 1033)

It works like a pull-down menu: the icon for it might read "label" and the choices to scroll through for selection: "autistic," "video gamer," "mentally ill," "bad life," "gun enthusiast," "Neo-Nazi." Similarly, Margaret Price analyzes the rhetorical devices used in the *Virginia Tech Report* that frame him as part of a mental illness narrative without ever having to explain it by using paraliptic statements, a common feature in coverage of rampage violence: "Paraliptic statements suggest truths while simultaneously denying doing so. Saying to a friend, "I'm not even going to comment on how ugly that sweater is" is an example of paralipsis. As she argues, "the Report manages to establish a connection between Cho's condition and autism while also maintaining deniability for doing so" (Price 2011, 154). These paralepses function like compromise formations, making it seem like the answer has been found without having to follow it up with evidence or solutions to the problem it indicts. They are ubiquitous in the media coverage of each event.

Increasingly, our experiences in telepresent reality are twofold: mass mediated interpretations of events are ones that, as Kac says, "transmit information unidirectionally from one point to many points (television, radio, etc.)" (Kac 1998), but we could also add social media which now allow for, as Galloway says, the venting of all types of affective subject positions. Baudrillard might call this the "obscenity" of our communication. Neither, it seems, allow for any kind of dialectic, as might be required in a civil society. Instead, the acts become transpolitical events, demonstrating the futility of any attempt at communication. As Carvalho writes, "I would go so far as to say that Seung-Hui sought agency through performed violent *détournements* for a society that appeared to him as incapable of listening and seeing anything but a media-constructed reflection of itself" (Carvalho 2010, 423). For this reason, it should not be surprising that many of the perpetrators have been diagnosed with communication disorders, whether autism or selective mutism, or depression *prior* to their acts and have spent much time being shunted from one ineffective therapeutic organization to another with little acknowledgment that they are primarily interpellated as stigmatized individuals in a supposedly normally functioning civil society. And there is no exit from this stigma: pharmaceutical companies can make drugs to help alleviate the side effects of the ones they made for your first (and all subsequent) behavior disorders, and they are everywhere; there is no "America," as Balibar said, where one can take up a new life. You can often only be medicated to "like" this static time and place.

For other related acts, like those of Hasan at Ft. Hood, the idea may come from having seen it in mass media (or from the repetitive recounting of violence that Hasan no doubt heard from soldiers as a military psychiatrist). Indeed, in a footnote Carvalho notes the odd similarities between the existence of Hasan and Seung-Hui. While the latter referred to himself as "?" in his writing and class assignments, in his dorm suite and online (even creating a MySpace page for "?"), Hasan was referred to without irony by his apartment/occupational peers as "Number Nine," the number on his apartment door, as Carvalho writes, "most acknowledged him as one would a prisoner, by a reductive numeric moninker" (Carvalho 2010, 425, f.n. 13). Yet, the comparisons have been noted between Hasan and other school shootings since he targeted soldiers only, went to a vaccination depot on the base (where he no doubt knew he would find many soldiers in congress who were going to be deployed to Afghanistan), as well as his own impending deployment which most close to him have described as a trigger. He had tried to get out of the military but was given inadequate information.[2] As another army psychiatrist stated, "This is a guy who's been in a very protected secure environment and people are saying it's time for you to take your training wheels off and go," and "I think the die was cast before he even arrived at Fort Hood" (Cox 2009). For these reasons, it is difficult to continue to maintain the school/work/classical rampage distinction outlined by Böckler et al.:

1. "Classical" rampage: A usually adult perpetrator kills at random in a public place without immediately identifiable reason.
2. Workplace violence: Cases of severe violence at the workplace standing in direct connection with the perpetrator's work and/or psychosocial and other experiences at work. (see also Rugala 2004)
3. School shootings/rampage school shootings: These are mostly committed by adolescent perpetrators and occur at school or in a school-related place such as the schoolyard or bus stop. The location is specifically chosen, often for its symbolic meaning to the perpetrator who wishes to take revenge on the community, or to experience or demonstrate power. (Böckler et al. 2012b, 4)

This latter category excludes specific motives, as if it were obvious to the public why people shoot up schools (no need for a motive, we all get it, we hated high school and felt powerless: "revenge").[3] In the first instance, what is the relevance of maintaining a difference between the school and the workplace unless one can identify a specific motive for each of them? If the motive is specific then these are likely to be truly personal acts of revenge against specific targets in either case. This was certainly the case in 2002 when Robert Steinhäuser charged into his school in Erfurt, Germany, and targeted specific teachers and individuals, warning others to go away, even people he did not know. After Steinhäuser, U.S. media went gleefully amok ("finally, someone else has a shooting like Columbine! It's not just something peculiar to the U.S."), but they failed to see the critical distinction. After Steinhäuser, Germany would experience two more shootings in 2006[4] and 2009 that more closely resembled the methectic script we are following here. In the second one, authorities at the school were alerted to Tim Kretschmer's presence by a loudspeaker announcement in code developed after the 2002 incident, "Mrs. Koma (Amok) is coming," which means an amok shooter is on the loose and alerted teachers to lock classrooms to deny him entry. The term is similar to the U.S. version of "going postal," developed after the short run of U.S. Post Office workplace shootings/sword slayings running from 1986 to 1993 perpetrated by "disgruntled workers." In 2006, Bastian Bosse, like Kretschmer, a former student at the school he attacked, used smoke bombs to distract school inhabitants.

To return, why even make the distinction between workplace and school shootings? We have, thus far, been referring to them as civil society mass killings, followings Solty's observations of James Eagan Holmes. It is impossible to tell the difference between them in the contemporary era. This was finally the case in the San Bernardino shootings which also complicated the differences between terrorism and the workplace shooting; FBI authorities could not decide on a motive, desperately searched for a terrorist motive but found none in the end. We no longer have authorities in schools or workplaces, just, allegiance to protocol or the code. As to the distinction between adults and adolescents, they are really no longer useful as most of these acts have been by men in their 20s over the past five years, and at least two of them are probably "school-related" but ten years after the fact, as with Lanza and Olivieria targeting their former elementary schools. What situates them together is the similarity in the actions undertaken, the randomness (or seeming randomness) of the targets and the fact that none of them have had an "easily identifiable reason." Classical, finally, means of the past, and that's where those shootings should stay. It may be interesting to note that there was once a woman shooter who didn't like Mondays and inspired a song, or to insist that Marc Lépine be included because his acts were so offensive to our egalitarian sensibilities. These latter acts are isolated from one another, separated by years, sometimes decades, and completely distinct. They conform more to the classical shooting parodied in *The Jerk*, where the shooter pulls names out of a phone book and targets folks in public because he quit smoking and his wife left him. They conform to an era when the rift between members of civil society was not so atomized as to produce widespread panic and generate the mass media frenzy and cataloging that we witness today. They also did not encourage social scientists to study them, but were the subjects of FBI profilers or mass market true crime. And they no longer take place. They were not telepresent events. None of those perpetrators could imagine the media detailing their crimes, or turning them into a kind of antihero[5], reminiscent of Cho's "poetics" (we'll return to this in the next chapter).

My suggestion is to begin looking at the specific features of the acts themselves: do they target people randomly (perhaps with some filters applied, like civilians versus peers), in a specific place where optimal damage may be inflicted, and are they suicidal, or at least losing touch with reality? Finally, do they occur after Columbine? This is, as I have already argued, a decisive temporal break in the logic of school or rampage violence. It is not just that after 2006, some of them can share information about the acts through a heterogeneous social via YouTube, it is that after 1999, reality itself became *telepresent*. To live is not to make meaning but to be seen.

One last thought on video games. What about physical training and hand-eye coordination? The sheer number of rounds fired at the scenes in many of these cases far outweighs their accuracy: Columbine, 188 rounds; Virginia Tech, 174; Newtown, 154; and so on. Not to mention the number of rounds stockpiled beforehand and carried to the scene; in each case it is nearly triple of that fired. This is important because one of the common arguments about video games is that they perfect the shooter's skills, making him a better, more accurate shot. As we've seen, the ratio of shots fired to the actual harm done is fairly large, so these are not very accurate shooters. Also, each of them introduces some kind of version of their own "enabling acts," as Galloway says, whether it is a diversion, smoke screen (Holmes), trapping victims on a island (Breivik), in classrooms (Weise, Cho, Auvinen, Saarti, and Lanza), confronting an unsuspecting lecture hall from behind the curtain on the stage (Kazmierczak), and so on. There is also what might be called the big diversion: where shooters stage another scene elsewhere to occupy the police (Cho in the dormitory murders, Holmes in the elaborate bomb set up at his apartment, Weise in the murder of his grandfather and partner, Breivik in bombing the parliament building). The FBI agent that analyzed the events at Red Lake admitted that this could have been a diversion (to get police to go to his home and be preoccupied there) but also could not help but invalidate that premise by sticking to the strict definition of "pre-event homicide," which could also "prevent them from going forward with the shooting" (O'Toole 2012, 186). But as we've seen, if they mimic existing stereotypes about domestic violence or terrorism, there is little need for the perpetrator to worry about getting caught since they look more like an act of hegemonic masculinity or international conflict (in the dorm at VTU, it would look like a failed romance between the G.A. and a resident; in the case of Weise, his grandfather and his domestic partner in a murder-suicide). So, while we wring hands over the type of weapon (assault) or background checks (in the U.S. at least), this type of legislation will not stop these acts in particular. Making the case for policy change based on them is dangerous because it will backfire when they happen again. The best case for gun control is to prevent accidents, but this still does not deal with the over 200 million small arms already in circulation within the United States, nor with the other millions (est. 500 million) circulating the globe that are manufactured by the U.S., Russia,

China, Germany and France (in that order) (Martina 2013). In many ways, the citizen/civilian is like the impotent film viewer, unable to respond to what's happening, but caught in its processes. How we represent these problems in terms of power and control is important.

The difference between cinematic representation and gamic action is that in one, the viewer/user is, as Galloway says, "impotent" and cannot respond to what's happening on the screen, and in the other the user is active, moving through an unfolding milieu. So, to return to Cianfrance, he is making representations of violence in a medium, specifically film, that cannot represent violence in its current social form; that is, its every day *grinding* allegorical significance. Cianfrance is representing violence through narrative and image, something that no longer happens in a politically significant way in real life given our mass mediated realities. Oftentimes, this is the "unthought known" (Bollas) of commentary about media violence. Empirical researchers have a very hard time proving the connection between watching violent images and becoming violent. Society resists the urge to put violence, when it occurs, up against the the allegorical test: does it convey some kind of symbolism or meaning? Most of our cinematic violence is senseless; as people often remark about it, it is gratuitous and adds nothing to the story, or makes no commentary on contemporary politics and social issues. Increasingly, many Hollywood films for example, *are laughable* because of their gratuitous violence. As Galloway argues, one of the problems with analyzing social issues in the current control society is that we keep going back to representation, in still images, or images of violence. As he argues, the only (largely ineffective) response to them is affective, and affect studies are on the rise. Affect simply gets mapped back onto ratings: as in "you decide," in news and entertainment. So, let's attempt to put the violence and cruelty back into an allegorical framework where it might even be "figurable," that is, "accessible to our imaginations" (Jameson 1977, 845). Before doing so, it is helpful to have a contrasting example that allows us to link back up with our central concerns about the breakdown of civil society.

The theoretical framework for beginning my analysis is Stanley Aronowitz's twinning of Kosovo and Columbine since its starting point is looking at the social contract and its necessity for upholding mediation between agencies in democratically constructed political systems. In the next chapter, I detail the cruelties perpetrated by Seung-Hui Cho, the disgruntled English major at Virginia Polytechnic University, who reopened the wounds of Columbine and declared in his manifesto a war on the rich and purported to leave a generational legacy to his "brothers and sisters." Before that, however, we look at the overlooked case of Jeff Weise and its similarities to Columbine and Breivik in Norway. Finally, we will look at Steven Kazmierzcak, another overlooked case (often mentioned, but rarely discussed) I would argue, because he disrupts our media categorizations so disturbingly, making the connection to cruelty and morality more central than all other perpetrators. In Columbine, the patterns in the rage are taken up, for Aronowitz, in middle-class format. Thus, the control allegories that we might look for later will be structured by a partial reading of his essay.

Kosovo/Columbine

There are two underlying similarities between Kosovo and Columbine that most commentators would not admit to seeing or believing. According to Stanley Aronowitz, both events are failures of a kind of middle-class social contract; for Columbine it is the middle class of youth in the suburban United States, for Kosovo (and indeed all of Yugoslavia, perhaps even more so for Sarajevo) it is the failure of the "second world" as a model example of the new international middle class that would have been created following the switch to market economies after the break up of the Soviet Union. It was imagined that it would uplift itself through a kind of international form of social ascription (of course with the help of the World Bank) into the first world, or at least its sphere of influence and values. By 1996, even then U.S. Secretary of State Albright was hoping to integrate Eastern European states even further into the western economy and cultural mindset by extending NATO membership to them during and following the bombings of Kosovo. Perhaps it would bask in the glowing light of the transatlantic alliance hoping one day to eventually be let in, but this was not the case in the spring of 1999—on either side of the Atlantic—where the alliance between two worlds was breaking down: the alliance between middle-class youth and schools and the alliance between second world nation-states and the international order of development. Now, nearly two decades ago following the events, several recent ones signal our interest in their link to capitalism, democracy and ideas about development that can be linked to profound failures: the domestic "treasons" triggered by the global war on terror and the massacre at Virginia Tech. What these events foreshadowed, however, was not an era of containment or integration, but one of outlaw politics, stigma and increasing forms of security that signal a loss of belief in civil society and capitalist culture. The outcasts created by these events are more and more convinced that the exit option is preferable to any kind of negotiation, remediation or mass communication. It is in this chapter that I will lay out just how a non-cognitive form of action, an action delinked from the rationality expected of democracy and the tolerance presupposed by civil society but nonetheless one that is communicable to its would-be adherents traces out the very patterns of rage for its audience: future actors. The tracing out of this non-cognitive action prepares the reader for our discussions in Chapter 6, where we confront the technologies of the virtual and their use by citizens and soldiers to immerse themselves in realities other than the physical. Those who take the exit option also immerse themselves in the virtual in order "to know" the vulnerabilities and weaknesses of their enemies: those who live in civil society without mediation, negotiation or mass communication but pretend as if they do. But first, let's examine just what it means to take the exit.

Taking the Exit Option

Stanley Aronowitz persuasively argued this case of middle-class social breakdown in "Essay on Violence," where he compared Kosovo, specifically the NATO intervention in Kosovo, one that violated prior international security arrangements and then existing international law with the episodes of school shootings that signified an abandonment of middle-class refusal of violence as a means to resolve disputes in the United States. This can also be expanded to other cases in Norway, Germany, Finland, and Brazil. Contrary to "conventional wisdom" (read: received sociological opinion), he argued, Columbine represented the deconstruction of the boundary between the use of violence in the United States and the agents who are thought to use it with just cause. We tell ourselves a story, he writes, that only the lower class or the poor use violence as a means of resolving disputes because the systems of justice designed to arbitrate for citizens is unevenly applied against their interests. Knowing this, the poor have no reason to follow the dispute mechanisms in society or to use the law to solve problems amongst themselves or other social class actors. Likewise, those of color are more than likely to come to the conclusion that the use of violence is appropriate over white Americans because the law discriminates against them in the settling of disputes and in policing and legal modes.[6] This is the useful distinction that Protevi takes from Delueze and Guattari by placing it between molar and modular actions. Aronowitz is on the molar plane. And, of course, he admits from the outset, violence is most likely to be used against women of all social classes as a means of keeping them from changing places in the system or experiencing freedom in a way they see as appropriate.[7] In sum, because the male white middle classes have the illusion of liberty as provided by the social contract, they must play the game without violence.

However, the middle-class social contract was breaking down since it was not even the outliers that we admit occasionally use violence from the middle class that are the ones using it, the "extreme individual cases of severe mental imbalance such as serial killers, wanton pedophiles, angry lovers, and unusual family disputes" that give truth to the lie that middle-class citizens have renounced violence (Aronowitz 2000, 217). To clarify, the middle-class social contract is precisely this: "In exchange for renouncing force as a means of resolving differences, individuals and groups submit to the rule of 'law' which assures justice and restricts the arbitrary exercise of authority" (ibid.). Thus, whenever one of these properly middle-class (male) eruptions takes place, we find the media trying to contain them either to the category of "psychopath" or "enemy combatant," depending on where they can fit them in, at least in the United States. Now that each case seems to include perpetrators who are legally adults, these categories become even more important, as we've seen with the Tsarnaev brothers and James Eagan Holmes. Middle-class citizens are increasingly "opting out" of the terms and conditions of the social contract which demands they renounce violence. Historically, they have, following Hobbes taken up this social contract and renounced violence in any form to resolve disputes. For this renunciation of violence, they receive in return three options or choices for dealing with their subjection that he borrows from Albert O. Hirschman which include "conferring loyalty on those in power, *exercise voice in criticism* of leadership, yet accept to remain within the system when they are defeated when calling for leadership change, or *exit the system* and give up any benefits or rights conferred upon them from it" (ibid.). Whereas the Health and Human Services report following the Virginia Tech shooting would have the public believe that the problem lies with a blockage of information flows between social service agencies, Aronowitz's framework retains the idea that citizens in democracies make "choices" about how to participate in the social contract. While all the evidence was pouring out of media outlets to confirm Cho's mental illness as cause for the shootings, the media could not help but compare the event to past shootings where mental illness reports were not so readily available, as in Columbine.

Eric Harris and Dylan Klebold were framed as many things: gay, racist, "failed joiners," juvenile delinquents and atheists, but the war on terror had not yet arrived, so a categorization like "information silos" could not yet make an appearance on the media scene. This was in spite of the fact that the public was angry that their diversion records were not followed up on by the Jefferson County police department, as well as the reports made by Brooks Brown's parents. *That* kind of reflex would only occur after American society was broken in by global terror events and threats and urged to trade privacy for information sharing among government authorities. Instead, Harris and Klebold can be clearly understood as having taken the exit option. Aronowitz argues specifically that they gave up on the middle-class social contract that rests on the refusal of violence for resolving disputes (So, in many ways, we can imagine them as having a choice because significant events that prompted legislation infringing on privacy and agency autonomy have made it possible for the public to put the blame on a lack of information, rather than the outright refusal of violent perpetrators). It is the media, police and other authorities who cannot admit they have *made a choice* in exiting. Had we had our systems more networked, the Jefferson County authorities may have been able to track them before they committed their acts (indeed, this is what almost all the analysts of this case agree upon). It is important to remember that the middle classes are caught within the system of democratic representation as alibis for the rest of the system's inequities. The bind that they were/are caught in is precisely this: they cannot give up the middle-class criticism option because they will remain caught in the system of oppression—there is no exit option for the middle class, for it seems their very specificity, as a class, is this promise to remain within the social contract; they must remain faithful, they are the alibi of the entire system. Furthermore, as we've seen with our obscenity of communication by mass media, their criticism is continuously co-opted by the mass media and other outlets; they do not have the benefit of feeling like they have been heard, unless it is within some kind of poll that is framed for the benefit of the organization that commissions it. Others are let off the hook, at the high end and the low end of the social class spectrum; exit options are morally accepted yet punished severely in the latter case and virtually celebrated as heroic acts of leadership (I would argue) in the former one. What is supposed to alleviate the burden that the middle class inordinately bears for the survival and longevity of polities based on rule of law and the social contract is that they can have their day in court and feel like they've been heard, even if the outcome is not favorable to their cause. This is the middle-class "subterfuge" in which they can protest through means provided by the governmental system and sublimate the rage and disappointment they may feel at being denied full satisfaction of their demands. The poor are disavowed completely by the social contract, and so the exit option is presented to them as replacement for the option of dissent or voice criticism, provided they go quietly to live in the gated corners of cities, covered from view by tourists, and kill each other, as has been happening in Chicago for over a decade with little national outcry.[8] They are to be neither seen nor heard, and contained to spaces where they cannot disrupt the public perception that democracy works, and as the rising prison rates affirm, they are increasingly physically contained to penal firms, privatized systems of incarceration without assurances of information flow and accessibility. The middle classes are seemingly thought to benefit from participation in the system of mediation, with little or no challenge to its authority. And yet, Aronowitz relents, "While a 'few' scattered instances of unexpected violence may not describe the activity of a whole generation of middle-class youth, there is reason to insist that coherent models of nonviolent social conduct are losing their moral suasion; rather they are increasingly projected by school and other societal authorities as a cultural ideal rather than a practical model" (Aronowitz 2000, 219). Here we get to the point of our initial excursus through Balibar: how can violent social conduct become a cultural ideal and what does this mean for publics who unwittingly believe they remain in a system devoted to practical models of behavior? What happens to cause the shift from using models of nonviolent conduct as practical models to projecting them as a cultural ideal? In other words, how do people who believe they live in a disciplinary society respond to the increasing idealism mandated in the control one? Is this the breakdown announced by Arendt that we outlined in Chapter 1, where authority no longer makes sense as a practical matter and "play" and "flexibility" come to dominate all of our relations, especially as they relate to social conduct? And, why do they do this? Is it because it's more fun or because it's demanded by our current mode of production? Furthermore, what happens when the play and flexibility comes at the expense of some and maintains a system of privilege for others? As Paton confirms in looking closely at the school shooting videos, as well as online user comments surrounding school shootings, that there is "another level of attachment [in the] construction of a critical stance regarding the failure of institutions, first and foremost the school, followed closely by the media as a system corrupted by hegemonic thought" (Paton 2012, 221). Aronowitz's framework too rests in the disciplinary society but gestures at a coming resistance to the control oriented one he cannot outline, given the parameters of Hobbesian thought used in his essay. Yet he moves on to make the link more explicit by binding these seemingly random events to war (as conflict writ large), or what I would more precisely designate as asymmetric conflict; that is, between radically unequal parties with a completely different set of goals and existential needs (Mack 1975; Arreguín-Toft 2005).

The rest of Aronowitz's essay sketches out an argument that links the U.S. government's inability to take criticism from the middle classes by noting that

"The Gulf and Kosovar wars provide convincing evidence that visiting terror against civilian populations in order to invert public indignation against their own governments, rather than the putative aggressor, is becoming an acceptable aspect of warfare" (Aronowitz 2000, 225). In this way, Aronowitz sees one form of collective middle-class rage being displaced onto another group's exit strategies as a form of containment and punishment. Up to this point, Aronowitz's reading is important because he further elaborates how the schools and the authority structures in the schools (with media complicity) have heaped blame onto parents for not controlling kids' use of popular culture, as well as the school's commitment to punitive measures and peer mediation (evidence of the governing structure's failure to assume responsibility for its side of the social contract). Aronowitz's model for violence fits perfectly within the spectrum of knowledge concerning social contract theory and containment: pushing someone into a corner with no exit option (and, as he notes, both Harris and Klebold and the Serbs had *decided to exit* the system but were not allowed to do so either physically or representationally because they were stuck within the hegemonic governing structure of the American public school systems and the International Monetary Fund, respectively) is the double bind of compliance, and it breeds shame and rage. *It breeds shame because the subjects are forced to act as if they are agents in a free system that gave them a choice in joining the social contract without the reliable protection of the sovereign authorities.* This shame, if highlighted by continued humiliation in public spaces such as schools or the international community, spirals out of control into rage as students are publicly assailed and taunted with their powerlessness by those who have not only the protection of the authorities, but also have the captive attention of the mass media in what passes for the public. The American public[9] only witnessed one side of the Kosovo conflict, just as they did with Columbine, where the jocks emerged victorious as the new prototype for behavior, the "cultural ideal" of the American alibi reassuring the continued functioning of the social contract. This new model of citizenship was produced by the events at Columbine and Kosovo. Just as international relations scholars map the NATO intervention as the first instance of an overt changeover in the representation of interventions by strong powers, Columbine justified bullying of non-normative middle-class students in favor of the callisthenic celebrity of sporting and the presumed authenticity of the deep Christians. Only later in 2004 would the public see in the case of Pat Tillman's death by friendly fire and government cover-up just how desperately the government needed athletic heroes to represent this successful contract and merge it with the global war on terror (e.g., that captive fan base). Tillman was a superstar football athlete who traded his 3.6 million dollar contract renewal to join the military and serve in Afghanistan. In the public perception, only one athletic endeavor can surpass NFL stardom: military valor in war, and throughout American history scholars and public intellectuals have pointed out their exchangeability (Shapiro 1989). Now, however, we must resume our ongoing analysis of Aronowitz in light of subsequent shootings following Columbine as it helps make clear the connection of all these events to civil society, not just schools, workplaces or other spaces.

The first problem that emerges with a middle-class social contract framework is that it relies too heavily on a supposed justice inherent in democracy. While it can be agreed that one important aspect of this framework is how it exposes the lie of middle-class renunciation (and one cannot miss how "pity" for the poor can be easily translated into hatred and distrust à la Nietzsche and Balibar's remembrance of Foucault's Nietzsche[10]), it still does not explain how large majorities of the middle classes continue to seemingly scrap violence for really poor forms of mediation. Furthermore, how the liberal sociological argument that only the poor engage in criminal (violent) behavior is dangerously close to justifying scapegoating of the poor, especially when combined with policies of privatization.[11] Aronowitz's argument, while sociologically sound, fails to respond to many other potential causes for middle-class unrest, such as economic and social deprivation and Baudrillard's insight into the transparency of evil and the breakdown of our systems of representation. For example, how can students count on what he concedes is the "improbable outcome" of trusting "the remnant of progressive reformers who have enough vision to see that the educational system cannot expect to win the loyalty of youth unless it concedes some power" (Aronowitz 2000, 226). Presumably this would mean expanding our representational repertoire to include non-normative behaviors at school, and giving the disaffected a voice that is publicly acknowledged to have merit, whether or not the outcome approximates justice for the wronged party.[12] This overlooks the important argument that schools (and social service agencies in general) are mediated by curricula and protocol that are composed for corporate desired social efficiency agendas, focused as they are on behavioral control and the expansion of traits that facilitate consumerism. It is only the non-normative behaviors and identities that can be exploited for market expansion that can be tolerated. Indeed such non-normativity is often recouped by advertising soon after any violent media event that showcases it.[13]

For Aronowitz, the wars on television were an outlet for the rage of the middle-class adult populations in the United States that were in turn oppressing the youth in public schools. These televised events substituted as excuses for the government's lack of authority in matters of school policy and function while relaying satellite feed of the bombing of the "real" aggressors in Kosovo. While the structural soundness of Aronowitz's essay is nearly perfect, it is designed to convince a nostalgic readership already convinced by ready-made explanations that conform to progressive era logic (e.g., the dramatic war between rich and poor, the social worker/teacher who "cares" really exists but is bogged down in bureaucratic minutiae).[14] Certainly, the public school systems and the IMF generate as much profit as one another while maintaining the largely incorrect public persona of social welfare institutions; however, this does not mean that they have a purpose in the current control era other than acting as containing structures or holding patterns. For example, the idea that restoring an imagined legitimacy of the school and the rights of minorities simultaneously will resuscitate the middle-class contract is suspect in light of ongoing trends in both forms of governmentality and technologically-driven authority structures. It may even be another nostalgic iteration promoted in the mediascape to forestall truth-telling about the actual breakdown of interagency cooperation and authority of U.S. justice systems. The problem is that we need a way, as Galloway argues, to represent politics in the current version of the control society which functions according to "protocol." He writes:

> In *The History of Sexuality*, Foucault contrasts the older power of the sovereign over life (one characterized by the metaphysical concern of either the absence or presence of life) with a new node in which life is either created or destroyed: "One might say that the ancient right to *take* life or *let* live was replaced by a power to *foster* life or *disallow* it to the point of death" (1978, 138). He continues: "the old power of death that symbolized the sovereign power was now carefully supplanted by the *administration of bodies* and the *calculated management of life*" (138–40, emphasis mine). Foucault's treatment of bio-power is entirely protocological. Protocol is to control societies as the panopticon was to disciplinary societies. Protocol is more democratic than the panopticon, but it is still structured around command and control. (Galloway 2004, 13)

It is, as the subtitle of Galloway's book maintains, "how control exists after decentralization," and the power that thrives on this decentralization is what Hardt and Negri call "Empire" or what we have been simply calling corporatization. This means that there are no retroactive moves that can be made to reconstitute social contracts; only social movements going forward have the capacity to be "read" in this telepresent environment, and the simple fact of forwardness does not ensure progress that is positive, indeed it frequently means abjection, expulsion and implosion. In addition, the widespread yen for action figures to choreograph the drama of "progress" makes the idea of empowering and respecting downtrodden social workers fall flat in the mediascape. It makes more sense to view liberal models of citizenship as "dead artifacts" we rehabilitate in public discourse to maintain the fiction of political will, whereas in reality the people who most yearn to participate in the system of liberal democracy are the ones who run it, and even then it is only for the purposes of simulating democracy. Liberal citizenship, whether parsed into active categories of participation, assembly and belief in temporal progression or passive ones that figure around consent and acquiescence to popular authorities or freedom from government influence, is no longer accessible to most, nor is it desired by the public except as a simulation to achieve basic needs. Living under a system of forced integration, most people do not want liberal citizenship for it provides no model for living an individualized, creatively-inspired life and instead offers little autonomy and much compliance with value systems that steal precious time and shame them for failing to meet expectations that were not set democratically, but have been choreographed by elites, the media and experts. For Aronowitz, we can bring back the "practical model" of ethical behavior and abandon the moral ideal once we have *protoloco-logical* agents to manage the process, only they would not be informed by the language of idealism but practicality. Ostensibly, these agents will be able to carefully discern guilt and responsibility alongside the important claims made by aggrieved parties. However, in the shift to post-9/11 security concerns, the former codes that managed political correctness gave way to "patriotically correct" thinking. Under this type of thinking, whatever transgressed the "homeland" was considered traitorous from criticizing the leadership of the country to questioning safety guidelines. More often what is now patriotically correct is also more in line with Lockean property interests rather than a Hobbesian consensus about violence. What confuses Americans about the difference between Hobbes and Locke is the intertext of Rousseau provided by American public education, as we saw with Arendt in Chapter 1.

Stylizing the Exit Option: Mimetic Violence, or the "Columbine Thesis"

Before going into the individual cases as contrasting examples of "exits" from the middle-class system, it is important to underscore some departures from Aronowitz's framework. One detail that the essay leaves untouched is the way in which many of the violent exiters stylize their events through the appropriation and deployment of popular culture. First they identify with a film or video game that resonates with the particular environment or situation they see themselves as forced to participate in and want to exit. Films with revenge narratives (*Old Boy*) or resistance movements against aggressive or totalitarian forms of control (*The Matrix*) are especially popular. So, it is partly film and television that animates the rage found in episodes of school violence or in treacherous loyalties to causes aimed at the destruction of American sites of common life. But it only gives a *narrative form* to the acts where none is forthcoming, or the perpetrators have been barred from explaining their acts in the media. Filmic identification is an interesting component to the mimetic behavior of school shooters, but it fails to apprehend motive and capacities that are mobilized to complete such acts in real time and space. Film is the medium through which such acts are communicated to the public, but the most important features of the acts are demonstrated in their targets (real people in civil society) combined with the promise of digital technologies of the posthuman age. What shooters are actually doing is using filmic poses and accoutrements (weapons, urban assault gear, camouflage, trench coats, poses, etc.) to perform for the remainder of the American public still left behind in televisual land. Moreover, I partially agree with Vincent W.J. van Gerven Oei that, at least from Columbine through to Holmes, the poses assumed and the stylizations are ironic and aimed at a public who will split when faced with their acts: one the one hand, observing that what they represent (especially in their still photos) is what the audience desires, while carrying out acts they cannot endorse and find morally abhorrent. This is a public who consumes film, the largely passive medium for constructing stories about how life transpires in its ideal moments. Details left out of most theoretical analysis of popular culture's use in everyday life, even in its most spectacular and violent forms, provide a convincing explanation for how the shooters in particular use digital and video game technology to actually carry out such acts. We have heard the arguments about video games wearing out the midbrain (Grossman & Christensen 1995, 2004) and how video games are said to lead to the deterioration of ethical norms concerning violence and other forms of hatred and injustice. However, most of this analysis has zeroed in on the content of the games and not their form; that is, what they enable the user to do that is dramatically different from other forms of virtual culture: act. In other venues, such as distance education and entertainment for adults, we hear endless commentary about how empowering the "Web 2.0" revolution is for democracy and citizenship by allowing people who lack physical access to schools or travel to meet and educate one another. Somehow when it comes to video games (users play them online with people all across the world), the storyline changes: kids don't want to go to school anymore, or exercise (hence, *Dance, Dance, Revolution*) or pay attention to their immediate surroundings. This is hypocritical because no one wants to respond in real time any longer.[15] And when they do it is as if in a game, which is called "gamification." Jesper Juul's recent essay on video games making us all intentional losers is instructive. He points out that the logic of gaming now pervades many of our social interactions and productivity schemes. We apply the logic of assigning points and assessing performance throughout the world, especially where the market dominates social and political realities. This may give us a clue as to how to figure control in the current era. Consider his reading of the 2008 financial crisis:

> We need to think more closely about why games work so well: at the very least, good games tend to offer well-defined goals and clear feedback. This gives us an objective measure of our performance, and allows us to optimize our strategies. If applying this to nongame situations sounds tempting, consider how the 2008 financial crisis was caused in part by large banks and financial institutions making their organizations too gamelike by giving employees the clear goal of approving as many loans as possible and punishing naysayers with termination. This was a case where the design that works so well inside games can be disastrous outside games, even if we think of the well-being of the companies involved. (Juul 2013)

This was not just the case in the U.S.; it was Ireland (remember John McCain trying to point to that country as a financial model for the U.S. in 2008 presidential debates?), Iceland, the Euro Zone in its entirety, and even Brazil was able to hold out until it recently emerged that people could no longer take the austerity imposed to save Brazil's relationship to the market. What many people learned is that governments and firms were playing games with their futures. Why renounce violence for that? What Juul is saying, which is similar to Galloway, is that games are increasingly becoming the allegories that structure our "outside the game" life. This includes our ideas about civility and tolerance. In games, as Juul points out, it is legitimate for another player to purposefully subvert our goals, but in reality this would be unacceptable. However, I would argue that we have not questioned this gamification enough, to the point where an entire new world order is built around worshipping the game of global capital, while each person's attempt to thwart another's chances is ignored (and often celebrated on reality television). I think this is what Larkin may be trying to get at when he discusses celebrity, that is, in some sense we worship the "winners," overlooking how impoverished our own lives become in the process. And yet, we still have ongoing media coverage exclusively centered on narrative, the visual representations of violence and making them cohere to larger national narratives about politics and violence. Appropriately, we are now witnessing the battle of the crypt keepers on network news programs that are caught between their loyal audiences of older generations that need to have their violent stories communicated through references to film and older developmental paradigms, and the younger generation who reluctantly take in television news and when doing so want to see only themselves reflected back on the screen.

Because ratings require that television news secure a wide audience, it prefers analyses that focus on the filmic references in shooting episodes and make this form of popular culture the trigger for the rage. I have argued elsewhere that the rage is fomented in reality, not in the fictional accounts of film or literature, nor in the content of video games. Even though initial news reports about Virginia Tech claimed that Cho favored the game *Counterstrike,* these comments were later deleted from online reports, and the official crime scene list did not include a gaming console.[16] As E. J. Carvalho has persuasively argued:

> The heightened imagery of violence that Seung-Hui scripts for the psychic residue of his aftermath is most definitely the product of artifice. His extensive familiarity with new media forms—cybercultural social outlets like MySpace and Facebook—enable him to manufacture a social metanarrative and yet create a political performative space where he renders false 'profiles' of images to temporarily stand-in for the Seung-Hui we now recognize as the Virginia Tech shooter. To Seung-Hui's advantage, these images attract our attention (as he intended they would), giving us a sense that he wanted to belong, and, incidentally, they also act as accelerant for his performative constructions on this front. (Carvalho 2010, 416)

School/Civil society violence perpetrators *want the public to think* their acts are mimicries of film plots as this form of popular culture remains dominant as a system for conveying meaning about nationality and citizenship in the American context, as well as others. The unexamined saliency of these arguments forms in the popular mind the notion that these forms of expression should be censored, and this leads figures from the entertainment industry or from the peace movement to hang their analyses on a particular backdrop as motivational for violence. For example, Aronowitz's decision to hang middle-class violence on structural inequality alone, without looking at how traditional political communication can no longer take place. What theses analyses fail to see and lose touch with in terms of the actual events of violent exiters is that they are primarily directing rage against the *forms of mediation* that have been employed to bring them back into the middle-class social contract: the psychological counseling, forms of detainment, forced self-commitment, legal arenas for disputes, official school policy, and pharmaceutical solutions (drug them into complacency). These forms are evident in the array of objects they appropriate and combine for stylizing their acts of revenge and exiting the system. They are never original acts because the options are always drawn from a set, just as one pulls down a menu option and selects from programmed lists.

One aspect of the larger problem that distracts from more important concerns is when the media lead experts and industrial officials move away from the acts themselves to a position of defense against larger social and political movements, such as opposing war (MoveOn.org) or a humanitarian defense of it.

Aronowitz has provided a nice sociological framework that satisfies many conditions to explain school violence episodes by making it allegorical for larger international political conflicts, such as the war in Kosovo. Other authors covered in this book have attributed violent episodes to a culture of violence as evidenced in the domestic militarization of citizens under the GWOT (Global War on Terror) as a contentious historical process of conflicts without mediation leading back into the Cold War (Kaldor 1998) or to industry alliances that make war a form of entertainment delivered to a desensitized American public that consumes such scenes daily (Der Derian's media infotainment network, 2001). It is not enough to causally link domestic episodes to larger conflicts or political battlegrounds, and the theorists who have done this have not furthered collective knowledge of what is actually happening in the space between the domestic and the international that is achieving events of "teeth-gritting harmony" unprecedented in the twenty-first century. Relying as they do on disciplinary interpretations, that is interpretations that rely on a larger *source* as cause of *symptomatic* episodes and behaviors, such as militarism or mass violence, such analysts reify the cause/effect relationship between events that name a primary institution or knowledge framework as an independent variable. What links them is new media.

Rather the independent variable in the case of shootings is indeed the shooter, but not as "evil," "gay," or "psychotic" (i.e., one that can be ferreted away from public scrutiny as an outlier brought about by fate or bad genes), but as an agent who constructs the transpolitical spectacle of his own demise, expertly using knowledge of public attention and media complicity to stage revenge against the systems of mediation that have humiliated him, not because he accepts their codes of operation, but because he rejects them, that is, out of spite.[17] School shooters are rejected and mediated by systems of power they do not even believe in or care about (mentally they never entered them, so the question of exiting is ironic). They are outcasts. This happens after having been thwarted by other players in the real-life game. The bullying and the disavowal of it by the entire society contribute to this rage. I think here about the football coach at Columbine who told his players to "be nice" to outcasts and other non-aligned students only so they could increase attendance at games and could continue to play in a better stadium, not because civility adds value to common life in a democracy in and of itself. Increasingly, our instructions for how to be civil coalesce around an explicit reward system (Juul's points) characterized by a narrow range of actions and options we mistakenly consider offers of expanded "choice" without a larger purpose or goal, i.e., Balibar's Gewalt. As Juul maintains, "games are not a pixie dust of motivation to be sprinkled on any subject" (Juul 2013). This gaming logic is dangerous if it is carried out without much thought for its repercussions in the real world, in larger groups of people where the implications are far more serious. One could think of the stress on military recruiters in this way where the logic of gaming is also applied in terms of increasing the number of enlistments without acknowledging that no one with full knowledge of the war or economic alternatives would join to fight. Now the situation will be "solved" by drones, another telepresent solution. I do believe these perpetrators are a kind of canary in the coal mine, but not about violent masculinity; they warn of the future destruction of civil spaces by the logic of this particular game of global capital.

Knowing he commands proficiency in representational cultures that do not inhere to disciplinary modes of communication, the civil society mass killer manipulates them to leave the public traumatized and confused by the nature of his acts. And yet, the media and special interest groups can use such episodes to generate debate and subsequent ratings by attaching themselves to inadequate explanations. More time is wasted explaining them using prevailing disciplinary logics than is devoted to reading them as symbolic formations of gaps between two systems of communication, action and political power. As Murray Edelman noted about the political spectacle, it "would, if it could, keep everyone's energies taken up with activism: election campaigns, lobbying, repressing some and liberating others, wars, and all other political activities that displace loving and creative work" (Edelman 1988, 7).

Not even in the more thoughtful coverage do we find an explanation for how and why the exiters stylize their crimes in this way or that and what the choice of representational objects, poses, clothing, notes or video tapes say about what they believe they are doing in these acts. Instead they are exploited for their use in larger political causes generally unrelated to their intended aims. Such moral short circuits provide the media with the freedom to interpret traumatic events how ever they like without censor by the public. But they are in Edelman's analysis (derived from early Baudrillard) the way that the indifference of the masses is represented. As an example, words that are used to signify crimes against people we don't know or have ethnic affiliation with or are remotely connected to are now routinely labeled crimes against humanity in the absence of a real (tangible) victim who forsakes their own vigilante justice (renounces violence) for mediation in the penal system. However, now the assumption is that every crime is a crime against everyone. The assumption is that the public has an interest in these kinds of crimes when they are not personal or ideological but are leveled against a category, civil society, for the misplaced level of perspective characteristic of the age. These kinds of reactions can do nothing in the form of justifying public interest in them, but they do not have to justify what they do to the public, only to elites and executives. My argument is that the thinking public needs and deserves a better explanation to diffuse such acts from happening long before they get to the rage phase. For Aronowitz this meant intervening at the conflict stage through dispute mechanisms, but I would argue that we need a nuanced analysis and critique of these very *practical* mediators because they can be a very real trigger to rage[18] and often form a complex part of the narrative of violence stylized by exiters that I prefer to break into streams of communication and motive, each one accomplishing a different desire in the act. Similarly, those public figures whose analysis of these events are taken seriously often use them as a pretext for their political causes without much forethought for the consequences of doing so, of applying one interpretation to a situation where it had no merit other than persuading audiences in a cheap and underhanded way to your commercial and academic cause.

Formats of popular culture are also peculiar to the exiters. They signify to us the *hidden script* of domestic violences as they are expressed in public crimes; school shooters attempt to take their private problems and make them public. This is no different from the domestic affairs of a state taking on an international character in suicide bombings. This is why Aronowitz makes the comparison between public forms of mediation in the U.S. and the International Monetary Fund, which acts as the mediator internationally for many of the domestic concerns of nation-states. While most Americans labor under the assumption that they simply dole out free money to undeserving people, they are never educated about the kind of power such institutions wield and the kind of profits they generate, ones which never return to the American public. Such institutions bypass the authority of the state, just as social service agencies bypass the authority of parents, where they administer and directly control the everyday lives of citizens. These mediations exploit and shape people's personal, private lives, such as their ability to find work, buy bread and milk and care for their health. They do not go to the state for mediation of their disputes, instead they go directly to the IMF—that is why so many riots have occurred protesting this institution. This is one of the effects of shifting to a control society while relegating the disciplinary institutions to the dustbin of history: empowered agencies can bypass systems of mediation to directly affect and control populations that are unrelated to them by national origin, civic solidarity or class affinity in the system. These agencies do not even have to demonstrate proficiency in delivering or administering mediation services. Populations are detached from their symbolic sovereign moorings, yet still find themselves caught in broken systems of justice and distribution. *We still represent disciplinary societies but we do not inhabit them.* Thus, the claim that we should understand any international conflict as a source for domestic unrest is misleading—the hierarchical system of power characteristic of disciplinary societies has been punctured by free market excursions and control over populations across national boundaries by numerous types of agencies (banks, criminal networks, privatized security firms, educational corporations, media outlets, not-for-profit advocacy groups, religious interests, etc.). Indeed it is more appropriate to say that international and domestic acts feed one another through their contact in the media, whether in their displacement and framing by television or in their networked contact through digital feeds. The television media's role is to frame such events so as to compartmentalize their effects. Just as the film industry produces a largely passive narrative designed with neat (idyllic) closures to complex social problems or heroic tales of individualistic sacrifice, the television media provides framing of complex events around issues and debates that can be easily attached to existing experts or domestic lobbies.[19]

Nowhere was this hijacking of the problem more common than in the comparison of Columbine as a subset of the NATO war in Kosovo. In a world where democratic states retreat from responsibility for maintaining the social contract it is illogical to think of school violence or terrorism as a subset of wars between states or peoples. The media continue to frame it that way except when law enforcement officials label it otherwise to secure their own importance (as we'll see in the next section). School violence represents a war between peoples just as terrorism does, and it is no longer just the state that suffers for its own misdeeds, it is the very people it is charged with protecting. Many people do not like the comparison because suicide bombers are perceived to be poor and their crimes are said to represent an ideological cause to reduce the gap between rich and poor countries and between the hegemony of Christianity and capitalism in world institutions, and the relegation of Islam to the margins, as well as its pronounced discrediting by many as a religion of terror. Yet I would argue that they are not much different and that suicide bombings and mass school shootings only are rendered different by the presentations of them by the media and subsequent reactions to these depictions by the public. For example, the film *Paradise Now*, a fictional drama about suicide bombers in the Israeli occupied territories, focuses on the process involved in preparing to undertake a suicide bombing by an average Palestinian man who is surrounded by a loving family and friends, whose acts are inexplicable when read against a personal biography of normalcy where a love interest holds sway and a job is frustrating but nevertheless satisfying; the main stopgaps on the person's life are the road blocks imposed throughout the film on every street in the occupied territories that make it difficult for him to conduct his otherwise normal life without obstacles. The persistent theme of obstacles that block an otherwise normal life also haunt the personal trajectories of school shooters who are blocked from paths they have chosen and are denied alternative routes. Just as Said must stay at other people's homes when roads are closed in *Paradise Now*, so must school shooters be rerouted out of normal pathways of being in order to protect the safety of the rest of society. The continued recognition that one's path is blocked or one is detained in order to protect the civil society presents a problem, especially where authorities are repeatedly issuing false statements that it is for the detainee's *own* good that he is being contained or searched. This argument has shades of equality in it; the authorities claim to be treating everyone equally yet singling out certain people through profiling and surveillance—again, for their own good. The dual application of safety rationalizations is problematic as a young person is at once a threat to society but is held for his own good. This persistent needling and rerouting by authorities produces a form of resentment so powerful that it can no longer be contained by such systems of incarceration, nor can it be held off by deflection—in the end, the rage that forms in these spaces of mediation goes somewhere and the crimes that reflect its patterns are exhibited in the very form of suicides bled into mass murder. The person will hurt himself and others to spite the authorities. This hurt must be public in order to further threaten the very spaces that are protected. This is why explanations for both suicide bombings and mass shootings that focus on popular culture as motivating are another form of deflection from the nature of the problem.

What constitutes justification for such separate analysis between school shooters and suicide bombers is the notion that one set of transgressors possesses access to popular culture while the other seemingly does not. Sublimation of rage can be rerouted through forms of popular culture into productive forms of expression and participation in "free" societies. The problem, it seems, is that suicide bombers do not live in free societies nor have access to the means of cultural reduplication to sublimate their rage. Let us not forget the educational backgrounds and wealth that produced the terrorists in the 9/11 hijackings. This kind of analysis may be duplicitous but is nonetheless ubiquitous. Once a certain explanation for violence or war is articulated that constructs an impossible problem to solve, it becomes the default for all subsequent problems. There is good reason for this: it allows the political class to maintain the status quo. One such argument is found in actor Tim Robbins's response following Columbine that stressed that the Clinton administration should not have been allowed to blame Hollywood for media violence while it was processing a war in Kosovo. For Robbins, the argument about Hollywood films constituted scapegoating. He even went so far as to claim on *Charlie Rose* that he may even believe that Hollywood allows kids to sublimate their rage in appropriate ways whereas a "real" war like the NATO intervention in Kosovo constituted an opportunity for the kids at Columbine to feel justified to try out their rage in real attempts.[20] But why does only the act of war and its televised presence allow for the "trigger" to enact Harris and Klebold's rage, whereas the Hollywood films were keeping it under wraps? Harris and Klebold no more experienced the reality of Kosovo than they did the reality of *DOOM* or *Natural Born Killers*. Here it is important to recall Galloway's "fidelity of context" argument: it is not the kind of violence mobilized in these games per se, but whether or not they pass the test of social realism.

In this analysis we find a profound ignorance of the dispute mechanisms and their role in fomenting rage that, while it may be sublimated by popular culture for many, and even used as a means to replace reality in the extremely immersed, Robbins rendition of the problem emerges as a kindler, gentler form of the argument that anyone outside the sphere of U.S. interests must "hate our freedom" when in reality they probably just despise their own mediations. It does not explain the violence because if hatred of the other is what motivated such acts of violence, it would be sufficient to remain alive and find other more satisfying ways to torture the other or luxuriate in one's fantasies of mistreatment.

There is almost an existential need to produce the violent suicide as revenge against other people when in reality it is revenge against a particular form of existence. Other people stand in abstractly for the society at large that allows such miscarriages of justice; to the bomber or shooter they are like sheep herded together, indifferent to their surroundings. The popular mind cannot separate these two things since the urge to exit the system is always interpreted as a rude gesture towards the hospitality of civil society. The belief that popular culture is so helpful that it can act as a therapeutic cap on physical violence is evidence of the culture's increasing acceptance of it with caveats about age appropriateness linked to censorship. The "security of concealment" adumbrated by Hannah Arendt emerges here as another concept applied to youth and violence, as well as issues of visual propriety (what can and should be seen)[21] and the ethics of development (what can and should be known); these two facets of contemporary life in the United States are merged, yet the research and expert opinion (even popular opinion) concerning both is bi-furcated into two separate modes of inquiry. Popular and common opinion tend to focus almost exclusively on visual propriety with little or no interest in explaining how (a question of epistemology and therefore what should/can/is be known or understood about visual images of war) these images affect youth development or sanctify the excessive reliance on the national rating system that is far from informed by seasoned field research on development, character and national identity. Again: wherever shame is mobilized, there is rage. We will return to these issues at the end of this long section, after a short foray through less publicized attempts at violence, as well as some analysis of the coverage of Virginia Tech and the issues it has sparked, particularly with regard to mental illness and the carryover of high school rage to college as in the "second generation" of school violence perpetrators.

Although Aronowitz deploys a few Enlightenment narratives to understand contemporary youth violence, especially the emphasis on the discrete failures of the social contract for middle-class youth, he is genuinely concerned with government structures that can redress or reactivate failing social contracts. Robbins's argument is different because, unlike Aronowitz, he proceeds from the thesis of militarization. What this means is that governments militarize populations and present them with violence as an ideal through their own military excursions. Robbins is more concerned with how war becomes the trigger for the rage, and how a lack of leadership and restraint demonstrated by leaders translates into immoral behaviors in young people. Robbins's view coincides with that of social movements for progress that claim that war or violence in any form is wrong and must be stopped. Aronowitz concedes there will always be violence and conflict, we just need better mediators for grievance. It is important to note that neither perspective takes into account the changing nature of ethics in our society and its relationship to telepresent reality. Moreover, there is a lack of apprehension concerning the use of virtual technologies in the social movements themselves. They are instead celebrated. Indeed, these very same technologies transform the movements' aims without their conscious knowledge; they operate as shaming mechanisms. They begin to exert control over the subjects who believe they are autonomous. As Baudrillard has written of the virtual (a phase of experience mostly middle classes enjoy): "In the virtual, we are no longer dealing with value; we are merely dealing with a turning-to-data, a turning-to-calculations, a generalized computation in which reality-effects disappear. The virtual might be said to be truly the reality-horizon, just as we talk about the event-horizon in physics" (Baudrillard 2005, 40–41). How does one discern "practicality" in this except as an unconvincing alibi for the conversion to data of human aspirations? For example, is it practical to mobilize support against war by making it *easy* for people to oppose it? As MoveOn.org became the default consciousness of the progressive Left throughout the last decade, little circumspection surrounding the effect of these revelation tactics and extreme headlines was examined by progressive reformers. The space devoted to nuanced criticism dwindled as the twenty-four hour news cycle pre-empted any attempt at in-depth coverage of an event. Even at present there is excessive, constant coverage, but it is delivered in the form of sound bites and ill-constructed comparisons, data assertions that find adherents less because they make sense than because at the time they feel good or are reassuring in anxious times.

What I am suggesting is that we should read these events more closely to see what the exiters are trying to communicate (for I agree with Aronowitz that they are indeed "exiters"). Beyond this, we have the benefit of retrospection and can see that what would tie them together is this telepresent reality where they could get the ideas, find the script, and follow its appeal, which would serve to make them become a global phenomenon, which Aronowitz still could not have seen in 1999 when his essay was published. I would put the exiting option more on the claim for exiting, with the immediate precipitants to action being the unfairness they perceive they experienced during forms of mediation. The precise effect of this mediation is not a rational calculus about violence or nonviolence, but is actually rooted in the shaming experience of humiliation, an experience created by the sociological worldview. In the sociological worldview we find important concepts that incite shame and humiliation for those who fall under them: norm, integration, consensus, appropriate socialization, etc.

As the culture of the U.S. and other states become even more conformist under globalization (and the increasing division of labor and specialization designed for a consumer market as indicative of a failing economy), people can find any number of ways to exploit people's feelings of inadequacy to sell products and services, and do so to extreme levels.[22] Whole new psychological disorders pepper the *DSM-V* (*Diagnostic and Statistical Manual of Mental Disorders, Version 5, U.S.*), ranging from rage disorders to personality to restless leg syndrome, and marketers will invent more ways for those diagnosed as inadequate to improve themselves according to the unwritten code of normalcy that fluctuates alongside the profit margin, not scientific or developmental codes or markers. The effect of all this shaming is certain to spiral into a bad situation as whole groups of people carry shame around for lack of integration into a system that is selling a form of happiness as wholeness, especially where what represents this wholeness is civil society, an institution of democracy that no longer exists. What now represents American civil society to itself and the rest of the world is this very consumer culture, and it will come back to shame the nation in the unfair ways that shame presupposes.[23] When we take these exit cases to the media, as the exiters inevitably do, we can see new forms of communication that are created by virtual technologies that never fail to be misread by the media framers and publics they entertain. As these cases become more high-profile media cases, the role of shame and nationalism becomes increasingly important, albeit in a novel manner.

The National Wave of Shame Is Ironic

Thomas Keenan's reading of the mobilization of shame as a conceptual event that can be read by public audiences is interesting in this regard since it focuses on the misplaced expectations that such audiences have with regard to shame. As Keenan maps "shame" beginning with the American experience in the Vietnam War and connects it to the Kantian Enlightenment strategy, which supposed that citizens could be shamed out of heteronomy; that is, they could be informed by news coverage of the war's failures, calculate their costs and sacrifices and make a practical decision to stop support for it. Yet, he finds that the response to feeling shame can also be read as an act of defiance, of revenge against the moral authorities that would judge such acts as shameful. As he writes concerning shame as a tactic deployed by social movements or media for progressive causes, "Mobilizing shame presupposes that dark deeds are done in the dark, and that the light of publicity—especially of the television camera—thus has the power to strike preemptively on behalf of justice. With a wave, these policemen announced their comfort with the camera, their knowledge of the actual power of truth and representation" (Keenan 2004, 446). The "wave" were the acts of the soldiers in Kosovo to the camera with full knowledge that their crimes will be captured on film. In this case, representation, according to Keenan, doesn't matter because the effect of the shame is that it becomes a badge of pride. Moreover, the soldiers are able to use the camera to communicate their revenge to mobilize new adherents to their cause. He quotes Keats while explaining the wave, which I read as indicative of many of these publicized attacks:

> The wave announces—it performs, it enacts—that there's no hiding here, nothng in the dark, nothing to be ashamed of. And it demonstrates this for the very instruments that are known for their revelatory abilities—the wave says, "Expose this, this is what I am exposing for you." Like the hand at the end of Keat's strange little fragment "This Living Hand," the waving hands of Mijalic each say, "See here it is, I hold it toward you," and they do what they say. (Keenan 2004, 446)

Shame, like hate, is also an emotion that circulates in an economy charged with new iterations; it produces unintentional a/effects. In fact, it can even be used to justify vengeful acts, especially when those who are shamed are given no exit option from the system of integration, from the game. Much like the Seung-Hui Cho videotapes, many of the perpetrators know that in the age of telepresence the best way to communicate is through the screen. If it doesn't get into the digital feed, it does not challenge our enlightened presumptions. This is what happens to shame in a hyper enlightened age, which is to say hyperreal.[24] It is easier to rationalize such acts by fellow citizens by finding a national past for the individual that refuses to live in the present, as we saw in Chapter 3 with Breivik. We also saw this in Chapter 2 with the review of Larkin's book that claimed parts of the U.S. had yet to be enlightened. Too often, the possibilities for responsibility proliferate in this very enlightening media, and any kind of shameful lesson to be learned gets re-directed (to use external forces to make an individual change behavior) at the outcasts in the name of national responsibility. As Farid Abdel-Nour explains:

> In its popular form, the language of national responsibility is invoked as an accusation directed en masse against Serbs, Americans, Israelis, Palestinians or Turks for having perpetrated some unspeakable act (possibly in the distant past) against their accusers. Such accounts of responsibility serve to prepare the groundwork for indiscriminate "collective punishment," "terrorism," or any number of other forms of "retaliation" against the accused nation. *When such an idea is invoked, individuals are treated merely as exemplars of their national group. The nation is hypostasized and national identity essentialized.* The history of the last hundred years spares us the task of having to imagine the monstrous acts that this kind of logic can be used to justify. (Abdel-Nour 2003, 696, emphasis mine)

This explains why Weise, Cho, Hasan and others[25] were covered by the media as un-American when in reality the path was well-trod before them by high school shooters during the late 1990s. The media and academic split occurs by national affiliation and the artificially imposed line between high school and early adulthood (as all of these men were in their late teens or early twenties). In regard to challenges to the U.S. government by essentially middle-class "terrorists," such as Timothy McVeigh and groups like those assembled at Waco, Texas, the mass tendency is to shuffle them away into an aberrant category of pathologized individual or misguided (yet political zealot). This may also explain both the media and academic tendency to overlook the Northern Illinois shootings, as we shall see in the next chapter. Steven Kazmierczak was doing everything right (in school, socially), and he was white. Mingus and Zopf place this bifurcation within racial lines, arguing that "Being White Means Never Having to Say You're Sorry," and that the media reactions (which mirror the public) make non-white examples into "exceptions":

> The 'exceptions that prove the rule,' of course, are those involving incidents where the shooter is identified as non-white. This occurred both at Virginia Tech and at Fort Hood where race suddenly became not only an issue, but one of such paramount importance that others who shared a racial identity with the perpetrator became victims of racial interpellation (Chong 2008; Hall 1980), forced to apologize or, worse, made to live in fear of retaliation. (Mingus & Zopf 2010, 66)

Subsumed under the logic of collective identity, these persons become the prototypes for future transgressors. It is not just that this containment is physical and exists as policy only for those who can be predicted to engage in mass violence, it is really the question of *psychological containment* that the public demands, as people seek to distance themselves from the markers of identity displayed by domestic terrorists like McVeigh. As Abdel-Nour shows, the nation becomes the container for a threat that is produced globally in the protocol of the control society that manages capital. This alleviates the burden on citizens in having to imagine that they too are implicated in the structure. This was clear in the reactions to the Abu Ghraib prison scandal, where, as David Griffith recounts, Americans were more than happy to agree with Donald Rumsfeld that "the pictures should not have been released," as the events occurred "a long time ago" and therefore were "of little consequence for understanding any American responsibility for violence committed in its name" (Griffith 2006, 157). Galloway uses the Abu Graihb scandal to illustrate something about the very nature of representation. In questioning the link (he says) between images and violence, we are hitting our leftist heads against a wall:

> It is only natural to wish for *some* mechanical link between images and violence. It would be a noble pursuit if it were not demonstrably false: the photos from the Abu Ghraib prison were released, or they were not (and nothing changed); we grieved and we protested in the proper channels, or we did not (and still nothing changed). Representation *happened*, even if one feels anxiety about the outcome. The problem is that adequate visualization of control society have *not happened*. Representation has not happened. At least not yet. (Galloway 2011b, 95)

Curiously, the American response is to construct another problem (e.g., too much time had lapsed/more visual propriety). Yet, as Žižek contended, this was the "obscene underside" of American culture of belonging, that is, of civil society. The crisis was not framed as a moral one but as a crisis of propriety. And, like "urban decay" which has simply continued, the American polity has added new chronic social problems in the form of authority and hierarchy, crime and violence, and responsibility. As Edelman remarks, "the willingness to suspend one's own critical judgment in favor of someone regarded as able to cope creates authority" (Edelman 1988, 20). However, the old references in the form of "evil" remain, while the media generates even more attraction to them, despite the public's will to divert attention. In the contemporary era, this has meant that politicians and private contractors work together to find temporary, anxiety-alleviating solutions to complex problems. Ironically those who are temporarily rendered powerless in these cases of violence are not the traditionally disempowered or poor who are completely neglected by these overt mechanisms of power, they are the middle classes. The media provides the framework for deciphering who might be a potential terrorist or school shooter, then, in democratic form, the public is asked to be the eyes and ears of law enforcement to turn persons of suspicion into authorities. However, the way the media has constructed such profiles, they have focused almost exclusively on the stigmas of national or religious identity and mental illness, leaving the rest of the homogeneous social free to act as violent and rageful as they like with little surveillance. Where this separation by national affiliation and mental illness cannot be applied, the media resort to class discrimination, as often happens in the case of soldiers who are brought to trial for heinous crimes that the public would rather look away from. This has certainly been the case with Abu Ghraib and other cases of military personnel who were indicted for rape and murder while serving abroad, and in some cases those who return to the states commit domestic violence against family members. Griffith further explains how the public disavowed claiming responsibility or concern for it by reviving the *old* sociological argument demolished by Aronowitz where we come to "expect nothing more from people like Graner and England who we imagine to be from tacky trailer parks in dead-end hollers," and he notes that it's a "tragic plot," that is, as Edelman argued "inevitable": "The hero can do nothing other than what he was born (and raised) to do" (Griffith 2006, 135). If this is the case, what are the mostly middle and upper class perpetrators of civil society mass killings being "raised to do"? Meanwhile, as was argued earlier, the inevitable solution is profiling when violence and trauma are rendered "senseless" "inexplicable" and "random." Moreover, profiling is the optimal response to these types of crimes because:

1. There is no person remaining to hold responsible (school shootings that most evoke this response are ones where the perpetrator successfully commits suicide at the end) or
2. There is no remorseful or believable person to hold responsible.

For this latter problem, we can return to Keenan's astute perception of "criminals" who know they are being shamed and refuse to play along. Instead, they use their knowledge of the enlightened viewers' presumption of guilt to reverse its effects by making a parody of it. Much like the soldier's wave, Cho flaunted the public's presumed need for shame and humiliation from him by staging a video articulating his revenge so no one would misunderstand or frame it according to their own imperatives. *To date, no authority has willingly put forward a motive in the Virginia Tech massacres.* In this way, the narrative of school violence that follows Columbine has *learned* something important about the public's reaction to it: that it will contain it using visual censorship. The only way to get the message across that shame and responsibility are not forthcoming is to capture it on screen. It is only after a violent act has taken place that the public and media begin to dissect the perpetrator's national background, searching for any other reason for "why" outside the obvious one that part of what motivates the act is a profound identification with the telepresent ethos to shed responsibility at the moment one is caught in the act. Profiling is the modus operandi of the complicit media. Restricted by a series of options for interpreting behavior, law enforcement personnel increasingly cannot compute what behavior means that does not flow from profilers' charts; hence, everyone becomes a "psychopath." One reason for this is that punishment is an education in crime. What our concerned mediators fail to see is that we are in an era of impunity where punishment is no longer viewed by its object as therapeutic and leading toward a future goal; instead it is an exercise in humiliation that labels such transgressors' as pathological. There is a hidden script of knowledge operating here on a non-cognitive plane. At once aware that the system is broken and offering no rationale for the painstaking work of joining it, such persons find themselves in partnership with others as deviants to the system, finding ingenious ways to overcome its blindspots and demonstrate to those invested in it just how vulnerable they actually are. This is their form of participation.

We have reviewed Aronowitz's claim that the explanation for random school shooting lies in the failure of a "middle-class social contract" where middle-class people would have access to an "exit option" from punishment by sovereignty and law. Does this mean that class values somehow matter to an analysis of the use of violence by such citizens? Insofar as one can discern the boundaries of the middle as a class, it would seem that the only virtues they share in common are virtual and linked to their status as those citizens believed to have a reason to participate in the system; that is, that they benefit from it in some way despite the fact that they sacrifice violence as a means of solving conflict. In an era where conflict is not acknowledged, where difference is medicated and compulsive conformity is the norm, the breakdown of civil society is evident. As we shall see later, this has given many individuals a new argument in favor of carrying concealed weapons in public spaces of civil society, such as university campuses, airplanes, and other spaces. A related argument accompanies the logic of privatization and individualized answers to security. With conceptual roots in middle-class hyperreality; that is, the simulation that there is a middle class, and by extension, a civil society, keeps citizens in the game. The very dynamics of this game actually contributes to even further destruction of the remnants of these institutions. Play is seductive. We have to remember Galloway's concern (and others) that the new mode of production stresses "immaterial labor" and the "increase in cultivation and exploitation of play—creativity, innovation, the new, the singular, flexibility, the supplement—as a productive social force, play will become more and more linked to broad structures of control" (Galloway 2006a, 76).

5

Of Rogues and Fans

"True crime is crime fact that looks like crime fiction," Mark Seltzer tells us. And he is right. Trying to separate the fact from fiction through the vehicle of the mass media is nearly impossible. It is also what invites many into the narrative of crime as fans. As he writes, the:

> Interestingly paradoxical relations between true and false crime points to the manner in which crime in modern society resides in the interval between real and fictional reality: the uncertain, mobile, conditional and counterfactual reality of a 'reflexive modernity,' which includes the self-reflection of its reality as part of its reality, and as one of its defining attributes. This is reality bound up through and through with the reality of the mass media. Put somewhat differently, true crime points to the media a priori in modern society because the technical infrastructure of modern reflexivity is the mass media. It points to the fact that the real world is known through its doubling by machines, the doubling of the world in the mass media that makes up our situation. (Seltzer 2008, 26)

This can help to explain why there are so many "fans" of civil society mass killers. This is one thesis that has been put forward focused erroneously to explain why the women who find such perpetrators attractive or are willing to protest their innocence in the face of mountains of evidence to the contrary. A more clinical explanation, often cited in the articles covering this fandom, labels it hybristophilia, or "Bonnie and Clyde Syndrome," which is a sexual attraction to bad men. The less clinical or current theory was put forward chiefly after the

Boston Marathon bombing when Dzokhar Tsarnaev's cherub-like face appeared on the cover of *Rolling Stone* to the consternation of the Twitterverse, it went something like this: these young women will never be with a famous man, like an actor or musician, therefore, these vilified guys might seem like a possibility. They imagine that they might be able to get close to the spotlight through them because they will be willing to take them there, being outcasts and all. The first thing to be said about this thesis is that it begins with the "loser" assumption. This is part of gamification, the ideology of gaming itself. It says that all of us want to be famous, in the spotlight, so some of us pathetically choose the most vilified creatures in the mediascape to fetishize in remote hope we'll get close to them, and by association, the spotlight. What Seltzer points out, and I would agree, is that in "reflexive modernity" it is impossible to separate fact from fiction. In many ways, as we have already seen, as video games become our new form of fiction, and reality is increasingly erased under the hyperreal mediascape, we cannot make a critical distinction between real people and their media presentation. Put another way, liking a serial killer or bomber is a lot like identifying with a character in a novel. It's fairly harmless, except for in these cases where the sensational media make it out to mean something more than it actually can be. It is also clear that a lot of this fandom is ironic. James Eagan Holmes has a following on Twitter and elsewhere called "Holmies" who wear plaid (usually ugly plaid clothing) because he apparently wore a plaid jacket into the theater that night (like the Joker). They drink Slurpees, due to an online video of Holmes in high school revealing his life-long dream is to own a Slurpee machine (Slurpees are slushy drinks trademarked by 7-Eleven convenience stores). They also dye their hair red (like Holmes appeared in court) or draw and find red-headed avatars online to represent him. In a lot of these Twitter comments users perform a kind of parody of him. Sure, they say "he's kinda hot," but that's because of the juxtaposition of Holmes's act and his appearance (he isn't as bad looking as we might expect someone to be who does something like this). He reverses our expectations. As well, many of these "young" people use Twitter to actually talk to each other like it's in-person communication. People say things like that in real time, all the time. It's a way of reacting to something you don't know how to react to in a sane way. To make a joke, admit something odd but true.

A related problem is that these crimes are so heinous—they touch us at the core of our democratic assumptions, the right to assemble freely in public spaces—the expectation that not only will people be civil, but they won't try to murder us, that it would be difficult to believe someone might do something like this. This explains the conspiracy theories that have emerged surrounding not only Columbine, but more recently the Century movie theatre spree and Sandy Hook Elementary. Fueled by conspiracy sites like *InfoWars*, these theories suppose that both Holmes and Lanza were poisoned by government officials to hide their fathers' secret information, no doubt uncovered just prior to the acts. These theories suppose that Lanza and Homes are contemporary Manchurian candidates, drugged or programmed to commit these acts by government officials who are trying to cover up crimes. Or, more specifically, Alex Jones suggests that the Sandy Hook massacre was staged. He was one of the first to argue that the Oklahoma City bombing was an "inside job" by the U.S. government, and Jones and others on the far Right, as defenders of states' rights in the U.S. and extreme despisers of the federal government (especially when it is headed by a democrat), have generated a considerable fan base over the past two decades (the Tsarnaevs are said to have visited these sites frequently). Moreover, the success of these conspiracy sites is ultimately tied to the decline in civility in U.S. public culture, as well as the overall decline in living standards. These conspiracies are not fueled only because people lack rationality (that's part of it, we no longer value reason where affect trumps it) but because hyperreal media do not permit rationality (again they feed on "ratings," which is a measurement of "affect"). In order for something like a reasonable explanation to be revealed, there would have to be a baseline reality to measure it against and decipher its validity. Mass media, as a proliferation of interpretations, does not allow for a baseline reality. Thus, we are left with conspiracies, fans and general nonsense in our reporting *ad infinitum*.

To return briefly to our concern with citizens unable to accept that these crimes have either taken place or that the killers committed them, it is important to look at the narratives of their fans. The controversial *Rolling Stone* piece on one of the alleged Boston bombers, Dzhokhar Tsarnaev, points to his close friends from high school and college who could not believe he could do such a thing. Immediately after he was identified on the camera footage at the marathon and a citywide manhunt was underway, the younger Tsarnaev's close friend, Troy Crossley, launched a Twitter campaign "Free Jahar" (his nickname in Massachusetts), unable to believe he committed the bombing. Crossley is hailed as the next Alex Jones, a new generation in conspiracy building. The two main arguments by these groups are that the backpack in the media footage (released to the public to identify the bombers) is not the same color as Tsarnaev's in later footage, and that the pictures released (against policy) by the Boston police officer trying to counter the so-called positive image on the cover of *Rolling Stone* do not show a throat wound, as authorities indicated he had when they took him into custody. This wound was said to explain why he could not speak or talk about the bombing for several days, even weeks. A *Boston Globe* article summarizes even more of the fans' ideas that go into government involvement:

> There are those who believe the bombs and blood were staged, that the amputees and others injured were actors in some kind of Hollywood production designed to justify martial law. Others acknowledge the carnage but say it was perpetrated by a secret squad of special operations soldiers. And there are those who insist that inconsistencies in early reports, erroneous statements by public officials, and unreleased evidence from prosecutors—among other things—reflect anything from a government cover-up to an effort to frame the suspects. (Abel 2013)

There is a radical contradiction in the way these fans function and the way that critics who want to stop these acts think about them. Critics maintain that the fans actually admire these acts; they do not. They don't believe in them. Actually, they more often believe that the government is behind them rather than the perpetrator. At the end of this chapter, I will assess the three events that I cover against the theory of the antihero, a protagonist originally from poetic literature that breaks the rules, has some bad qualities or generally withholds justice in his character. He is nevertheless held up as an ideal figure. The fans (and they are not just female, as Nathalie Paton reminds us) of these killers are not, I suggest, interested in them as antiheroes. This is contrary to many media experts who argue that we should stop reporting about these events, or, at the very least, report on them in a particular way, to avoid more of what they call "copycats." Since, as I have already argued, these are not copycats but additions to the ongoing game, a form of participation, it is difficult to say if the reporting does anything other than give the next attacker a way to think about how to either reveal or obliterate himself in front of the American public. It does not, however, deter someone who identifies with the cruelty. As we have seen, that is not forged in identification with hatred alone, but prior to it, in modular society. I will return to this and explain obliteration when we get to Kazmierczak, who I think took the opposite tack of Cho and left almost nothing behind, at least no manifesto. Whereas Cho seems to have been desperately trying to reveal himself to anyone who would listen, finally taking it to an extreme level, Kazmierczak, in contrast, was trying to hide another side of himself, even in the final exit. He nevertheless participates in the ritual act.

Looking at three U.S. cases, this chapter looks at media framing of the Red Lake, Minnesota shooting, the Virginia Tech shooting, and finally, the often understudied and therefore overlooked case of Northern Illinois University, where a former student attacked and killed 5 students, then shot himself as the campus police closed in on him, in February 2008. Other cases previously mentioned occur in between these, for example the two shootings in Finland both occur in 2007 and the ones in Germany in 2006 and 2009, and Brazil and Francophone Canada, as we mentioned in the introduction. I invite other scholars proficient in those languages and more familiar with those media cultures, ones I have already readily cited in the past chapters, to compare, contrast or dispute the connections I am making here. I am focusing on these cases because two of them get overlooked (Weise and Kazmierczak) I think for the reasons outlined in the last chapter about national responsibility, but also, as we shall see, for reasons intended by the killers themselves. The reason the Seung-Hui Cho could not be ignored was that he committed the largest number of casualties ever in a mass shooting, and he sent a media packet directly to television outlets (other perpetrators possibly fearing their messages would not be aired, went directly on the Internet and their messages were eventually taken down). Jeff Weise was indeed figured as "other," as often happens with regard to native American citizenship, but also documented psychological disfigurement in his family life, and Steven Kazmierczak's identity obliterated all the past ones: he was white, middle-class, from a suburb of a major city (Chicago), a successful student (winner of the Dean's award at NIU), a published author (fourth author), had many friends, who remain baffled by his acts, and had a serious (yet former) girlfriend he lived with in Champaign, Illinois, where he was attending the University of Illinois as a graduate student. Report after report finds "no motive" in the Northern Illinois shooting, and few researchers cover it. This is curious. Perhaps because it doesn't fit the media's established categories, it must be overlooked. However, I think it is the most central case to date, and prefigures the tragedies authored by James Eagan Holmes, as well as Adam Lanza in particular. While I am not covering these extensively here, I will follow up at a later date after trials have ended, and a respectful amount of time has passed.

Rogues, Red Lake and Citizenship

Overall, Virgin Land enabled the American people to replace the fact that the land was already settled by a vast Native population with the belief that it was occupied. And the substitution of the national fantasy for the historical actuality enabled Americans to disavow the resettlement and in some instances the extermination of entire populations. (Pease 2003, 4)

While the technical definition of "rampage" would accurately describe a shooting that leaves 10 dead, it was a poorly chosen word to describe a catastrophe on an Indian reservation. Portrayals of "rampaging Indians" fed hateful stereotypes in books and movies for many years. Yet, I've seen the word used in many media around the country to describe the Red Lake shooting. (Parry 2005 qtd. in Byrd 2007, 317)

Who are the others of brothers, the nonbrothers? What makes them separate beings, excluded or wayward, outcast or displaced, left to roam the streets [rues], especially those of the suburbs? (Derrida 2005, 63)

Derrida opens the sixth chapter of *Rogues* by commenting on the commonplace use of the term *voyou* in France to designate wayward citizens, or those who have fallen off the normal path in society, particularly in the French banlieues (suburbs), and always defined in relation to that path from which they have strayed. These are the Parisian rioters that Žižek accused of committing impotent *passages à l'acte* in 2005, much discussed in Chapter 2. To be sure, Éric Debarbieux, in his study of school violence in France, has hesitated before the impulse to define violence, especially school violence, exclusively in relation to the popular notion of school kids in France, particularly immigrants (Debarbieux & Blaya 2002, 33–54). Searching for a wider definition that does not associate perpetrators with revolutionaries or terrorists, Debarbieux eschews any notion of school violence that would make these spectacular events fall under the category of violence examined by Benjamin (and commented upon by Derrida), "the 'great' criminal" who has "aroused the secret admiration of the public" (Benjamin 1978, 281). Those designated as "other" or the other of the brother in democratic thought (that is, western, industrialized nation-states) give one pause—a certain reservation must be issued—when speaking of the other of democracy. The presumption is always that the other is comes from away, but what happens when the other is the mistreated and ignored host?

On March 23, 2005, on an Ojibwe reservation in Red Lake, Minnesota, seventeen-year-old Jeff Weise followed in the path of other American school shooters by opening fire on students at the local high school from which he had been expelled several months earlier. He actively preyed on random students, following them to classrooms in which they locked themselves according to the school lockdown policy, shot the glass in the door window out and unlocked the door, allowing himself into the room to then open fire, indiscriminately shooting students, and a teacher. "Random" and "indiscriminate" are important words for describing Weise's act as he did not target specific individuals, nor did his calm, smiling face belie his intent to shoot at the bearers of an attitude: those who take themselves as the "people of gods" mentioned by Derrida as Rousseau's impossible wished-for democracy; an intolerable communitarianism (Derrida 2004, 110). Weise himself called them "zombies" and described their world as "so misinformed, ignorant and close-minded, it makes your life a living hell" (Hewitt 2005a). Zombies are the undead; they remain suspended between life and death, trapped on earth, in a state of "unrest." Zombies are also a category in philosophy that represents beings without consciousness. They are an interesting way of characterizing the influence of global consumer culture on formerly vital beings. In much the same way that so-called rogues in international politics have criticized G-8 countries and their hypocritical treaties, especially concerning nuclear development, Weise was critical of contemporary American culture; he argued it drained Native culture of its specificity, noting that hardly any people on the reservation spoke the native language. As globalization has come to dominate most forms of social reproduction, some groups feel they are being eked out of existence. It is at the point of cultural reproduction, identity and difference where the Breivik, the American Neo-Nazi and the Native American share some concerns.

Why is it "difficult" to be a Native American Neo-Nazi, as Jeff Weise claimed? That is the question this section will answer indirectly by looking at how identity is captured and examined in media accounts of violent episodes, as well as how identity is configured by media in the present day. The only controversy that Red Lake seemed to solicit in the American press was the notion that now "it can happen anywhere" and by faulty conclusion "we are all equal." The Southern Poverty Law Center expert Mark Potok remarks that minorities in the United States have all belonged to hate groups focusing on race, and that they identify with the power struggle and achievement of the "oppressor." He further notes that this "bizarre phenomenon" results in people "joining movements that aim to exterminate them or people like them" (Wilgoren 2005). I think Weise's own words to the Libertarian National Socialist Green Party explain the interpellation into fascist admiration best, "I guess I've always had a natural admiration for Hitler and his ideas, and his courage to take on larger nations" (Davey 2005). In fact, as anthropologists have highlighted, any deviation from "indigenous identity" as set out in constitutional and human rights arrangements threaten to deprive a subject of land, sovereignty and welfare rights. These arrangements are made by referencing "deployed alliances" made by "local descent groups" that are "a family tree organized on the basis of some rule of kinship, marriage, and descent, rules that situate persons before they are born in a generational flow of people, affects and goods; place them under certain fixed obligation and duties; and provide them with certain rights and responsibilities with regard to that flow. For it is important to remember that the deployment of alliance as the ground for self-action is not merely, or even necessarily, a function of indigenous social life, but a mandate of state law" (Povinelli 2005, 160). Not only did Jeff Weise have to fit a certain identity model within the community of the Red Lake nation, a specific group of Cherokee, the Ojibwe, with a long history of resistance to outside influence, he had to fit another one that spoke sense to the larger American political imaginary about the limited category "Native American." It is under this pretext that the term "rampage" is (unfortunately) unveiled to the American public. The term implies a hot anger, whereas most eyewitnesses to these events come to the same conclusion: the killer as cold, methodical, staring straight ahead, unyielding. If this is revenge, it is planned, methodical, and unyielding. And, as we move into the latter half of the decade, it is not against the original target, but some representative of it.

Outcast

This is starting to become a concern for me. This dangerous loner thing. It's never accurate. CBS described the kid as a loner and then brought on an "expert" that amplified that comment. I wanted to throw a brick through the TV. I hope anyone who saw that will contact them about it. I did. Loners aren't dangerous, outcasts can be.

We need to stop the bullies that create outcasts. But then, we only have to look at the current state of our government to see what a monumental task that will be. Capitalism equals bully. Or at least this ever more Hobbesian form of capitalism does.

—Chaska (March 26, 2005, Online chatroom, "Democratic Underground")

He was a loner, in part, by happenstance, his parents having vanished from his life because of quieter tragedies. Emily Parkhurst, who like many other residents of the Red Lake Indian Reservation knew nearly everyone killed or hurt in the shootings, said Mr. Weise's father shot himself to death four years ago. Not long after that, Mr. Weise's mother was in a serious car accident that left her using a wheelchair and living in a nursing home. "It was a lot to handle for a kid with no one to guide him or help him," Ms. Parkhurst said. "Nobody took the time to get to know him either."

—Davey (2005)

At the school site, the event unfolds much the same way as the Columbine event. We hear reports that Weise was smiling the entire time, paused to ask a student of their belief in God, and, in a weird twist, strangely approved of that faith, if the report is to be believed. The firing was random and indiscriminate; Weise does not have enemies in his sights, rather the enemy is perhaps the space of the school itself, what it represents. As we learn later he fought with teachers about the decline of native identity through the intrusion of American culture, such as rap music, drugs, and baggy clothing. We are not able to view a video of the event as in the case of Columbine; the video camera did catch Weise walking through the hallway, but there are no cameras in classrooms where he targeted his victims. Also, Minnesota law requires that schools have an emergency evacuation plan only; security cameras, guards and metal detectors are not required (though Weise passed through the detector at the high school). Weise purposefully cited several shootings, though the most obvious one to the casual observer was Columbine.

So, this "rogue" of Red Lake had veered from not just one path but many outlined in the media depictions of the shootings in March 2005. As Derrida has argued of the deployment of rogue in English, it can also apply to animals and objects, not just to people as in the French version of voyou (Derrida 2004, 94). When rhetoric is deployed to frame an open political situation to the benefit of the sovereignty of the nation in which it takes place, whether by media or politicians, we should maintain a healthy dose of suspicion. As Derrida has outlined it, rogue is one such term. Examples include de Villepin's choice of "social unrest" as a way of describing violence in French suburbs or the American media's depictions of young, alienated men that go on "rampages"; the stress is less on what is deformed or out-of-whack with the governing structure (democratic sovereignty, which Derrida rightly problematizes, and I would add the corresponding versions of multiculturalism that come in to play to preserve the fiction of self-determination under this structure) than it is on the deviants who take public attention away from the problematic source of governmentality's breakdown and inability to keep in check the "bullies that create outcasts." It is indeed difficult to keep the bullies that create outcasts in check when the government and its repressive state apparatuses are model leaders for this structurally similar form of bullying.

This is when the term *rampage* enters the larger national discourse. As Leavy and Maloney argue, the two famous images from Columbine, that of the students running outside the building covering their heads, and of the bloody boy dangling from the second story window became "iconic" and represented not only Columbine but school violence. They also suggest, after a detailed content analysis of the news stories after both events, that one reason was that Columbine "normalized" school violence around race, whereas most stories surrounding Weise were foregrounded by his troubled past, including the death of his father. They also suggest, and this is the trajectory we suggested in the introduction, that though we can never know, one reason Red Lake may have failed to produce a "collective trauma" in the United States is that the war in Iraq overshadowed any coverage, combined with the lack of iconic images (Leavy & Maloney 2009, 290). However, Red Lake did allow for the (perhaps) media debut of a new term: rampage. The new framing by the media describes Weise's act as a "rampage" a term borrowed from sociologist Katherine Newman who defines it as a "new kind of violence," and these events are a:

> special kind of attack quite unlike the more familiar revenge killings we hear so so much about. Rampage shootings are defined by the fact that they involve attacks on multiple parties, selected almost at random. These shooters may have a specific target to begin with, but they let loose with a fusillade that hits others, and it is not unusual for the perpetrator to be unaware of who has been shot long after the fact. These explosions are attacks on whole institutions—schools, teenage pecking orders, and communities. Shooters choose schools as the site for a rampage because they are the heart and soul of public life in small towns. Rampages tend to take place in rural and suburban settings— they rarely occur in urban areas—and rampage shooters are predominantly white boys. (Newman 2004, 12–25)

The media presents these acts as unfolding in a way that might fit the description of "rampage." This is not what we hear from survivors and witnesses. The general impression that comes from them is that the shooter, unlike Harris and Klebold, is methodic, deadly quiet with cold eyes. The media, with its unrelenting focus on iconic images (like the ones at Columbine), its detailing of the shooter's past and other interview tactics, creates the indelible impression in the mind of the viewer, that this person must have been "rushing about," "angry" and "frenzied," all words that technically define a rampage. Rather, most witnesses conclude that they were controlled in their movements, their faces betraying no emotion, and no speaking (how can "angry" be conveyed without language?). *Superficially*, these acts resemble a rampage, and while Newman is correct to note that the students plan these events for quite some time (including stockpiling ammunition and weapons), the main difference is that in none of the latter three shootings did the students plan to live to see the aftermath, nor did they care about who had "been shot after the fact" (Newman 2004, 12–25)

There is also no evidence in any of the reporting that Jeff Weise had attempted to join groups at school and failed. He is characterized as a loner who wore the official Columbine-esque clothing, acted "weird" (read: Goth) and drew weird pictures. These don't seem to be the practices of a student attempting to join or conform to the homogeneous social. In fact they seem like behaviors specifically designed to ward off communal involvement. Our chat room thinkers are on to something here: there is a difference between desiring community involvement and not desiring it, and there is, at minimum, a nominal distinction between *being a loner* and *becoming an outcast*; something must act as a catalyst for affirming one's status as "outcast"—indeed, the community rejects the loner who never applied for admission. Weise had much to say about the homogeneous social that he witnessed on the Red Lake reservation, and Jodi Byrd contextualizes the national press by arguing there was Neo-Nazi activity all around the area:

> As the media focused on the Nazi rhetoric in which Weise participated online, the transformation of 'Native Nazi' into the Columbine narratives of 'neo-Nazi' all served to mask not only that, in Minnesota, one finds the headquarters for the National Socialist Movement (America's second-largest Nazi organization) but also that in the months leading before the Red Lake shooting, communities in and around the Twin Cities saw a rise in Nazi flyers after a Hmong man was accused of killing six white hunters in Wisconsin. (Byrd 2007, 315)

As she asks, "The question as to how Jeff Weise knew about Nazism becomes, in this context, 'How could he not?'" (ibid., 316).

Startlingly absent from Newman's analysis in 2005 is any mention of bullies. Weise comments on bullies in his online postings, and we are told by media reports, that they are relatively ineffective where he is concerned because he is so big (without current photos released to the public, we cannot assess Weise's size but are told that he had grown very tall and stocky in recent years). Weise says the attempt to bully him is made by students at school but to little effect:

> You encounter a lot of hostility when you claim to be a National Socialist, but because of my size and appearance people don't give me as much trouble as they would if I looked weak. I already had a fist fight with a communist not to long ago over me being what I am (I also won), but it was worth it. I don't try to hide what I am from anyone, if they're going to start something over it then fine, I'm not backing down; Nor am I hiding. I try not to be aggressive in most situations, I'll use force if I have to, but I'm not about to go out and pick a fight. I'm mostly defensive, I'll defend myself if someone tries something but other than that I'm a peaceful person. (NSLG.org, 2004)

A loner is someone who chooses to be alone, and while the loner may indeed be "socially incapable," there is a kind of implicit recognition by the loner of this deficiency and a self-segregation from groups. Reports have Weise "lazy about school," frequently absent, a loner, who wore eyeliner and a Goth trench coat, listened to Marilyn Manson and walked down the hallway looking straight ahead without making eye contact with other students. One counselor remarked that "no one had taken the time to get to know him" (Davey 2005). Another student, quoted over and over again in the media reports had said, that as she tried to flee from Weise into a classroom with him banging on the door, she thought, "I didn't know if I was going to be a target. … I thought he might have shot me because I have a lot of friends" (Gottfried & Prather 2005b). In this way, Weise's act is similar to the other shootings with some notable differences. However, the questions now become not why do some students fantasize about shooting up a school and yet refrain from doing so while others clearly take up the challenge in real time, but why does someone like Jeff Weise, with so many environmental and familial factors working against him, choose the school as a site of violence instead of some other space on the reservation? Why mimic the other shootings? Clearly, Weise's problem was not just the kids at school and friendship, but a larger problem in his mind about the destruction of Native culture by the larger society whose version of civil society was imposed (he thought) on the reservation, to its detriment. Why put the same questions to victims who wear similar clothing and have similar tastes (e.g., Neo-Nazi websites, Hitler)? While no one will like it, it's clearly a parody of Columbine, an addition to the ritual established there, one of subverting the public's intrusive need to ask "why?" While not denying there are other "pre-event" factors that led up to it, his personal life, his treatment and expulsion from the school (possibly for his racist views) and the understandable depression that would result from this predicament, it is clear that Columbine was probably not just chosen as a copycat way to exit, but that he knew it was probably the only way to draw attention to the reservation. Could he have known the trial elders would close the reservation to reporters and that the FBI would be called in to investigate as a federal matter under U.S. jurisdiction? Maybe not. After all, Harris and Klebold thought that Oliver Stone might make a movie out of their story. We are still on the terrain of depressed teenagers with limited global perspective, but much telepresent savvy.

The media in the U.S., shocked and muted by the tribal council's closure of Red Lake to reporters, consistently made links between Weise's disaffections and his father's suicide following a standoff with tribal police in 1997 (about which they constantly commented that his paternal grandfather was involved with the armed standoff that ended with the suicide) and his mother's alcoholism that led to a car accident during which she suffered severe brain injury and was placed into a nursing home one year later. However, in an interview with tribal activists, they pointed out that most people at Red Lake Nation had lost a parent or had parents with drug and alcohol problems. Contrary to what mainstream media attempted to depict about Weise, he was "normal" where Red Lake conditions were concerned. As Byrd echoes:

> While Weise turned his self-hatred outward in moments of unforgiveable violence before killing himself, many American Indian youth on reservations, who do not receive mainstream media attention, turn to alcohol, violence and suicide because, in the words of First Nations hip-hop group Warparty, 'genocide makes [them] live their native lives deadly.' (Byrd 2007, 325)

The conclusion of simple mimicry or copycatting as an explanation for the Red Lake shootings is also foreclosed by close analysis of several aspects of the school attack. There are several deviations from Columbine (that might be seen as improvements on the serial narrative I charted in my last book on the subject of media coverage and public reaction to school violence), and they are relevant to a discussion about how remote technologies have transformed the "social" in ways that challenge critical social scientists' means for understanding them. There is no room for an easy answer, no one interpretation that will suffice—this is how Jeff Weise conveyed it. While the press was content to note similarities to Columbine (the most cited aspects were the scope of the killing and the Neo-Nazi connections, while some made the connections between particular acts of mimicry: smiling while shooting, asking a student if he believed in god then not shooting him (Sarche 2005), I would argue that pre-event specifics in this case more closely resembles the Springfield, Oregon shooting by Kip Kinkel in 1998. Kinkel's spree unfolded in much the same way as Weise's, and began with a similar event: the killing of family members. Where Kinkel shot both of his parents inside his home at separate times, Weise shot his grandfather. Also, Weise was in a home schooling program, having been expelled from school for violating an undisclosed policy, although the media speculates it was an attempted school attack since Weise relayed to this an online site, but argued that the charges were false (he was framed). In another twist, Weise then took his grandfather's bulletproof vest, squad car and two guns (a shotgun and a .40 caliber pistol), in this case echoing the shooters at Jonesboro, Arkansas, specifically Andrew Golden, who with the help of his partner, Mitchell Johnson, broke into his grandfather's cache of weapons for use in police work as well. Kip Kinkel had convinced his parents to help him amass the weapons he would use to kill them and students at Thurston High School, whereas these boys had to steal them as did Weise.

When Weise arrived at the school, he confronted two unarmed security guards (the reports on what happened next are contradictory), a man and a woman; the woman fled to warn other students, while the man would be fatally shot twice by Weise in the ensuing confrontation.[1] Later, after George W. Bush had been excoriated by the media and local officials at Red Lake for failing to comment on the shooting, he valorized this security guard as a "hero." In a move for self-definition, tribal leaders argued he was a "warrior," in contrast to Bush's hero. Angry over Bush's lack of response to the shooting and his brief hiatus from vacation to intervene instead in the Terri Schiavo case, tribal members called to remind the White House that there was a shooting. Clyde Bellecourt, a Chippewa and national director of the American Indian Movement issued a strong statement: "From all over the world we are getting letters of condolence, the Red Cross has come, but the so-called Great White Father in Washington hasn't said or done a thing" (Connolly 2005). Bush, it seems, waited until his weekly radio address the following Sunday to frame the event in light of ongoing operations in Iraq (the heroes giving their lives "for freedom's cause." The Red Lake condolences were sandwiched between two Iraq honorable mentions, highlighting the struggle to overcome "death" completely and that, through prayer, "even death, itself, will be defeated" (Bush 2005). Nothing, it seemed, could overshadow the war in Iraq, and perhaps even Bush wanted to downplay the shooting because of the later scandal surrounding republican affiliates Jack Abramoff, Ralph Reed, Jr. and Grover Norquist who were arrested in August of that year for cheating several Indian casinos out of money while representing them as lobbyists. This is not how Bush would react to the shooting at Virginia Tech where he could make political overtures. Although George W. Bush had avoided for years going to the funerals for victims of his Iraq war, he arrived with his wife, Laura, ready to make a speech and then do interviews with the network broadcasting news anchors who had assembled in Blacksburg for the event. Bush was at a critical time in his presidency. His Iraq policy was opposed by the majority of the public, and the democrats appeared ready to fight Bush on his failed policy (Kellner 2007).

Virginia Tech

> If the culture was not at fault, that meant figuring out what might have fixed Cho. Though none of the identities disappeared entirely from commentary on the Virginia Tech 'massacre,' they were in short order subsumed under a new category. In an act of historical recapitulation that would make Foucault proud, morality gave way to medicine as the prevailing explanatory paradigm. Cho, it was soon established, suffered from mental illness and his rampage was a consequence of a broken mental health system. This identity has now trumped all others.
>
> —Jones (2009, 74)

The only way to survive a rampage attack is to play dead. Playing dead in this formulation is a way of faking out the aggressor who is intent on taking as many lives as possible. And the aggressor is usually engaged in his own form of deception: faking being alive. As the police report later demonstrated, Cho fired more than 170 rounds of ammunition in just shy of 9 minutes. Those students and faculty that found themselves in Cho's line of sight at Norris Hall survived by playing dead or blocking doors so he could not enter the rooms they inhabited on that Monday morning. The campus shooting that occurred at Virginia Tech demonstrates an incipient form of violence that corresponds to a peculiar domestic frustration that then flows outward to an indifferent society. This rage is remarkably similar to that of suicide bombers: inexplicable, impossible to predict or diffuse through traditional means, and aimed at groups of people unknown to the perpetrator except as representatives of a culture or political form they oppose. Yet, at the same time it is truly democratic, "equal opportunity hatred" really, targeting no one in particular except perhaps a collective attitude: the rich kids for whom nothing is good enough, according to the manifesto. We have already heard from E. J. Carvalho who believes that Cho, particularly through his media packet, was attempting to parody media, and construct a pastiche of popular poses (tropes on *Old Boy, Taxi Driver, The Heathers*, etc. were embedded in the poses). It is here at Virginia Tech that evidence of the transpolitical nature of these events becomes clear not only with the media packet but also with the disturbing choice of targets (still no personal connections have been made between Cho and the two deaths at West Ambler Johnston Hall or the Norris Hall shootings, where engineering and technology students were predominant). Only that, possibly, "One clue exists in Cho's final selection of courses. He was taking a sociology class called Deviant Behavior, according to interviews. The class met on the second floor of Norris Hall, where most of the shootings occurred" (Gardner & Cho 2007).

"Ishmael Ax," it was reported was what Cho wrote on his arm in black magic marker, knowing he would destroy his face and identity at the end of his rampage, just long enough to throw the authorities off his scent and allow time for the package mailed earlier to arrive at NBC headquarters. The name there again, except it read A. Ishmael on the corner of the package. As Douglas Kellner clarifies:

> But on the evening of April 18, NBC reported that the package with the multimedia dossier was addressed as sent from "A. Ishmael." The latter literary spelling of the Old Testament and Koranic "Ismail" could refer to the opening of Herman Melville's classic *Moby Dick*, where the narrator begins with "Call me Ishmael." This reading would position the shooter as on a revenge quest, as was Captain Ahab against the White Whale, Moby Dick. But it also positions Cho himself within the great tradition of American literature, as Ishmael is the narrator of one of the United States's great novels. Another Internet search noted that the literary character Ishmael is also "tied to James Fenimore Cooper's novel *The Prairie*, Ishmael Bush is known as an outcast and outlawed warrior, according to an essay written in 1969 by William H. Goetzmann, a University of Texas History professor. In Cooper's book, 'Bush carries the prime symbol of evil—the spoiler's axe,' the professor wrote." [23] (Kellner 2007, no pages)

The package in question contained the clips that confronted the NBC executives with a moral dilemma: do they show them or not? Cho knew that they would show them, and he wanted them to have to confront that decision and to feel the resentment of a public who did and did not want to glimpse into his tortured soul. This was the *exit option* with self-awareness of how it was implicating the public, the media and the university. In the end, it won't matter as the mother of character Eric LaRue, a fictional school shooter who lives to explain his murder of three boys during gym class, because, "[sic] what you did didn't change how they feel. It changed how you feel" (Neveu 2007, 80). Like *Harmless*, Neveu's play in a similar genre, a moral confrontation ensues between the public and the perpetrator where the public is asked to confront its own want of being, its responsibility and its implication in the patterns of rage. The inner turmoil caused by extreme bullying or the rampant fear and suspicion of creativity or of otherness is directed outward finally in *Eric LaRue* at the boys who bullied him. In *Harmless* in a soldier's creative writing assignment, one that a professor, university president and army psychologist all decide is "harmless," despite their intense hand-wringing mediations in the president's office. Three months after this play debuted in Chicago, and two weeks after the massacre at Virginia Tech, a high school senior in junior ROTC, prepares an essay for his creative writing class in suburban Illinois. He writes:

> My current English teacher is a control freak intent on setting a gap between herself and her students like a 63 year old white male fortune 500 company CEO, and a illegal immigrant. If CG was a private catholic school, I could understand, but wtf is her problem. And baking brownies and rice crispies does not make up for it, way to try and justify yourself as a good teacher while underhandedly looking for complements on your cooking. No quarrel on you [sic] qualifications as a writer, but as a teacher, don't be surprised on inspiring the first cg shooting. (qtd. in Poulsen 2007)

"CG" stands for Cary Grove, the name of the high school Allen Lee attended. The writing assignment was supposed to be "creative," and the media reports that Lee was a straight-A student. The school board met to discuss the essay after the teacher reported it, and they voted to notify the police who arrested Lee on a disorderly conduct charge.

He was subsequently dropped by the Marines, causing a media spectacle. In the aftermath of the Virginia Tech massacre, experts noted that "zero tolerance has gone awry as policy" and that creative expression was under fire. It's no wonder then that this shooting in particular inspired controversy over creative writing as Cho had been removed from a professor's course and tutored individually due to his effect on the classroom. We later learn that he was bullied in middle and high school and that his mother sought help for him at local churches to deal with his communication problems. Carvalho's essay makes the pointed critique of Cho's upbringing in Seoul, South Korea; as a poor and possibly shamed family, they left to come to the U.S., and his parents worked constantly to put their kids through school. He mentions U.S. foreign policy toward the region, the economic shocks and the experience of being an immigrant in the U.S. as important factors which underlie the political import of Cho's multimedia manifesto, especially its references to martyrdom and Christ. While these are all valid considerations in what led Cho to become alienated and probably do shine through in his media packet, I would look much closer at the event itself, to the mediations at VTU and elsewhere in the psychiatric community. My guess is the psych hold set him off.

We will go there soon, but first it is important to reiterate: the exit option is when a citizen who has been a party to the middle-class social contract decides to opt out of participation, where that participation means a renunciation of physical violence to pursue grievances through forms of mediation in the legal arena or the institutions of civil society. I have in mind here the strict Althusserian versions: the school, the church, workplace, etc. Yet, Aronowitz's depiction of this space of mediation excludes an analysis of mediation in the psychiatric arena and how this arena provides a different kind of mediation, one that is judgmental and identity threatening in a society where mental illness is stigmatized.[2] It is also completely aligned with the repressive state apparatuses, like the police and other crime control agencies. Furthermore, avenues for mediation *delinked from civility* expand in times of privatization, where the government retreats from social welfare funding and allows corporations and private counselors to make assessments and mediations regarding problem individuals. In an era of subcontracting, where every available service is provided by organizations delinked from the sovereignty of the state, a social contract no longer holds. Participating in forms of mediation no longer means reintegration into something resembling civil society since that formation barely exists. Instead individuals subject to them are forcefully assimilated into ways of being and knowing that shift from one market expectation to another, and often they are abandoned in the middle of trying to attempt them. While scholars of politics have been perfectly willing to accept the decline of the state or its implosion into micro forms of policing and containment that co-opt privacy through surveillance cultures, zero tolerance boards, a decline in the social wage for the poor and underserved and a criminalization of social problems, why is there is a disturbing lack of acknowledgment that this will have an overall impact on civil society?

In the next few paragraphs, I will map this disjunctive traipse through the disconnected structures of mediation and dispute resolution. Where one system ends, another does not begin to continue the rehabilitation. This is, however, not something that can be fixed through reform as many would have it. Indeed any reform that has taken place in these institutions (at least in the U.S. and Brazil) has done so from the perspective of the market. Reform is a euphemism for market and corporate takeover. Moreover, without a way to imagine what civil society should look like outside the consumer model, how can social service agencies hope to help fragile individuals cope? This is, I think, the question Balibar wants to answer, but true to his Althusserian roots, is apprehensive about how to fix the problems left in the wake of the destruction of the ISAs (ideological state apparatuses).

Following Columbine, little by way of planning had been achieved, and in terms of continuing the U.S. national narrative of serial school violence, the mutual pact created by and between these shooters is distended in time, and any citation through media outlets had seemingly ended. Until the shooting at Red Lake, Minnesota, in the spring of 2005 where Weise had carefully planned and stylized his rage (anticipating the security guard, aiming at faces, succeeding in killing himself), the episodes seemed to be waning. That is until Virginia Tech, which many dubbed a "College Columbine," both confusing and merging the two events and spaces of spectral violence. I would argue for a subtle change to this and call it "Columbine Goes to College," where the new twist in the narrative is in continuing the rage or prolonging it through to the college experience. My analysis views the problem as a continuum, not as discrete events picked up by the media as they happen. Cho's rage was so violent and focused (chaining the doors shut and choosing a building with specific exit vulnerabilities, especially the second floor [a lot like Columbine]), directed at impersonal targets who represent the society he loathed, but were not directly of it (the students and professors in engineering and foreign language replaced the students in English and his own dorm). By staging two particular aspects of the event to throw off police investigators and buy time for more to take the message to the public, Cho calmly made his way to the local post office to mail video clips of himself stylizing his exit, striking poses from movie covers such as Oh Dae-su with his hammer in *Old Boy*, referring to "Eric" and "Dylan," reading aloud the manifesto in various tones (sad, elated, abject) and calling future generations of school shooters "his children" and the "weak and defenseless." The staging of the murder-suicide also meant that campus police would be detained on the other side of the campus, or off interrogating the boyfriend of one of the victims on a Virginia freeway outside of town—all thoughts that must have preoccupied Cho as he made his fifteen minute walk across the drill field over to Norris Hall. This careful planning is akin to the kind of power exercised by the stalker, someone who continually cruises under the radar of polite society and terrorizes civilians in their everyday lives. And yet, everyone left him alone. No matter how weird he got, he was just ignored even more. This is the fate of the adult in the control society. Whereas the child or adolescent that doesn't fit in is the site of a national preoccupation in the control society, the odd adult is usually shut out or ignored completely. Even Cho's alleged stalking is not reported.

Stalking

One of the most striking features of the case made against Cho by the media and other professors at the university was his odd, and at times, invasive behavior in classrooms, and his known propensity for stalking women outside the classroom, using the Internet and MySpace pages as a means of gaining knowledge of female students interests and their whereabouts, taking pictures of them in class while wearing a hat and sunglasses, and referring to himself through writing as only "?". Though the public was not made aware of the specifics of Cho's stalking episodes, except that his victims felt "weird and uncomfortable" by his attentions, the media highlighted the fact that none of them pressed charges.[3]

We have to look at the diversion staged by Cho at Ambler Johnston Hall. Whether or not Virginia Tech is responsible for failing to make a campus-wide alert is not our primary motive here, however, as we shall see, this particular staging is important.

At 7 a.m. a young woman heard a thud and went to investigate. Unable to open the door to Emily Hilscher's dorm room, and finding no reply to her queries, she returned to her room, packed her bag and left for breakfast, apparently in shock. When police were called twenty minutes later, they interviewed Hilscher's closest friend who told them she had returned with her boyfriend from a weekend getaway (and she had at 6:50); he also owned guns but was reportedly not violent. While there are conflicting media reports (and no official police or Virginia Tech report) as to what transpired during those hours from the shooting at West Ambler Johnston Hall until Cho's entry into Norris Hall much later, the way the police investigated Hilscher's boyfriend and failed to issue a campus-wide security alert has been criticized by many, including the victims' families who have sued in civil court, as well as the national inquiry by the Department of Education. Unable to find a motive for Cho's rampage, in the end the university's appeal to reverse the decision was granted in the spring of 2012 by a federal judge. This reversed the Department of Education's fining of the university for the maximum amount of $55,000 for violations of the Clery Act for failure to report the incident to students in a timely manner. Without a party to hold responsible for this heinous act, even if it was tangential responsibility, the nation decided on mental illness. That, however, did not mean the campus police's initial assessment was not biased:

> The public construction of Cho began as police responded to the first shooting, those of Ryan Christopher Clark, an African American residence hall advisor, and Emily Hilscher, a first-year white student and member of the equestrian team. Blacksburg Police, when told that Hilscher's boyfriend was a gun owner, appear to have brought to their investigation certain assumptions about college-aged young people but also about the volatility of of sexualized interracial relationships. Virginia Tech had experienced racist incidents in the recent past; the shootings at West Ambler-Johnston might have been another, more explosive, incident of racial intolerance. It seemed only likely to the police that a romantic relationship had morphed into sexual jealousy fueled by racism and resulted in domestic violence, as the off-campus, gun-owning boyfriend was assumed to have reacted violently to an apparent, (though eventually determined to be non-existent) relationship between Clark and Hilscher. In light of these assumptions, university officials believed the incident was an isolated one limited to people enmeshed in interpersonal conflict, and so they did not issue a campus-wide lockdown and classes proceeded as usual for a Monday morning. Racism and sexual violence, despite educational campaigns to eradicate them, were part of campus culture in April 2007 and provided the context for the muted response to the first shootings. (Jones 2009, 68)

This essay, entitled the "Thirty-Third Victim," is written by a faculty member from Virginia Tech. It should be noted this kind of analysis does not appear in the 2010 report issued by Governor Tim Kaine, the "official report." Instead the report centers around Cho, and when it touches on the Ambler Johnston incident, backpeddles considerably on the issue of the campus police response. Unfortunately, most of the discussion centered on the university's compliance with the Clery Act. This is a campus security measure passed as a 1990 amendment to the Federal Education Act of 1967, following the death of Jean Clery. Clery, a student at Lehigh University, was raped and murdered in her dorm room in 1986. Immediately following the shootings at Virginia Tech, Catherine Bath, founder of CampusSecurity.org, a non-governmental organization provided with federal assistance from the Justice Department, appeared on MSNBC to discuss one of the most traumatic effects of this particular event: that students were not notified in a timely manner that a "shooter was on the loose." What was clear to anyone watching the coverage by campus police chief Flinchum was that they believed the first incident at Ambler Johnston Hall was a domestic case, and therefore warranted no further warning to students on campus. One can see why this is disturbing to Bath, since she supports and encourages compliance with the Clery Act through her foundation which insists that campus police report crime statistics to the Department of Education, as well as make the public aware by announcing them to the university public. The Clery Act, which is administered by the DOE, also publishes the names of institutional violators of the act, and Virginia Tech had been one in the past (but so are many, many U.S. universities). This kind of legislation also works on an enlightened logic: that if students are aware of violent crimes being committed on campus, they will take extra precautions to protect themselves.[4] What I am more interested in here is the way this diversion is seemingly planned.

Cho fooled them. He did. And yet, while they should have kept an open mind about Ambler Johnston (instead of jumping to the aforementioned racialized and sexualized conclusions), they also could not have known they were part of a foil. Just as the media reported after Red Lake, "While many newspapers touted school surveillance as necessary after Columbine, journalists took a very different position at Red Lake. "But you know how far do you go … If a kid comes in—at Red Lake there was a guard at the door and he was shot first. It's ridiculous. Who would ever think a kid would come in and do that? You can't prevent everything" (Hansen 2005: 1N, qtd. in Leavy & Maloney 2009, 287).[5] Trying to imagine what the next shooting will look like would test anyone's humanity, and who would willingly go there? However, in the context of 9/11, this kind of imagining became the sole preoccupation of public policy. Cho's act would only lead to further containment, profiling and networking of public records.

Making It Real

Can fifteen years of imaginary training actually be put to use? It can.

—Oh Dae-su, *Oldboy*

In *Oldboy*, the South Korean revenge film adapted from a screenplay originally written in the genre of Japanese manga, the main character Oh Dae-su, has been locked in a room with only a television for fifteen years. He does not know why he was kidnapped on the street fifteen years earlier, but from the television broadcasts of the outside world, he knows that his wife has been murdered and in his absence this murder has been blamed on him. He can only rightly suspect that his captor, whom he does not know, has murdered her in order to frame him. Once he is let out of his private prison, he greets several menacing looking young men on the street who call him a "dickhead," and this begins the scene where

Oh Dae-su, having been locked up with no outside world contact, or physical contact with any living things, has to test whether or not all the mental preparation and virtual imagining he has done while watching television (mostly fighting) will be, as the quote above suggests "put to use." Of course in the film, it works; he holds his own against several men, and in several more scenes in this revenge film, particularly a scene entitled "One versus Many," he overpowers a mob with only a hammer as a weapon, and this pose would be made even more famous on American television networks and YouTube by Cho's pose with a hammer over his head, looking menacing to the camera in the days before his shooting rampage at Virginia Tech. While it is simplistic to believe that films "trigger" rage (Webber 2003a), it is important to consider what the film characters that school shooters choose as tropes communicate to the public about their rage, its duration, and its objectives.

Old Boy is a classical Oedipal tragedy. For Dae-su, he is confused about why he has been taken prisoner and released since he is given no explanation, and later we find that he is being tortured in a cat-and-mouse game by a former high school classmate for spreading a rumor that led to the shame and suicide of another female classmate. Is Oh Dae-su an antihero? Hardly. He is a sad, tragic figure who has his memory (intentionally) erased at the end of the film (through hypnosis), much like Oedipus has his eyes gouged out. What is initially appealing about this character is the way that he can get his revenge after having been isolated for so long, his weakness turned to strength through, wait for it—watching television. And yet, at the end, he cannot escape the way that he has been deceived by his nemesis; in tragedies everyone loses. These shootings are just that, tragedies. *Old Boy*, however, adds a new twist by making Dae-su an agent in an otherwise virtual prison. Once freed, he finds that proprioception works. He is able to overcome his bodily weaknesses through the sheer strength of mind and body working together. Dae-su does not have a gun; he fights off his attackers with a hammer, and the dramatic display in the film is not literal. Instead we see his shadow dancing against the bodies of the other men as he wipes them away from the viewers' vision one by one. *Old Boy* was a critical success. It won the Grand Prix at Cannes in 2004. Roger Ebert loved it. It's not a film that presents gratuitous violence. It has very violent scenes, but they mean something within the context of the larger story being told. It's a story about revenge, bullying and incest. Dae-su warns the viewer who not to be in high school: a gossiper. Cho himself seemed angry with his roommates after they called their parents to report him to the authorities due to his long commented upon "strange behavior." As a counselor from Virginia Tech explains:

Cho's social isolation and alienation continued at Virginia Tech; while he lived with roommates and attended classes regularly, he never formed any ongoing social relationships. His limited attentions to several young women perceived as weird or threatening while projecting self-hatred; for example, he left the following quote from *Romeo and Juliet* on the white board outside a young woman's room:

> By a name
> I know not how to tell thee who I am
> My name, dear saint is hateful to myself
> Because it is an enemy to thee
> Had I it written, I would tear the word

Her father contacted the Virginia Tech Police, who interviewed Cho. After being questioned, Cho sent a text message to a roommate, stating, "I might as well kill myself." The father of this roommate reported his suicidal ideation to campus police, who asked Cho to return to their office on the evening of December 13, 2005. (Flynn & Heitzmann 2008, 2)

"?"

No one can say for sure when Cho began planning his attack, since no one knew him. Certainly, one could date the actual planning by when he purchased the guns as the authorities often do, but this is not a reliable indicator given the detailed planning that goes into them. Alongside his impending graduation with no job prospects, as well as his alienation from the English department where it seems he invested at least some of his psychic energy in the dream of writing plays, this betrayal must have stung. The added banality of being the subject of so much concern (by the police, a judge, counselors and dorm mates) that turned into nothing would have really smarted. There is, however, a defense that can be made here. Due to a lack of funding over the course of the decade, VTU's counseling services (like those at many universities) had been dramatically cut. Due to insurance considerations, and, yes, federal privacy policies, no one in his family knew of his psychiatric detainment. Also, no one followed up with him after. He was supposed to contact a designated counseling agency after his release. Flynn and Heitzmann also detail that Cho was seen as an adolescent and had made writings that imagined a "Columbine-like" school attack. He was bullied in grade, middle and high school. At VTU, it seems he was mostly ignored. All these factors combined must have motivated *not the act itself*, but the parodies in his self-presentation in the packet mailed to NBC. Critics and experts read it out literally, but I would argue that he was mocking the media and everyone who had ever made him feel bad in that video. The only people who knew that were going to be other people just like him. Apparently, as we will see Kazmierczak was one such person. In the U.S. anyway, mental disability is seen as a liability and something to be feared. As has been noted throughout this book it is also seen as something contained to the individual that has not been in any way the result of the environment or social reality.

As Price argues, people think of psychosocial disabilities (like the one Cho had, selective mutism, intense shyness) as being "hidden" or "invisible," but she counters this by pointing out that "such disabilities may become vividly manifest in forms ranging from 'odd' remarks or lack of eye contact to repetitious stimming. Like queerness, psychosocial disability is not so much invisible as it is apparitional, and its 'disclosure' has everything to do with the environment in which it dis/appears" (Price 2011, 18). The hat and sunglasses may have made him feel hidden. After all, we tell ourselves that students have to attend the classes we teach and must participate in a certain way. That everyone "feared" Cho because of his odd behavior is telling in terms of Price's choice of words to describe a disability's manifestation: apparitional.

Here again we see the cruelty that precedes the violence. The violence re-enacts the cruelty, but it does so against the representatives of that cruelty. If it were revenge, it might have taken place in another part of the campus. This makes it even more cruel, "To kill me, did they strangle you, ye singing birds of my hopes" (Nietzsche, "The Grave Song"). This is not just an idealization of hatred or an impotent *passage à l'acte*, although it is *of them*. The people who taunted Cho know who they are: the message has been received somewhere down the line. And it's not fair to blame one single factor, or group of people for this event. It is one outcome among many, including imprisonment (1 in 10 U.S. soldiers is now in prison, mental illness diagnoses have increased fivefold in soldiers, and pharmaceutical drugs are the only answer). The truly relevant question might be: why aren't more of these happening?

> One affirmative judgment in reflecting on this event is that virtually no one acted irrationally. People chose what they thought was the best option for their survival or to protect others, and many tried to prevent the shooter from gaining access to their room. Unfortunately, *a shooter operating at point-blank range does not offer many options.* (*Mass Shootings at Virginia Tech* 2009 92, emphasis mine)

For Cho, the great equalizer was a gun, a .22 Walther P semi-automatic handgun. He shot many of his victims several times, returning to the same rooms. Gun enthusiasts were surprised that someone could commit so many fatalities with such a "weak" gun, but others pointed out that at close range, with people trapped in rooms with little cover, the gun was lethal. Cho made it real. With an idea in mind, put there by perpetrators that went before him, he added to the script: establishing a diversion to occupy campus police, chaining the doors shut, methodically going from room to room—silently—shooting at other Virginia Tech students and professors. This had been planned down to the last detail. A "crazy" person (however one imagines that person) does not plan like this. Cho may have had mental disabilities but they did not, as the public and the VTU community seemed to believe, *impair* him completely.[6] As was argued in the introduction, in each event following Columbine, "they add diversions or subtle changes to the script that allow them to increase their numbers, not through skill, but through close up interaction." They are modifying the game.

As we will see in the last section on Northern Illinois, Kazmierczak took every precaution to erase himself from the final act, in spite of the fact that he had many friends, a girlfriend, and family members he kept close and professors who mentored him. Cho, by contrast, had no one. He was able to construct himself in that final video for weeks on end.

What is often overlooked in analysis of school shooters preparations for events is their fascination with carrying out acts not previously achieved, such as "blowing up the school" (e.g., Harris and Klebold). These fantasmatic scenarios are no longer satisfied to stay in the imagination but are begging to be "made real." They take on a life of their own, independent of the subject so privileged under modern, praxis-oriented ways of understanding action. It is the object(ive) that seduces the subject to make it real. This explains the creative writing crisis we witnessed following the Virginia Tech incident. When it was not amplified by the anxiety produced by connecting Cho's plays or soldier's blogs on the Web and videos produced of atrocities in Iraq on YouTube, to issues of censorship, it does not cohere to what was previously understood as practice: the implementation of institutional imperatives without much thought (e.g., also non-cognitive). Practice might seem more similar to proprioception than praxis, and this is because it is its direct antecedent. Let me explain.

Recall our discussion in the introduction of Kac's celebration of telepresent technologies to achieve progressive projects. Kac grafts a utopian format of consciousness onto a telepresent medium: we can have presentism on screen, and it will resort in a subsequent praxis in physical spaces (e.g., meet online and then take off clothes in the street). As the screen replaces the street as a space of change, the agents in the process are rendered inert: not acting becomes a way of transforming the dominant narrative of any given political movement.

Most of the events forecast by the media are outliers in comparison to everyday experience, but as people increasingly mediate through the screen instead of physical public spaces, they are saturated with a continual barrage of shocking events, those that inspire an affective arousal rather than reasonable reflection (Massumi 2002; Connolly 2002). Furthermore, as we move away from cognitive frameworks attuned to rational reflections on empirical events that unfold in real time to give focused attention to immersed environments where trauma and counterfactual evidence appear in symbolic forms through pictorial representations (e.g., these are increasingly non-narrated presentations), we find a lack of imagination, a dearth of critical thinking and a enthusiastic acceptance to let virtual content provide the shape of our psychic lives. Most often, we find conspiracy, a profound suspension of belief in the presentation before our eyes. Clipped images inspire the widespread fascination with surgically enhanced bodies, polling data supplies opinion rather than reflecting it, symbolic references communicate complex ideologies and political platforms, and tropes establish common ground between people and network their social interactions. According to Baudrillard, all these advancements in the virtual are equivalent to the procession of the good and are dedicated to the extermination of evil, where he reminds his readers that extermination means to deprive something of its own (we presume natural or fated) end.

Northern Illinois University

If we bracket his massacre as the work of an evil lunatic on drugs, we'll miss yet another opportunity to genuinely examine what life is like for most Americans today, who live in that terrifying gap between the official propaganda about a nation of happy fun-loving Number Ones, and the reality of mediocrity, petty malice, and a flat physical setting that reflects the malice and mediocrity of its town elders.

—Ames (2008)

Mark Ames, a writer on the American version of "amok" called "going postal," angered a lot of people in his article on *Alternet*, especially leftists who might have agreed with his larger points. I agree with the characterization that is cited above, however, I part ways with Ames's analysis of the NIU shooting, which, in part, argues that *these* kinds of shootings only take place in "mediocre" schools like VTU or NIU because life in these towns is so terrible. Ames, in trying to make a social class argument about the shootings, ends up repeating the "What's the matter with Kansas?" argument that parallels our earlier insights about the South and West by Jeff Kass. Many towns in Illinois are a mess, and that's because the state is completely in debt and taxpayers are in revolt. Outside of Chicago, Illinois doesn't have much to attract outside investment other than corn and soybean fields. Ames misses an opportunity in his article to comment on just how such towns become decayed and how this happens all over the country, not just in these areas. More likely, Kazmierczak suffered from the stigma attached to mental illness, and while overcoming it time and again, knew it would always return. So, I'll stay with the "Number Ones" argument, which is really what we've already outlined as the homogenous social. If any one of our perpetrators can be definitively placed in the heterogeneous social after Columbine, it is Kazmierczak, and it is not because of race but the stigma associated with mental illness.

Steve Kazmierczak admired Cho's act a lot. But, according to David Vann, so did his close friends from college and discussions about Columbine and other acts were commonplace (Vann 2011, 52).[7] For Vann, the only biographer of Kazmierczak's life to date, his trouble started early in life with a troubled home, watching horror films with his strong-willed devoutly Catholic mother, and suffering from a lack of presence of his father (there, but not in "control" over his mother's bad influence). However, he recounts that two particularly telling incidents would seal his fate as an outcast just before he entered the ninth grade (or in the U.S., high school). In one a neighbor tells their common friends that he saw him having sex with his dog (one he is rumored to have treated pretty badly). When he is confronted, he tells his friends he was teaching the dog "dominance" but does not deny that he did it. The second incident is that he stole a bunch of things from his friends and someone taped him admitting to it and played it back to him. To make matters worse, he challenged that person to a fight and everyone began to reject him. He was properly "stigmatized." This was the summer before he began ninth grade.

He subsequently joined Goth groups in high school. He went into a group home. Following this, he tried to commit suicide several times, his parents had him put on lithium, and he was eventually sent to a psychiatric facility and later a group home, where he was denied many of the normal things most people take for granted. He spent one year in facility then graduated from high school in 1998. After this, he entered a psychiatric facility again, this time a group home where he began to self-injure. He was eventually kicked out of the group home. This and the earlier revelations about his adolescence might explain why none of the fans want to include Kazmierczak; they even reject him. However, I think he fits this model better than any of the others, especially where Columbine is concerned. Here is why.

According to Vann, Kazmierczak suffers and triumphs over and over again in his life, in spite of the fact that no one is rooting for him. Instead they are afraid of him, worried that he will hurt himself, them or others. In Vann's depiction we might find a good deal of kindred spiritualism between Kazmierczak's mother and Adam Lanza's, whose untimely death prior to her son's attack on Sandy Hook Elementary School in Newtown, Connecticut, inspired one mother to write a controversial essay in the aftermath entitled, "I am Adam Lanza's Mother." Not his mother, his father or even his sister really trusted him, according to Vann. He was a complete social outcast, and it was unclear when he finished high school what he would do. Living in a group home, he took himself off of his medication and began to exercise and provide his own structure in order to eventually free himself of the place (where his parents put him, not where he voluntarily entered) by being kicked out for "lying and deception." About what is unclear. He next worked his way up to joining the military while living with his parents and stays for just shy of one year until they dischargd him when they found out that in the past he had been in a psychiatric facility (just like Eric Harris). He was deposited back in Elk Grove, Illinois (a Chicago suburb, hardly "rural"), by bus to his parents' home on February 13, 2002, just one day shy of the anniversary date of his attack on Cole Hall six years later. As Vann puts it, "No notifications to anyone that he might be a danger to himself or others, just dump him, as the Army does" (Vann 2011, 43). Just prior to that, they had put him in "the Army nuthouse as a precaution against any suicide attempt. They tell him he's possibly a danger to himself or others" (ibid.). It doesn't seem to matter once he's no longer in their jurisdiction. It's the same story with Cho who was such a danger when a student's parents alerted the police, but once examined was no cause for concern. My point here would not be that these individuals should have been "locked away." What is the message the society sends to someone when they penalize them for something so serious and then they surreptitiously drop them? I would also not advocate that they share private information among agencies. To what end? So they can more readily drop him from enrollment at the university? Information sharing doesn't have an objective. To drop someone is pretty cold and indifferent, but it is pretty much the protocol that governs what's left of our civil society institutions.

Kazmierczak then worked several odd jobs, went to a community college and eventually transferred to NIU. Initially, he was awkward in the dorms (like Cho), and suite mates refer to him as "Strange Steve." He has tattoos he will later hide under long-sleeved shirts, yet, by and large, as Vann details, he found a girlfriend, became a model student, even a teaching assistant, worked on publishing an article with a major professor, and later found another girlfriend. It actually sounds a lot like what Ames thought college should be like but wasn't for students at NIU:

"The college years should mean a flowering of everything good: freedom from parents, expanding knowledge, new experiences, fun, friendship, and perhaps most important of all: a newly vibrant sex life of the sort that Hollywood had promised, all set in a lush manicured campus full of granite buildings with Doric columns, and some kind of state-of-the-art sports arena" (Ames 2008). On this reading, the only thing missing for Kazmierczak in DeKalb was the beautiful campus and sports arena (if reports are correct). However, this is the case for the whole country. Has anyone been to O'Hare or JFK lately? Bridges are collapsing due to the lack of infrastructure in the United States. Trying to take a shot at the rich by humiliating the poor is pretty cheap. Ames's critics are right about that. However, it is true that Kazmierczak probably had to hide a great deal of his other self from others. Although his close friends and girlfriend knew of his past psychiatric problems, as well as how they influenced his lack of confidence, his need for structure (he felt he wasn't getting at NIU, according to one friend), etc., it became increasingly clear that managing his illness got more difficult when he moved on to the University of Illinois in 2007. Even though successful there and living with his girlfriend, he took himself off of medication (prior to that, he had been off of it for five years during his stint at NIU and just prior, according to Vann). His mother died in September 2006, and later his father tells him she never forgave him, apparently for trouble he caused as a teen and later in life. The NIU Report marks this as Kazmierczak's point of departure too, and an independent psychiatric profile (this time, not by the FBI) argued:

> Unfortunately for Kazmierczak and others with such problems, remission from psychiatric conditions like Schizo-Affective Disorder or Major Depression with Psychosis does not mean cure. Rather, *without reconciliation of the problems that led to the conditions or realignment of the brain chemistry that might have contributed to their cause, reoccurrence is almost inevitable.* The individual is most at risk for a return of the disturbance at a later time, especially at the point of another life transition or in response to an event or series of events that again challenge the individual's mental and emotional integrity. (NIU Report 2010, 31)

A new school, a new town (he did well at U of I too), he then quit and took a job at an Indiana prison. Vann reports that Kazmierczak began seeking out casual sex online (even though he still lives with his girlfriend, at this time it is unclear if they were broken up and what each of them thought of this; *they did remain close*). As for the planning, as we said earlier, most reports choose the day the weapons are purchased as the onset of planning, but it goes way beyond that to ideation. We can see in this case (if Vann's depiction of Kazmierczak's open acknowledgment about admiring Columbine, and Virginia Tech are accurate) that it may have always been in the back of his mind, like Cho, like Hasan, like Lanza and on and on. As Kip Kinkel said, "when my hope is gone, people die." We might instead begin to look, as Price argues, at the "social" aspects of "psychosocial" illnesses with a view to how suicidal ideation has been transformed by cruel experience. Often these perpetrators are found to have experienced social forms of cruelty that have no meaning attached to them. More often than not it is a result of not fitting in, but also of not wanting to fit in to the control society.

Kazmierczak began to deteriorate after his mother died and he could not reconcile with her. When he learned what she believed about him at the time of her death, he knew he could not hope to change that aspect of this life, his past. He begins to cast aspersions at his sister (giving her coal for Christmas and refusing to speak to her). He shows his medical records to his roommate, and this, apparently, is a big step for him. The way Vann presents him receiving them from his father is as if Kazmierczak has never seen them either, and doesn't remember what he was like during those years of suicide attempts, and delusional depression.

Vann's book is called "creative non-fiction," which means he embellishes a bit where pieces are missing. He also reads himself and his own experience with suicide into the larger story of Kazmierczak's life. It's an interesting genre because it admits not everything can be verified as true, and cops to its own investments from the outset. Unlike Cullen's portrait of Columbine which does the same thing, including ventriloquizing the two perpetrators, Vann's admission and biographical revelations allow the reader to decide where truth and fiction part ways.

But Vann also reads too much of his own life into Kazmierczak's as if he were a "type" we should have all detected. Kazmierczak's attraction to the military is presented as a character flaw since Vann sees the military as an irresponsible institution, with no qualified explanation. Also, those around Kazmierczak are suspected of holding back or not having noticed what Vann presents as weird and creepy interests: Marilyn Manson, Craigslist hookups, Nietzsche's *Anti-Christ*, past school shootings, and popular but violent films. All interests shared by most normal twenty-somethings. At times, Vann's need to stop and raise a question about the ethics, or what I might call personal taste, of Kazmierczak's pop culture references reads out as Pollyannaish. For example, Vann makes a bigger deal than he should out of Kazmierczak's love of *Saw* movies ("the largest grossing horror film franchise of all time," grossing 730 million; Wallis & Aston 2012, 352). Featuring a puppet and a disgruntled man who enacts revenge on people for crimes and sins, the main character forces the guilty to decide whether they live or die, and in doing so, teaches a moral lesson. After all, these films are the sign of the times. "The disgruntled, middle-class white male professional, who fits in a long tradition of male characters *fed up with democratic institutions*, determined to set their own rules" (ibid., 356, emphasis mine). Aronowitz anyone? They continue, "Rather than continue his help at a communal, grass-roots level, Kramer [the moralist] turns to rightist ideology and vigilantism, selecting those individuals whom he believes are responsible for the decline in societal standards as his test subjects" (ibid.). By contrast, Vann reads SAW itself as an allegory for the military.

> All of Jigsaw's killings are strictly regulated by time limits and "rules." In the Cole Hall shootings, too, timing and strict control of behavior will help provide order to an insane act. Steve will walk calmly down the aisle shooting his victims, some of whom will be too paralyzed by fear to flee, with no hesitation. Like the military, the world of *Saw* offers behavioral control without any reference, grounded on absurdity. Unmoored from society, parroting the rules. (Vann 2011, 82–83)

Um, what society? Vann is correct to go back to the military. As we mentioned at the start, it provides structure in a world where both it and any kind of meaningful leadership or authority are lacking. However, Vann betrays his own bias: endlessly invoking the military as a space lacking any morality or social perspective. While I'm not myself a giant fan of the military (or militarism), it does provide a discipline lacking in the larger society, at least one that is socially recognized. As Althusser would say, as the ISAs (ideological state apparatuses) decline, the RSA's (repressive state apparatuses) become the default containment structures for less independent individuals (Althusser 1971). For someone with a mental disability, like Kazmierczak, this kind of stability and structure are necessary. Having to seek it out in civil society is a worthless quest. And in a control society based largely on "law and order" responses, which work perfectly well with outsourcing to corporations, there is no one to take responsibility, there is no chain of command; no democratic arrangement, only protocological organization, like Galloway argues. Grossman mentions this at one point, but I don't think he quite reads it through contemporary culture appropriately. While I would agree that in a functioning democratic civil society, someone or a group of people would be responsible for any number of things, in a control society, one is punted from one modulation to the next, *each new representative unaware of the last one*, or what they promised or punished. As Galloway says, each "node" in the system makes its own decisions provided it continues to speak the same language as the others.

The reason why Kazmierczak ended up at the University of Illinois at Urbana–Champaign was because the Department of Sociology was gradually phasing out Criminology, although The NIU Report suggests this is a confused idea that Kazmierczak had, with no basis in reality. The report states that he was concerned that he would not be able to continue, but that the Sociology Department had actually expanded its course offerings. The report does not mention that it expanded the type of courses he would be uninterested in taking and would not help him complete his sequence for the masters in criminology, only sociology. Here is how the report cites Kazmierczak's opinion (in a different place, in the independent psychological evaluation):

> Ok, so you want to know the truth about graduate school? At NIU for my first year of graduate school I was a teaching assistant for statistics (with a focus on sociologic research methods) and although I liked my teaching assistant position (i.e., grading, working one-on-one with students, teaching the occasional class), I absolutely did not enjoy the graduate program. This was mainly due to the lack of quality students. I am far from arrogant and consider my self-humble, but some of my fellow students there were not there for anything besides a piece of paper and always complained about assignments, the ample readings, etc., which really annoyed me. (NIU Report 2010, 39)

This is the corporate university. We know these students. They are in graduate school because the market does not supply them with good paying jobs. Kazmierczak had become invested in the university as a site of reason (to counter his demons, no doubt) but also as a place where he could redeem himself after his abject humiliation in front of peers and his family's rejection, fear and continued unwillingness to trust him as "cured." These are difficult things for even the strongest of people to overcome. The idealization of study, of inquiry, of research and teaching that Kazmierczak evinces cannot possibly match the unbridled nihilism and points gathering of his fellow students ("piece of paper"). This situation is not unique to NIU; it is everywhere in the United States, at least. Yet, see how it literally reverses the conjecture of the independent psychologist: s/he assumes that Kazmierczak felt *illegitimate* contempt for fellow students, but I would argue that it was simply *disproportionate*. He wanted a disciplinary society, not a control one. The report further speculates that Kazmierczak took his rage toward his family and directed it at his surrogate family, NIU, that he felt "let him down." Whether this is the case, who knows? It's certainly evidence of the breakdown between civil institutions, and provides stark examples of the "dismemberment" that Balibar describes in Hegel's transition to the new identity, one that is centered on "identification" "but is controlled in advance by the state or the 'higher' community, so that the result is *guaranteed*, since it has been prepared for well in advance by the ethical formations of civil society" (Balibar 2002, 31). Here we find no "guarantee," and even in disciplinary societies the subject could be rejected but most likely on seemingly ethical terms (e.g., not completed the requirements of study, lacking rigor, devotion, etc.). Here we find "phase out," where no ethical formations exist to guarantee the "result." Thus far, all of the perpetrators in this story have been languishing somewhere in between institutions, in a void, or perhaps an abyss of civil society.

Prior to his act, Kazmierczak left Champaign and reserved a hotel room in DeKalb where he maintained contact with Jessica Baty (and others) until the night before the event. She thought he might have been suicidal as he asked her all kinds of questions, the size of her ring finger, etc. He sent her a packet containing an engagement ring and some other items, including his marked copy of Nietzsche's *Anti-Christ*, which he had previously borrowed from her. Kazmierczak removed both the SIM card from his phone and the hard drive from his laptop. I have already made reference to the duffel bag. Others close to him theorize that Kazmierczak did not want people working in the hotel to find the ammunition, and that is why he glued the bag shut. He parked his car close to the building where he first took a criminology course several years earlier. He entered the building and proceeded from the back of the stage in Cole Hall to the front. He carried a shotgun in a guitar case and a handgun tucked in his pants. He began shooting, no expression:

> Some crime scene witnesses indicated that when Kazmierczak had emptied the shotgun and walked down into the audience with his handguns he shot only at those running out of the room or trying to hide under their seats rather than those who remained frozen in their chairs. If this was true and had been planned by him, one can only speculate what "game" Kazmierczak may have been challenging his victims to play. (NIU Report 2010, 43)

He continues to add to the script we've already been examining here. His act, however, is not received in the same way as Virginia Tech or others. There are no fans. There are no theories. Political lobbyists do not bring their issues to DeKalb, and the report speculates that this event is more like a typical university/workplace event that is focused on revenge. It may also be that Kazmierczak's average identity, white and middle-class, were not ratings grabbers for the media. Furthermore, there is the way that Kazmierczak authored it himself, by hiding as much evidence that could lead to speculation anyway. Plus, there's friends, *who care*, left in his wake. He is not a loner. As the report makes clear:

> All references to offender motivation made by the FBT BAU-1 were necessarily speculative, as there were no letters, videos or manifestos left by the shooter providing an explanation or rationale for the attack. (NIU Report 2010, 20)

6

Remote Projection and Militarized Subjectivity

A Different Iteration

This chapter examines the transformation in civilian subjectivity brought about by U.S. participation in virtual war. Many theorists have noted the similarities between war and other national pastimes such as sports and business. Still others have examined the role that a modality of war plays in promoting certain kinds of subjectivities that reinforce the necessary citizenship behavior to support war efforts or rationalize the failure to meet military and political objectives (Boose 1993). Usually, but not always, these subjectivities are transformed through preferred gendered and racialized norms that leave imperial ambitions of war-makers unchallenged, if not supported. By looking at how subjectivity, social control and citizenship are transformed through the remote projection of force displayed in U.S. technologies (war gaming, simulation, disinformation, satellite surveillance, etc.) this chapter presents a new thesis on ego formation using recent interventions in political theory that highlight the role of proprioception in the "posthuman" or age of the "automaton" (Hayles 2002; Massumi 2002, respectively). What current technologies target are neither discursive normative strategies nor identitarian positions but the body's compulsive and habit-driven capacities to assume risk in uncertain physical environments against odds.

Remote Projection

In hunting the long process of universal history coils up and bites its own tail.
— Ortega (1972, 136)

The enemy we're fighting is a bit different than the one we war-gamed against, because of these paramilitary forces.
— General Wallace to the *New York Times*, qtd. in Dwyer (2003)

In following the twentieth-century trajectory of history most famously framed by Kojeve's interpretation of Hegel, then Fukuyama's bland application to formulas of modernization and democracy via the "end of ideology," one is led to the conclusion that the U.S. might have reached a point where it should be able to *reflect* on its war time practices. By the end of this chapter I will have made a case for U.S. foreign policy being *beyond reflection* by examining the normative assumptions made by war planners, as well as the transformation of forms of military and civilian subjectivity brought about by virtual war. A comparative interpretation of the phenomenon of virtual war has yet to be offered. To do this, I read a Spanish philosopher famous for defending hunting as a virile sport using existential philosophy. Most commentators on virtual war agree that the U.S. militant missionary foreign policy was designed to fill the space opened up by the collapse of the Soviet Union and the inordinate amount of power that shifted to the U.S. at that time (e.g., the debate over "unipolarity").[1] Huge military spending left the U.S. with resources to challenge small states that refused to conform to Fukuyama's thesis and become democracies. Virtual technologies allowed the U.S. to retain a superior advantage over these small enemies by reducing soldier casualties, the one limiting factor on presidents who wish to enforce regime change and fight terror. For Ortega, the hunting instinct is always deep within men and they need only the environment of nature and the element of risk to bring out their animal selves. For the U.S., it was the retreat from nature into the virtual combined with aversion to risk that brought out the predator in search of lesser prey. As General Tommy Franks processed the initial "shock and awe" component of the Iraq invasion in 2003, he must have known that he was internet hunting and not engaged in any incursion resembling traditional war. The most pervasive interpretations of total war are that it is fratricide: brothers killing brothers. In asymmetric conflict, there is the "West" and its other. The battle between good and evil was born again I will argue in a particular understanding of "gaming."

Ortega's philosophy on hunting has been chosen to frame this chapter's discussion of remote projection in warfare (as was practiced by primarily the U.S. central command but also by NATO) because his reflections most accurately match many of the assumptions made by our authors of virtual experience who will also help explain the transformation of subjectivity that takes place during virtual warfare. Before detailing these departures and commonalities, I would like to outline the direction of this chapter and its ultimate claim. In contrast to modern warfare, posthuman warfare is characterized not only by the technological advances applied to the situation but also the *modality of conflict*. Remote projection poses questions not only to technical changes in warfare (i.e., the RMA thesis), but also to the morality of war as practiced in this manner, not merely for its legal implications or geostrategic concerns arising from global inequities, but primarily in an existential sense: what is "at stake" in virtual war? Most theorists who have confronted virtual war have done so from either a moral standpoint (Ignatieff 2000; Clark 2002), a fiscal one (O'Hanlon 2000) or from an epistemological one (Virilio 1997; Der Derian 2001). In this chapter, I will review these arguments while contextualizing them in my larger discussion of how both subjectivity and corporeality were/are transformed during virtual warfare, specifically by the use and application of remote technologies to the conduct of war between radically unequal "adversaries." I argue that virtual war is not war at all but a new version of hunting, or more likely, gaming. This will not be argued from a moral standpoint but from taking a trip into the stakes, technological transformations and the nature of the activity itself. Posthuman conflict is not postmodern conflict. While the term *postmodern* is applied to many contexts and political situations in the contemporary era, posthuman describes the space of politics after humanism. War gaming is about challenging the individual to take risks against the self, to put one's self up against the odds (not fate, odds) in competition against one's own physical limits and resources. This is the allegory of the control society.

The Decline of Fatalism and the Advent of Odds

In many ways, Ortega's text on hunting (as well as others, such as *The Revolt of the Masses*) is an appropriate text for understanding the particular instance of virtual war introduced by the second Gulf War because his philosophy of life shares features with pre-modern thinkers, much like the neoconservative authors of the war. While many may argue that war with Iraq, like the intervention in Afghanistan, can be written off as an aberration in U.S. foreign policy and wartime strategy, it can be seen as a continuation with previous policies in wars throughout the twentieth century. What was different about that war was the new iteration in subjection that it encouraged soldiers to adopt, as well as civilians. This subjection means putting one's existence up against *odds,* and not at risk for a cause or larger social order. The difference between the two rationales for doing "war" is important. As past wars have been situated within literary genres of epic or tragedy, war-making over the past decade was cast as a winning bet with odds on the side of the aggressor. Fighting "terror" was not a quest initiated or determined by fate but rather the very odds the administration had set against U.S. troops.

The first assumption that Ortega shares with virtual theorists is a rejection of the Cartesian assumption of the primacy of the mind and many of the conclusions that flow from that assumption. Although he doesn't have the language to communicate it, Ortega believes that the psychoanalytic Real is ultimately bad (in the existential sense). As in his other writings he reiterates that the modern individual in mass society finds his existence modeled on that of one who is shipwrecked. Life is risk for Ortega and a heightened sense of anxiety and expectation flow from that fact. His defense of hunting begins with an exploration of what he views as the motive for the hunter and the contest between the hunter as predator and the prey or animals he pursues. As Heim argues, "Your active seeing originates the sense of precepts of what you see, feel and touch. Intention guides attention, and from attention comes sense perception. But art as aesthetics has disengaged the senses from the intentionality that builds worlds, so that art could become aesthetics, a free-floating play of the senses" (Heim 1998, 77). For Ortega, the hunter's vision is itself part of nature (Ortega 1972, 14). The hunter intends to put himself into nature as a diversion from the banality of life as work. Thus, the hunter is avoiding something in an active manner by putting himself into a situation where he will experience excitement and risk. As we have already demonstrated, critical thinkers now believe that perception is modified by new technologies of the virtual, going so far as to argue that they conduct surgery on the act of perception (Virilio 1997, 100–101). And yet, for Ortega we find pleasure in hunting because it is a diversion from modern life which is "empty," having to be filled with "occupations" or work, and when men hunt they are recharged with an adolescent vigor that takes them back to the primitive stages of evolution where their animal instincts return to them momentarily, if only during the activity of the hunt. This is gaming for old-timers. The following depiction serves as an important contrast between the gaming described in the last four chapters. This is important because as Galloway remarks, we often find we are immersed in an anthropological sense of ideology (which is perfectly acceptable for explaining this case, I would argue) but not very good at explaining more banal social violence that happens in everyday life.

Hunting is necessarily asymmetric as it is the "free play of an inferior species in the face of a superior species" (Ortega 1972, 111). He is careful to argue that every precaution must be taken to make sure that the "authenticity" of the hunt is maintained: the prey must be "overpowered," there is a "tactile drama" involved in capture, the game shows its fierceness, a struggle ensues, the hunter witnesses the blood and carnage of the killing—there is "orgiastic intoxication" and the hunter must experience an "uneasy conscience" about killing, despite the fact that the death of the animal is the proof of hunting although not its ultimate aim" (Ortega 1972, 109).

The prey's job is to "elude" the hunter, and this is what makes the difference between hunting and combat or fighting since in combat, "both parties have the same intention and similar behavior" (Ortega 1972, 55). This is an important distinction because once the parties are taken outside of their natural realm, it is a constructed situation and no longer hunting. Finally, there is no difference between man and animal as Ortega maintains that man cannot assume he has transcended his animality and he also has no reason to believe that rationality is proof of this.

The hunter is a kind of Socratic man when it comes to experience: "The hunter knows that he does not know what is going to happen, and this is one of the greatest attractions of his occupation" (Ortega 1972, 150). By contrast, virtual war takes the hunter outside of the aleatory structure of nature; that is, where events are unpredictable. Leaving aside the idea that nature is constructed, granting the supposition that nature is physical reality and has a separate existence from the "human" (Ortega is modern), virtual war is characterized by its very predictability; all moves are presupposed and written into code, maps are fed into programs, physical capabilities are quantified and "risk" is averted, at least that is the pretext of virtual war. Nature, and the unpredictable qualities of it are omitted from the war-gaming strategy for military success. As reporters commented on Frank's and Rumsfeld's initial war strategy, the two saw the Fedayeen and other insurgents as "little more than speed bumps on the road to Baghdad" (Gordon & Traynor 2006b). Commandeering the war effort from 7,000 miles away, General Franks threatened to fire a field officer who doubted his assessment of a speedy virtual victory; empirical verification was trumped by technological faith. Here we reach the vast difference between the hunting of Ortega—that takes place in nature and avows risk—and the gaming of the U.S. military that presumed risk was averted through technological application (and still does in the case of tactical drones). The only ones taking the risks were the soldiers on the ground, and they were doing it without a narrative to structure their experience, to make the war seem justified. As the finally witnessed opposition to the war indicated, the "orgy was over" as Baudrillard once said, and we should really have put our clothes back on and gone home much earlier. I would argue that this hunting excursion into the Middle East took place because of the over reliance on technological superiority and the scant attention to the human conditions real adversaries deployed to protect themselves. In this the U.S. high command was overzealous in its faith in technology, and this was the outcome of relying on teleportation, and the U.S. public was just as mesmerized by it.

Telepresence is the word that best captures the lure of remote technologies now in place as the primary mode of security in the United States and abroad. Broadly construed, remote technologies begin with the notion of protecting troops and security personnel from harm by random miscreants in open spaces. As the last chapters suggested, in the absence of values or discourses mediated in public spaces or of functioning civil society, the fear on the part of most of the U.S. population is that these spaces are ones of vulnerability to "innocents" who may wander into them. The predators who would attack these spaces, case them, and target those who enter are not given much description by those who want these spaces protected; they exist largely in the imaginaries of democratic populations, demonstrating the lack of confidence in democratic ideals and one over-certain of the effectivity of its liberalism. Where the Ten Commandments fail, remote technologies are preferred. The camera acts as the audience; to be "seen" by no one is the goal. As Michael Heim argues, the only barrier left between humans and the virtual worlds they increasingly enter is the screen (Heim 1998, 13). The screen moves subjects past the mirror and into hyperreality; indeed, the mirror might be the organizing trope for liberal humanism and Enlightenment thought. To move past it to the screen means losing the self-centeredness of humanism, shedding human features (the signifier and the signified of "human" slide apart). As Ronald Reagan found his image in the screen, so are increasing numbers of people (they also tend to share his bad acting). As technologies begin to enhance the view provided by these screens, the degree of realness of images that pass through them elevates transforming the experience of the watchers. Some have even argued that access to the screen is considered part of being a citizen, as the working poor stumble through their finances to come up with the cash to pay for cable while forgoing rent and other necessities. As Nikolas Rose has persuasively argued, in the society of control the "image of control by totalizing surveillance is misleading" because most theorists who endorse this interpretation take the surveillance and information technologies to be the independent variable, whereas Rose argues, like Galloway, that it is *control* that must be analyzed for how its mode of operation shifts: "Control is better understood as operating through conditional access to circuits of consumption and civility: constant scrutiny of the right of individuals to access certain kinds of flows of consumption goods; recurrent switch points to be passed in order to access the benefits of liberty" (Rose 2000, 326). As Galloway pointed out in his analysis of *24,* the television show that best narrates the entire decade and its logic of security, the mantra of liberation is no longer one of leisure, but "Just let me do my job!" (Galloway 2012b, 107).[2] One such "switchpoint" for lower and middle-class students who wish to go to a university, and then the much coveted "job" has been the military. Now such forms of control proliferate in the institutions of civil society. Our "cracked open" institutions have these "switchpoints," and some students and workers access the "benefits of liberty" easier than others.

Remote technologies are a means to protect the so-called protectors; they are an extra layer of security over an already powerful and sovereign subject, usually the elite subject. Much like a deer blind, where hunters hide in trees camouflaged by leaves and branches and shoot (usually bows) at deer and other non-predatory animals from above, maintaining a superior advantage over the animal in the process of hunting it, remote security technologies allow for a "global view" of the ground. Among the characteristics valued by these technologies is their ability to conceal the identity of the hunter (including his/her smell through the use of deer scents), provide enticements for bringing the deer into the clearing space adjacent to the blind (salt licks, rotten apples) and reduce the distance the hunter has to cover while making up for the weaknesses of strength, correcting for aim and improving the projectile powers of weapons. While this example demonstrates the opposite of the one for remote security forces (in this case the predator is using the advantages of technologies to shoot prey, not to protect the clearing and its inhabitants from harm), remote security enhances the predatory capacities of humans. Witness the rise in crimes in public spaces that are re-released to the public on television as was the case with teenagers targeting homeless people in Florida during the winter holiday season of 2005–6. Obviously, the surveillance cameras in these public spaces (bus stations, college buildings, etc.) did not deter them from committing crimes; perhaps they thought no one was watching. Indeed, like the Gulf War that "did not take place," the crimes were only watched as "after-images" once the actuality of the crime had been reported. Reports say that these incidents "shed light" on a growing problem of beating up homeless people, usually by white males under the age of twenty, and that this activity has "practically become sport among young people around the country" (Anderson 2006).

Having the advantage of higher ground has always been a valued principle in warfare. During the Vietnam war, Ho Chi Minh's forces were able to surround

U.S. troops from above using the natural topography in order to force a surrender. The debate surrounding the peace agreement between Israel and Palestine was hotly debated over the issue of the Golan Heights because these territories were elevated, giving the Israelis not only a land buffer from ground invasion forces by a bellicose Syria (or so they claimed) but also giving them an elevated advantage. Finally, there was the ethical issue raised during the first Gulf War of the superior aerial advantage of allied forces against Iraqi ground troops—the famous "turkey shoot" on the road to Baghdad—where allied soldiers were "picking off" Iraqis until Powell stepped in to halt the carnage, fearing (and knowing) that these acts violated the Geneva Conventions. While the first examples point out natural advantages provided by the vagaries of territorial elevation, the latter suggests that technologies, specifically remote technologies, have transformed the way that wars are fought by those countries who possess superior communications technologies, specifically satellite, laser and internet technologies by giving them the high ground in war.

Remote technologies remain the cornerstone of U.S. foreign policy in the form of drone strikes. The Powell Doctrine of an exit strategy for foreign intervention flowed from the lessons of Vietnam as much as it did the knowledge that the U.S. had these technologies to protect soldiers. The Clinton and NATO doctrines followed the same logic. The Bush Doctrine, with its three main components of preemption, unilateralism and strength beyond challenge, departed from the previous administration's view of foreign policy, but only in its quest to challenge the long respected right of non-intervention in international law and practice by rejecting multilateralism (or simulating it, Powell's United Nations speech). It also follows the initial strategy of power cited by Kenneth Waltz: to become the superpower who can afford to make mistakes that neither has to suffer for them nor answer for them (Waltz 1979, last chapter). Michael Ignatieff argued that the NATO justification for bombing Kosovo (to halt carnage there) rang hollow among most states outside the alliance and sounded more like "force majeure." Force majeure is not only absolution for events transpiring outside a party's control when bringing overwhelming force to bear on an aggressive party, it is also equated in its power dimensions as being the equivalent of an act of God. Force majeure is the legal term covering responsible parties for contracts; when they fail to protect or meet their objectives they are covered by an explanation that the event that disabled their ability to perform duties was like an act of God or natural disaster—it occurs without prior knowledge or is outside of human control. The religious overtones of the Bush administration and many of its cabinet did the same.

Proportionality

Ignatieff's analysis of virtual war warned the reading public about the ethical stakes involved in asymmetric war when he argued that states like the U.S. fight them to serve humanitarian purposes while trying to limit casualties for the soldiers that process them. When one side possesses superior military technological strength over the other, the war is not really fair, and there is a tendency for this type of war to violate the principle of proportionality in war. This principle, derived from European legal traditions, argues that only the necessary amount of governing power should be used to accomplish a strategic objective. Its purpose is to curb the excess of power that might be committed during a sovereign act; that is, to avoid an open situation getting out of hand. An open situation is when the outcome is uncertain, and for modern thinkers like Machiavelli, it was necessary to cultivate virtù to be able to assess the winds of fortuna and make the decisions necessary to bring about the desired end. However, for these modern thinkers confronting technological advantages were not the main problem. The gap between themselves and their adversaries was uncertain and virtù became an important concept precisely because predictability was not assured. In contemporary wars, the fear is that they may become "turkey shoots," with one side picking off the other safely, ensconced behind computer screens, gun sights or television screens. Without vulnerable troops on the ground in primary reality, the notion of risk is obsolete.

For Ignatieff, the Kosovo campaign was limited by the simple fact that it was processed by NATO and that the nineteen states involved in the bombing followed this principle using humanitarian law as a guide and strictly monitoring the purpose of and objective of each decision. However, cast in a different light, the wide gap between the NATO coalition and the Serbian military did raise questions about "equality of moral risk" in war. If the NATO coalition could not argue that they were risking lives in the battle while the Serbian military clearly was, was the principle of "kill or be killed" at play in this campaign? Similarly, these asymmetric wars do not "mobilize societies" that allow for them to take place, and therefore do not rise in the minds of the democratic citizens the stakes involved for one side of the conflict. Ignatieff, like most other theorists of war, comes to these conclusions through comparisons to former wars—the great ones, world and total wars. The power of World War II over the minds of thinkers on contemporary war is significant. In the U.S., we are taught that this is the good one, while subsequent incursions, while good enough, are not about self-preservation, equality of moral risk or saving helpless people from fascism. Usually they are explained as movements toward the eternity or preservation of democracy. World War II, however, challenged the moral turpitude of every person on the face of the earth (except the fascists), and they mobilized entire societies around the notion of cooperation to fight for a cause: fighting German fascism and Japanese imperialism. As much as the media and government officials would like to make foreign leaders ranging from Manuel Noriega to Saddam Hussein seem like drug dealers and fascist dictators, the similarities to Hitler or Mussolini seemingly end at the ink on the newsprint. They do not fully capture the personalities of the people they are designed to demonize nor do they convince publics that the threat is worthy of mobilization on the scale of the great wars. In these wars, Ignatieff tells us, even notions of masculinity and femininity were transformed for war mobilization, and we know this to be the case in wars of national liberation where people perceive their existence to be threatened with extinction and go so far as to include women in war and suspend religious beliefs that previously held women apart from men as reproductive citizens needing protection. Instead, women are encouraged to work in factories, use birth control, take on military roles, and even assist in terrorist acts. As he argues:

> In the total wars of the twentieth century, mobilization of the population sank deep roots in the psyche, helping to define the ideals of masculine and feminine identity and connecting masculinity with the idea of the upright carriage of the drill yard, the coarse jocularity of the barracks and strict self-control in the face of danger and death. Military ideals of discipline—vertical, hierarchical, unquestioning—exerted an influence well beyond military life—in school, prison and factory. (Ignatieff 2000, 185)

Male roles are also transformed in total wars. Prior to them, the notion of masculinity tied to heroism or valor is relatively unimportant, and a "warrior class" is largely unnecessary. R. W. Connell has gone so far as to argue that masculinity is constructed during war (Connell 2001, 218). Yet, most social critics have failed to take this analysis into civilian spaces: if masculinity and femininity are transformed during actual war, what happens to them during virtual war? What is the effect of virtual war on the onlookers? How does virtual war exert influence both within and beyond military life as a perverse form of social stasis? How do remote technologies for surveillance and warfare challenge our traditional notions of masculine subjectivity while deploying "warrior" narratives in the process? In the school? The remainder of this chapter explores these questions by examining literature about warrior subjectivities, military recruitment ideologies and virtual technologies. As the military began to replace the school as the institution of social reproduction for those students outside the middle-class social contract, and indeed those that exit the middle-class schools to become soldiers, what has been the the effect on American society? Militarization does not "leak" into society (Grossman 1995); it enters through diffuse technologies from disparate sources. It also bubbles up from the center of civil society itself, reinforcing the power of policing and surveillance structures already in existence to contain criticism of the failed social contract, the now "law and order" society. As it did for Galloway, it enters through software which allows for those "switchpoints" mentioned by Rose. Militarization is not an ideology, as some critics maintain. Militarism might be a cover one mimes or adopts to reap certain monetary benefits or access to rituals of prestige (Luttwak 2006, 48). There's certainly no shortage of that. Militarization, by contrast, is the process by which political cultures become dependent upon weapons and surveillance systems, access, and switchpoints as their primary mode of not only security, but civility itself. It is when socially reproducing the adherence to using weapons and deterrence systems becomes the default mode for organizing civility between peoples rather than *sittlichkeit*. These switchpoints are also determined largely by social class indices, such as a university education and, of course, normative evaluations by experts that certify one's membership in the homogeneous social we outlined in the first three chapters.

Militarization has become a feature of American public life through a new kind of perception deployed in increasing numbers of simulators used by the armed forces, video gaming technologies, the enhanced visuality of screens (that are everywhere broadcasting violence), surveillance technologies and the architectural transformations that make them effective, the limiting of access to public spaces, as well as the well-placed information media pieces demonstrating why publics should fear them. Surveillance technologies used in public spaces to deter crime, such as those in whole neighborhoods in Chicago, have transformed civilian practices. Contained to the home or on the inside of buildings, residents do not meet in public or show their faces, unless to harm. The murder rate is at an all-time high, and legislators in Springfield make Illinois the last state in the union to pass "conceal carry." Back in the middle-class world, taking the long march into the virtual world and leaving the institutions relatively vacant, young men in large numbers seek distraction in worlds where they are powerful, and feelings of inadequacy are addressed not directly through humane comparison, or a focus on dignity and humility, or the confrontation with authority figures, but where avatars make them super powerful controlling the fate of characters, imagining themselves as sexual predators or sublimating rage through the dramas that *unfold* in these worlds. Where the social ego may have once met the practical end of its omnipotence in castration anxiety, it is now deferred indefinitely through the temporal extension of this moment by remote technologies. Able to project the social ego that in actuality would have confronted a Big Other, the new transformation in subjectivity allows for a diversion from the Big Other to a whole new world in the interactive spaces of gaming.[3] Much like Ortega's version of hunting as diversion from industrial capitalism, this new form of diversion is from human *authority* and *reflection*. Instead authority is lent to technology and experts (Webber 2003a). This omnipotence does not yield a uniformity of experience. It does, however, agitate. And when confronted with the reformed bureaucracies of the civil society, one willfully defers to the corporate version, if it can be afforded. This is how the middle class is split apart at the center.

Consider the main forms of amusement (or diversion) that have become popular for U.S. civilians: gambling (the first form of gaming), extreme sports, video gaming and betting on professional sports (e.g., the NCAA tournament). They are choreographed by corporations. Cities no longer own teams or stadiums. Gambling is now perceived to be the new form of tax collection. None of these national pastimes rely on cooperation or discourse. They put the individual's capacities up against odds. The individual no longer relies on a social ego to survive in civil society but rather needs access to physical or technical *support* systems.

The central concept that makes them effective at enhancing these experiences, and disparages the actual world of physical reality is their reliance upon something forward-thinking scholars have added to their theoretical arsenals: proprioception. Proprioception strikes down Cartesian assumptions of primacy of mind over body and human over other life forms by placing the subject in a different experiential capacity. As Katherine Hayles explains of this, "force of habit that shapes embodied responses," it "is the internal sense that gives us the feeling that we *occupy* our bodies rather than merely possess them" (Hayles 2002, 299). Hayles puts the attractiveness of proprioceptive sensation up as a replacement for what C.B. Macpherson had argued was the possessive individual formed by late capitalism, where capitalism was the end result of the social contract theory's manipulation and training of the five original senses in Hobbes. The "training" necessary to form the possessive individual is no longer necessary as consumption and self-interest have been perfected. In moving past possessive individualism, where liberalism provides the alibi that citizens control their bodies how they choose (the "freedom from" tradition of privacy and private property), proprioceptive "interpellations" from the virtual environment control bodies rather than the possessive individual. While the Bush administration spoke of small government, the security and surveillance powers of the government and private agencies has grown into its own form of "positivist state." Moving past "late capitalism" (Jameson), people now enter into new worlds of virtuality that harness their autonomic capacities as standing reserves. As virtual technologies have developed, this new sense of proprioception is in humans that use them. For Massumi, proprioception "folds tactility into the body, enveloping the skin's contact with the external world in a dimension of medium depth: between epidermis and viscera. The muscles and ligaments register as conditions of movement what the skin internalizes as qualities: the hardness of the floor underfoot as one looks into a mirror becomes a resistance enabling station and movement; the softness of a cat's fur becomes lubricant for the motion of the hand" (Massumi 2002, 59). Proprioception acts as our own personal GPS (global positioning system), and technologies that target this sense do so without the consent of the "I." Vision is less important than is the relationship between the physical body and the environment (the smart environment) that interacts with it. Structural support now comes in the form of the physical relationship between the body, technology and architecture communicating the proprioceptive sense to our autonomic nervous systems.

If it sounds like the floor replaces the parent who holds the infant up while contemplating its specular image to create the "I" that will carry it through a structural narrative called "life," then proprioception may indeed be a new practice for such social control. Hayles notes that the military is particularly fond of exploiting this "sixth sense" in order to effect habituated bodily responses in virtual environments. The difference, as Massumi argues, is that narrative gives way to a "body without image" (Massumi 2002, 57). Not only is the body that reflects erased, but a new body on screen replaces it, one that can be seen from all angles in motion. On screen there is no body to have a reflection; it is there in all its non-orthopedic splendor. No longer a "lack" with a need to find completion in the other, this body without image needs only a screen to project it into another virtual world. Introductions are no longer made through narrative but screenings: it is, quite simply, the "rendering of phenomena into data" (Heim 1998, 66) and the subsequent rendering of data into image. Now projected remotely onto the screen (teleported), the user can have their body trained to respond to virtual situations that simulate physical scenarios, as in making the "climb over exo-cosmic topologies" (ibid.). According to Bergson, humans have always had the capacity to teleport the difference is that the modern imagination housed its image in the brain, the imagination of contemporary virtual users is stored in the drive, projected by the camera, saved on the cloud and capacitated on the ground in real time by the satellite. This is why the destruction of the laptop or cell phone, or the disappearance of the hard drive or the SIM card is traumatic to publics who want to know "why?" If we can now occupy our bodies it is because we now rent them rather than own them. Instead of being occupied with the world of work, as Ortega headily argued, we are occupants in bodies trained for hunting, gaming, of amassing points—the exploitation of the body and the immobilization of the mind and narrative thought. The body without image is "meat." The image projection can now be manipulated by the user; its sense of time can be inexhaustibly managed on a number of registers (temporal): rewind, pause, play, and spatial; cut, paste, color, enlarge/reduce, splice and mix. The spatial component of experience having been dealt with once and for all, all modern associations related to the weight of existence are now done away with (as long as the data is reliably stored, this is why file corruption is so disturbing, a traumatic encounter with the virtual). When Massumi writes of the body without image, he is at once announcing the death of the subject (of humanism, physicality, modernity, knowledge, reason) with an image reflected by a mirror. There are no more mirrors, therefore, the body has no image.

The Lacanian mirror must be understood in a number of different ways related to the notion of reflexivity. If the mirror (phase) once demonstrated the dismemberment of the subject, leading it to form a desire for the other to complete it in a fictional wholeness never attained but strived for ("never give way to one's desire"), then this subject was only barred in relation to the other or to *codes of conduct* stemming from the Oedipal drama: heroism, risk, mastery, nobility, authenticity, virility, etc. These are the pre-modern narratives that structure the neoconservative war rhetoric. The entire modern period was predicated on *codes of rationality and fraternity*: justice, objectivity, liberty, loyalty to a cause or progress, community. The subject was barred in relation to an authority figure to which it bestowed a kind of respect; recall authority is power that is respected or justified; it carries a certain kind of weight. It was barred by the limits of its chosen social ego. The assumption of mastery as life narrative forecloses self-forgiveness for failure; the assumption of virility carries with it the threat of impotence, and so on. The assumption of justice forecloses self-interest; of objectivity, it is personal whim that must be forsaken. Under codes of fraternity, one takes a hit for the "team," whereas today's army is of "one."

If the mirror provokes the formation of the ideal ego as narrative, the removal of the mirror can be interpreted to have major consequences for the way we think about a number of issues, not only war, but civic life. If there is no need for the mirror, having been replaced by the screen and other physical supports that overcome the recognition of orthopedic lack, and then also gone is a modern narrative of progress, developmental stages and future-oriented goals and ideals. Wars no longer have objectives, other than their longevity (Kaldor 1998). Also gone is the capacity for secondary revision, for correction and for therapy. There is no longer a need for history and the past to tell us who we are and place us in a teleological frame; history cannot explain events that take place in the mediascape nor in a discontinuous "life" with no narrative structure. Images replace the mirroring, and they're animated by proprioceptive sense which is, in turn, informed by data. It is not the case that, as critical theory would have us believe, bad mirroring is in effect (no good role models) and we simply need to find the corrective in the form of consciousness, discourse, reason or revolution. All these solutions presuppose a truly enlightened logic is at play in posthuman society. This logic is united in its Kantian belief that if a human individual is confronted, contained or exposed to its own behaviors it will reform itself; it will use its free will to transform the self, adopt reason to replace orders from authority and make the best possible decision for itself. That it will, as Thomas Keenan showed us in the last chapter, be shamed. Instead, the subject waves. Who cares who is watching? All of this was true while the mirror held an authoritative position in democracies. Or, as Rubenstein put it so neatly, "There is no longer the reflexive or critical distance between the real and its concept, between reality and appearance; rather there is operational miniaturization. The real is produced via the miniaturization of its model. Enlargement/reduction replaces the specularity of reflection" (Rubenstein 1989, 584).

In teleportation there is too much information, and there is no demand that the user craft a verifiable truth out of it; criticism as aiming at interpretation with stable meaning is no longer the aim of symbolic efficiency. A much simpler means of enacting social control is to target unconscious mechanisms to perfect bodily practices, movement, direction and scope of activity. Retraining the user's autonomic nervous system allows managers to avoid having to rationalize policy as it is simply incorporated into the programs. Resistance to social control no longer takes place because there is no mirror for the employee or soldier to look into to contrast with the person acting out directives. Cho doesn't look into a mirror when capturing his poses (like *Taxi Driver*'s Travis Bickle), he pours himself into the camera and mails the result to NBC.

Unlike Ignatieff's insistence that we think about war through the narrative of a (somewhat telegraphic) history, choosing those wars and mobilization strategies that best serve our need to figure out present forms of militarization, as if militarization boiled down to a *policy choice* made by governments about how to control civilians. Is this "within the limits and conditions" established by its corporate sponsors as Balibar contends (Balibar 2002, 33)? Instead we should think of it as an interpellative strategy that draws the subjects into militarization and ideologies of force by promising job training. While there is fierce competition between the school and the military as the recruiters maintain a right to access schools to find new enlisters for "life skills," that will "prepare them for the job market," it is clear that the seduction of violence (so neatly packaged in military fantasies of being a gamer who spreads democracy, etc.) was the key to military recruiting strategies. Once the soldiers arrived, however, they clung to neither justification nor rationalization but "junk." As the quote from ant article reviewing Iraq war autobiographies circa 2006 indicates:

> Three years after the beginning of the hostilities, the testimonies of American veterans returning from the Middle East are multiplying. Every conflict generates its own literary genre: epic for the Second World War, tragedy for the Vietnam War. And "junk" for Operation Iraqi Freedom. The material is composed from blogs, personal letters, raw details furtively thrown on paper between two patrols. The combat scenes oscillate between video games and gore fests. Garrison life provides closed-door secrets worthy of a reality show. Question of the times, the culture, and also of the context. Iraq inspires its conquerors to disjointed tales with no message, no direction, no laurels, no praise, and no critique. No diatribe against the US Army or George W. Bush, but no great patriotic couplets either. (Boltanski 2006)

> Just "me" and "my rifle" that "I love more than you." (Williams 2006)

Furthermore, the surrounding advertising culture in the U.S. supports militarization through the exploitation of video versions of violence, as well as the increasing attractiveness of extreme sports which only test the individual's capacity to push the limits of the physical body through training and risk. These "sports" also develop proprioceptive capacities using physical spaces instead of virtual ones. Recall, Massumi's examples of the floor as support. We can think of the numerous platforms for bodily training in extreme sports: the bridge for suspension, the concrete for skateboarding. Physical supports of all kinds now have a kind of determinate force to shape the body's movements, to control access to certain environments and then re-write the purpose of occupations. The de-centering of the human will and capacity for rationalization from this environmental and surveillance oriented political culture allows for the exploitation of the body's proprioceptive powers in automated directions. It also hinders the power of mind or "I" to object to human displacement. In the posthuman realm, the body, not the mind, is the real target of power. Thus there was the need for an effort to bypass logical thought or narrative explanations for war. The administration's rhetoric was a continuation of the political strategy of expediency long ago perfected during the Reagan administration, tempered but strategically used by Bush (e.g., Panama, Gulf War) and Clinton, but refined by Bush II for domestic uses, namely, the dismantling of civil society. As one prominent neoconservative strategist argued, the next administration would need to be concerned with

> "arresting the decline of American education, reviving a sense of citizenship and civic responsibility, and repairing vital national institutions such as the armed forces" (Lord 1999, 417). He was concerned that the next time there was a crisis and the president called us to sacrifice, will we be ready to do that? So the Straussians were talking about the need to infuse foreign policy with a moral language during both the George Bush and the Clinton administrations, and of course it came to fruition after September 11. (Xenos 2004, no pages)

What the neoconservatives and even Clinton did was inject the reality principle into virtual technologies (a reinjection of the Real into warfare). Where previously "liberal" approaches to foreign policy (grudingly) tolerated international law, such as the right of sovereignty and non-intervention, arguing that diplomacy and containment were viable strategies for cajoling non-democratic states to at least give appearance of holding democratic elections, the neoconservative strategy was to force feed democracy to the Middle East. For those who did not understand Der Derian's argument about "anti-diplomacy," this is precisely what he meant: it is not a normative argument about what "should" be done in foreign policy, but about the fact that empirical analysis and definitional comparison should show scholars that, in fact, anti-diplomacy means a militaristic approach to foreign policy. It means that conventional legalistic and normative approaches (especially Keohane's assertion that regimes across national boundaries could effortlessly apply a kind of passive aggressive diplomatic pressure) are not even considered by politicians and war makers. Like Ortega's philosophy of human nature, hunting and virtue, the neoconservative ethos is essentially *pre-modern*; they do not accept ideologies of progress that have to do with historical necessity or enlightened reason. Like Ortega, they see necessity only in *elite* leadership, in a class of warriors and leaders that will act as the vanguard party forcing populations to see not contradictions but to inhabit the virtual world of seamless democracy they were making through "regime change." Ortega's word for this elite is "select," a republican form of leadership that is not based on social class status or inherited privilege but earned through intellect and fortitude. These select individuals rule because the masses are incapable of reasoning, and when given too much power in democracy can revolt in the most regressive ways.

Militarization is a diffuse phenomenon produced by corporations and advertisers that seek to exploit the "orgiastic power" promised by violence.

Vicarious Pleasure

Ignatieff's comparison of the modern wars to virtual ones is connected by ideas about military conscription and nationalism. Evoking the levée en masse, Napoleon's great invention for taking over much of Europe, Ignatieff argues that mobilizing the entire population incites nationalism but may also temper it in democratic states. If the people do not believe that the military campaign is worth the risk of life to large numbers of citizens, they will not give the sovereign the nod to go to war. Forced conscription ended in 1972 in the United States, and there were campaigns to end it by pacifists throughout both world wars who argued that conscription militarizes a population's youth (specifically, in this case, young men) and hinders their development in conceptualizing peace (Dority & Edwords 2004, 12). It even leads to a denigration of the human condition, where people can no longer imagine themselves as humans worthy of dignity or capable of humility. In many ways, they argued that human self-perception was out of proportion with reality. In recent times, as telepresent technologies pass into common everyday usage, the population is largely dependent on the figure of the human as represented by programmers and media images. Scan the local paper, and one will find numerous examples of the confusion between categories like human and animal or even plant, combined with references to humans as machine-like combines with drone fetishism. Online personalities like avatars seemingly erase personal problems associated with being one. Indeed, the urge to find vicarious pleasure in the activities of other creatures is strong in a hyperreal society.

One might argue that passing out of the fantasmatic relationship to the Real and into the virtual challenges our traditional psychoanalytic categories for understanding personal motivation, enjoyment and even pleasure. Lacan's ego ideal/ideal ego distinction starts to look surprisingly dependent upon human relationships that occur in real time in the past, the "screen memories" that help to construct an imaginary, rather than with the images and objects we become fascinated by in the mediascape. There are several facets of virtual experience that make a re-envisioning of Lacan's formulations in the mirror stage necessary, not to mention the fact that it is heavily dependent on presumed stages of development that undergo a radical shift in virtual societies dominated by the temporal priorities of market productivity. This analysis will remain within the structure of the Lacanian topography for ego formation, asking how it has been transformed rather than engaging in a wholesale rejection of the theory. In the spirit of Baudrillard, I would ask whether or not virtuality allows the ego to pass through the mirror into another narcissistic space that is not a semblance of human identification but more likely that of human rejection animated by an environment of technological transcendence (recall Juul's depiction of the game where other player's constantly try to sabotage you). This speculative analysis will differ from previous normative debates surrounding the use of these technologies and their impact on human subjectivity; it is neither pessimism nor utopianism, nor realism, but an analysis of the transformation of the ego during repeated immersion in other egocentric spaces and the relationship to the counterpart. Pleasure is derived from vicarity, not identification or adversarial recognition. This explains our fans.

How does the counterpart motivate human behavior? For Lacan, we imagine a person or a thing, an object, to be watching us as we engage in activities that we have decided inform and reinforce our ego strength. When a specular image bumps up against our chosen fantasy space that doesn't cohere with our ongoing narrative, we have a properly traumatic encounter with the Real. Yet, as we pass through developmental stages in life, we imagine ourselves being watched or judged by the counterpart. Our success or failure in these practices is judged by the counterpart that we have chosen to watch, and this counterpart is imaginary, as in made up or hallucinated. There is also the function of being watched. In traditional ideal ego scenarios the subject imagines being watched; the narcissistic element should be obvious in that they imagine someone thinks they are important enough (or what they are doing is) to capture another's attention. Online the tendency is for people to believe that no one is watching them as a physical being but only the representation or screen image and discursive depiction they provide for others "out there" in cyberspace. Heim suggests that we can move from the tunnel-vision encouraged by use and limited technological capacity of current virtual projects into the "spiral" where presumably interactive gaming and programs would bring the spectators back into the picture. As he compares the two, "The tunnel sucks us further into technology as a forward-thrusting fovea-centered, obsessive fixation. The spiral moves us into virtual world that return us to ourselves, repeatedly deepening the experiences we have of ourselves as primary bodies" (Heim 1998, 76). We simply need greater bandwidth. In contrast to Massumi's portrait of Reagan as our new virtual model for automaton selfhood, Heim makes his retrospective move with the concept of this spiral and the world-building that flows from it. For Heim, we will simply leave the body behind but copy the social ego over to our hard drives; a whole new visual world built by cyber artists will accommodate our social egos in virtual spaces. One day, we will want an audience again; we will copy the mirror over to the hard drive as well. One central difference is that in the Lacanian mirror phase the transformation of the specular ego is the result of a structural demand (the Oedipus Complex), while in the virtual the automaton is the result of an identitarian demand: who are you? The answer to this question does not come by way of deep questioning, an inquiry into the soul or desire, but by means of adoption or purchase: I am whatever image I can afford to assume.[4] No longer determined by the specular image in the mirror, I can adopt an image for the screen, refashioning a self that has no physical limitations and no need for narrative coherence. "I" am obliterated. It's the ultimate goal of the suicidal exiters we've examined in this book. Heim leaves out of his analysis the idea of proprioception, at least the impact that it has in transforming our practice and by passing the "I" in the formation of experience. This is what is fundamentally at stake in the *volunteer* armed forces.

Somatic Compliance

There are two main ideas that I would like to map out in concluding this chapter. One, somatic compliance (as I am calling it here) is an effective means of encouraging a new kind of militarized subjectivity, the kind that doesn't question the purpose of a war or its stated objectives. This is most clearly found in a volunteer military, but there are many other examples (the flexible nature of work, the indeterminacy between work and play, between income and debt, etc.). I have looked at the military here since it has foregrounded our discussion so far. Two camps diverge on the question of the ethics of recruiting (ethics as in relation to the "Good"). One, the side against recruiting at schools is clearly identified with a pacifist agenda that is so entrenched that they have even argued against the presence of recruiters on law school campuses. This group, while noble in their efforts undercuts any kind of persuasive argument about the nature of military recruiting by taking such a hard line stance against any recruiting, even that of *adults* on law school campuses. Their position corresponds neatly with Laurent Berlant's claim about "infantile citizenship" in the United States as that which preserves itself against having its political virginity spoiled by the recognition of mature politics (where this is realistically marked with corruption, militarization, and unethical and illegal behaviors) (Berlant 1993). This is much different than Young's argument that since 9/11, U.S. citizens have been domesticated by security concerns acting as battered housewives. Rather, I see the American public as literally *infans*, that is, "without words," in relation to political authority, especially that of the military (*Harper's* forum 2006). This second camp—that of the silent majorities—had only the opinion of the military high command at its disposal. The real adversary to pacifists was (and remains) the military itself whose recruiting strategies focused on geographical areas with citizens who both out of desperation and political agreement with military service (e.g., red states) sign up, but also the recruiting strategies they employ aim at bypassing rational thought and going straight to compliance. We might even say that in this age desperation and political agreement are one and the same.

Recruiters may give students a "choice" to sign up for the military (and this is the main argument in favor of the justness of volunteer armies), but they do so without knowledge or availability of other options. As the schools are strangled financially by a decline in state and federal funding, they cut academic counseling services (and even general counseling services), and the recruiters show up in this environment and deploy arguments that counteract parents' objections (e.g., the Vietnam syndrome commercial) and to appeal to students' careerism and desire for adventure (Merrow 2005). This compliance is enacted without any kind of narrative drama or ideological justification; there is no future attached to it, and no past is appealed to for justification. It is, as critical thinkers like to say of globalization these days "immanent" (Hardt & Negri 2000). Wesley Clark restated the proposition in this way, "This administration has taken us on a path to nowhere— replete with hyped intelligence, macho slogans and an incredible failure to see the obvious" (Cassata 2006). As Boltanski rightly surmised, there is no need for an epic (and the goal is to avoid describing that war is as a tragedy), but the goal is to appeal to their subjective destitution by providing an image for them to assume. The idea that students were volunteering was a sham; were they to have had a real choice between several options we might considered this volunteerism. The idea of going to war without conscription also evacuated any purpose for the war as linked to patriotism or a narrative of duty to a cause or heroism that soldiers could cling to when the war became traumatic. Similarly, the open and permissive command structure encouraged by using virtual technologies to process information about events on the ground and in the air had the added effect of provoking even more anxiety than past wars. As Boltanski argued above by examining narratives about previous major wars the U.S. engaged (major in the sense of emotional and patriotic litmus tests), the Iraq war provided no convincing rationale for prolonged engagement, sacrifice or the formation of a social ego because the hierarchy of authority had dissipated (if one engages in a heroic or sacrificial act, they needed a superior to recognize it) and because the soldiers volunteered (they deserved whatever happened to them for not choosing some other option as a life calling). In other words, they gambled and lost.

Whereas in past wars, total wars, the command structure of the military could be clearly identified as hierarchical leading to blind obedience to authority and dependent upon leadership styles associated with justifying killing and war through references to fighting fascism or "kill or be killed" logic; today there is question about the role of new organizational structures in militarized states and societies and how these affect and manipulate certain forms of identification with killing and images of combat. Ignatieff charges that the latest RMA (Revolution in Military Affairs) encourages a move to "flat command structures" where hierarchy dissolves into equality among ranks, and soldiers can make decisions with information in combat without a superior's approval or direction. In many ways the problem with the current war is that there is a disconnect between field commanders and the strategic high command (just as in world wars, especially in the Asia-Pacific theatre). As the quote from General Wallace reveals, as well as recent information concerning the initial march toward Baghdad in the spring of 2003, high commanders did not anticipate paramilitary forces on the ground to battle with troops. They "gamed" a much different war than the one they confronted in Iraq. If the first Gulf War was a success on this front it was because its objectives were clearly stated (and yet, it is unclear that they were met politically in terms of foreign policy objectives). As Der Derian argued, all citizens could judge the progress of the war by were its "after-images" on screen.

Jane Fountain has found when interviewing military commanders using computer-based command systems that they tend to deskill operators from traditional leadership and decision-making styles that rely on "experience, intuition, wisdom and judgment" in order to "socialize them to automation" (Fountain 2001, 189 and 179 respectively). One consequence of this new style of decision-making has been that while it gives commanders access to information in the form of data at "dispersed locations" in the battlefield, this "freeing up" from being tied to the command post also created significant problems for the traditional authority structure that is hierarchical. Since various commanders can make judgment calls from remote sites with data that must be interpreted as information, they can be confronted with new battle developments that differ from the central command's assumptions and conclusions drawn during the simulated gaming phase (ibid., 173). Fountain further argues that the organization of the military is the optimal area to test her thesis on the application of virtuality to bureaucratic spaces since this is considered one of the main areas in which authority and control was of necessity. As we move onto the conclusion, we can see how such an environment played a role in how shootings took place throughout the decade.

Conclusion

What we have examined in this book is, quite simply, the way that violence and suicide as ideals play out in the control society. Galloway has linked this control directly through Deleuze to networking and information, through the ethical machine that is the computer. I am not calling for the eradication of these technologies; they can be useful. I am not blaming video games. In fact, I am not blaming "objects," and this is a key point. As a reviewer of Galloway's book *The Interface Effect* wrote, objects are not useful vehicles for understanding how power and control work. The focus on objects itself is ideological:

> But it's not merely that media studies has been focusing on the wrong objects; it goes wrong, Galloway claims, by sticking to the matter and form of objects at all. An interface, for Galloway, is "not a thing"; it is "always an effect"—a technique of mediation or interaction. The conceptual move here departs from the object-centered approach taken by critics such as McLuhan, for whom media objects are technological extensions of the human body; and his position differs, too, from Kittler's contention that media objects carry their own technical logics that only intersect obliquely and occasionally with human perceptions. Galloway draws from a different philosophical tradition, including thinkers such as Martin Heidegger, which "views techné as technique, art, habitus, ethos, or lived practice." In this view, media are not "objects or substrates" but rather "practices of mediation." While his approach risks casting too wide a net (what, we might ask, is not mediation?), it also promotes a form of thought that is open to ongoing interactions that unfold in complex systems. Thus, Galloway's method shifts attention from stable interface objects to dynamic interface processes. A computer, from this perspective, is no

> longer a media machine that standardizes and absorbs all other media, including print texts, audio recordings, films, and games; it is a process of translation among different states. (Jagoda 2013)

The computer, the interface, the network, these are, as Galloway says, allegorical for the way social control is lived in contemporary societies. Just what is different about them? Many thinkers contend that we are living in a "post" world. As Žižek argued in reference to the concept of a "post-historical" or "post-ideological world," such thinking can obfuscate our ability to think politically and urges us to act as if many complex questions are settled by democracy and capitalism. Others see a direct line to something called either the posthuman or the nonhuman as the sign of the times. As Katherine Hayles argued, "What is lethal is not the posthuman as such, but the grafting of the posthuman onto a liberal humanist view of the self" (Hayles 1999, 287). If the posthuman is understood simply as the temporal space of politics after the hegemony of humanism (an ideology in decline in U.S. public culture, and I suspect, elsewhere), where regimes of security are almost exclusively understood as technological, then public demand for algorithms to anticipate each and every potential need and threat have become the norm. As in, the preference for them is about protecting this liberal humanist self, which, it turns out, is really just the consumer self.

The U.S. media and a grudging public policy elite reacted to high-profile cases of civil society violence by squelching dissent, blaming objects (video games, the Internet, pornography, and secularism) for spreading a contagion of militarism to vulnerable youth; hence, the response was containment: lock down the schools, withhold freedom of speech and assembly for minors, profile adolescents, and engineer ways to monitor youths' use of technology. This was the "post-Columbine" world. At that time, there was still a comforting sense that while such episodes of violence were at the same time reprehensible and unpredictable (from this, inexplicable), they could be managed by policies that sought to contain youth from the objects that led them zombie-like to their miserable fates. This security and complacency would be challenged by Virginia Tech. It's not that the events leading up to it did not pose a challenge, it's just that they were still contained by media strategies that aimed to either frame them by a notion of "national responsibility," race or mental illness.

In every case there is *mental illness*. We have demonstrated that the social environment plays a large role in fomenting it; it is not from the individual alone. The difference, it seems, is the fate of the mentally ill in a society that is no longer civil. As poet and novelist Dennis Cooper puts it, "I feel that school shooters do what they do in an effort to square the botched equation between what sociologist Erving Goffman calls their 'soiled identity' and the fucked up reality that frames it" (Cooper 2007, 2011). Moreover, in these particular cases, the criminal justice system always deems the perpetrators to have been juridically sane at the time of the event, usually due to the evidence of long-term and extensive planning that goes into choreographing these events. And yet, we find they're not as successful as they might intend to become. There have been recent episodes that have introduced a change in the stylization of the act, as well as have increased the casualties. Following the Boston Marathon bombing in summer 2013, another attempt at a mass casualty shooting took place at the Washington D.C. Naval Yard where a severely mentally ill Aaron Alexis, who had been hearing "voices," opened fire on the workers there. Rather than kill himself as the police closed in, he engaged in fire with police until they shot him. The same thing happened with the older Tsarnaev brother, whose gruesome death ended after a shootout with police on a street in Boston that had been closed. The younger Tsarnaev touched off a similar fire fight after he fled the scene, only to hide in a boat and come out to police without violence. Finally, in December 2015, a married couple in San Bernardino, California opened fire on a Christmas party and training event at the Inland Regional Medical Center. After leaving the scene, driving around seemingly aimlessly, they were confronted by police on a California road, where they engaged in a firefight. This couple pledged allegiance to ISIS before their attack, setting off a media firestorm of fear about Islamic terror in the U.S. and ending with a standoff between the FBI and Apple Corp. over hacking the husband's phone to find evidence of a terror connection. In none of these incidents was a connection ever made. The media, especially Fox News, continued to report—recklessly and shamelessly—that these were acts of "terrorism," implying they were connected and indeed, ordered by ISIS commanders. They were not. They may have been inspired, but they were not connected. They were no more inspired by ISIS and other radical "Internet Imams" than they were by Columbine. All of these perpetrators would have been entering their teenage years when the Columbine event took place and living in the United States. Furthermore, Columbine was followed by a Global War on Terror, and Muslim Americans were repeatedly subject to discrimination and profiling and surveillance during this era. Moreover, the rise of "political homophobia" closely related to and emanating from radical Islamic notions of Western imperialism in the Mideast and elsewhere, where Al-Qaeda and its affiliates took control of rebel movements and aided in ensuring that many otherwise uninterested and peaceful citizens began to see the LGBTQI movements in the United States and elsewhere as Western inventions, like neck ties, not native to Muslim and other kinds of lands. This was also true of the Christian Right in the United States and other countries: Canada, Australia and Great Britain. Political homophobia has "gone modular" in that as the progress of LGBT rights spreads, it rises up as a political strategy used by leaders to deflect from unpopular policies, creating an imaginary threat (Weiss & Bosia 2013). This brings us to the shooting of the Pulse nightclub in Orlando and its perpetrator who emerges as a complex figure (like all of the perpetrators we have examined so far) for having been known to frequent the gay club for years, as well as use gay apps to cruise for men. Although he was twice married, Omar Mateen followed a known pattern of sexual confusion in that he assaulted his first wife until her family rescued her. It is true, as Soraya Chemaly says, that at the root of many, if not most, of these events there is domestic violence, committed both by and against the perpetrator, often both.

> This public violence is a direct outgrowth of tolerance for violence in homes. Boys and girls who grow up in these homes are four times—particularly the boys—more likely to be aggressors as adults. And so, when you look at a young man like this one, who went into this club and was clearly exhibiting patterns, very destructive patterns, before, you have to ask yourself: What could have been done to intervene earlier in the process? What was happening that inhibited the family from seeking more institutional help and support that would have been a red flag more broadly? (qtd. in Goodman 2016)

His father reported to the press that he was sickened by seeing two men kissing in Miami in front of his wife and son. One wonders if it was that: literally seeing what he had done secretly being done out in the open with no shame in front of his wife and son. It was a duplicity that could no longer be compartmentalized—a growing number of Internet sites and ISIS videos show gay men being thrown off of buildings and publicly executed or a radical Iman promising forgiveness if acts of violence are perpetrated against the "infidel." Furthermore, he had a father who probably never would have accepted him as a normative Afghani-American gay man, given his statements to the press that God would judge gays. This new iteration of the mass shooting script, which is profoundly American in character, is characterized by its end game as a shootout, dying in an exchange of fire. In fact, Mateen called the Tsarnaev brothers his "homeboys." Reminiscent of Virginia Tech and Columbine, he made several phone calls during his time in the Pulse nightclub to media outlets. To 9–11, he pledged his allegiance to ISIS, Al-Qaeda and Hezbollah (which really doesn't make much sense). He even called a local television station. The reports of what he was doing while holding the hostages for hours continues to unfold as I write this. This very day a blog post has gone viral for describing Mateen as "as American as apple pie." While these posts are important and serve the function of fighting back against media attempts to script him as a Muslim terrorist, they are not going to allow us to pull back the veneer of media self-satisfaction in order to examine these acts in a philosophical way.

However, we have seen that these episodes form a game. We have attempted to understand them from a multidimensional perspective. First, we looked at the experience of the perpetrators themselves (e.g., what are they experiencing in their lives prior to the onset of the decision to plan these acts down to their very minute details). We found that most of them are psychologically vulnerable. This condition, in most cases, stems from a series experiences in the social worlds they inhabit, be it in families, schools or workplaces, the media. These are institutions of civil society that mediate the citizens' relationship to others and himself. They are failing. These are the modulations; the processes and interactions that the perpetrators have with these institutions are modular, and they fail to contain his problems or cure them. In fact, they show him how inessential he really is. The perpetrators, by and large, are outcasts, not loners. In order to find this out, we had to listen to the work of people willing to investigate the other side of these stories, the side of the perpetrator.

This was our phenomenological foray into the perpetrators' experiences through the lens provided by Balibar, and by extension, Hegel. As Galloway writes, "For phenomenology, the solution to any problem is always found in the irreducible authenticity of the feeling subject" (Galloway 2013, 362). In contrast to many other approaches to these events, I have tried to empathize with the predicaments of these persons prior to their acts. They are all suicidal, and those that survive do seemingly break apart psychologically, their messages lost in what Žižek called "impotent *passages à l'acte*." Yet this is their (lack of) meaning for us, as spectators, survivors, victims and authorities. As told to the character/perpetrator Eric LaRue in Chapter 5, "what you did didn't change how they feel. It changed how you feel" (Neveu 2007, 80). It may be revenge, but it's not the kind of revenge that provokes the subject to stick around. I contend that its satisfaction is more immediate, and consumed in the act itself, and in the act, the perpetrator participates in something larger than himself, in a kind of ritual gameplay.

There are cases though, where meaning is attempted. In trying to decipher what they might have communicated, we highlighted the notion that many of the acts are cognizant that they will be received in telepresent reality where the message is less conveyed through an official manifesto than a parody of representational poses that mirror the society's expectations (e.g., violent films, poses, characters, etc.). Helpful here were the more thoughtful coverage of these events, as well as reactions to them by several critical scholars doing work on the political and historical background of the perpetrator, as well as critical analysis of the institutions (schools, universities, the military) that have shaped their experiences as disabled beings. Given the mass media setting in which they occur, they are transpolitical acts. The perpetrators always already know they are refracted through the media, and they account for this development. Witness the parade of "selfies" and posed portraits the shooters take of themselves.

The acts themselves correspond to a larger script developed at Columbine and transformed with each new mutation. They correspond to the logic of the game that we described with help from Juul and Galloway. From Juul, we learn that games are everywhere in the contemporary control society, even where it is probably unethical for them, like stock markets, political bargains and of course civil society. We noted the homogeneous social that is identical to the consumer citizen trained by postindustrial capitalism that produces heterogeneous elements (following Bataille and Sumala & Tikka's pathbreaking work connecting the four episodes in 2007–8 through YouTube and the Internet, generally). The fundamental difference between the operations of the control society and the disciplinary one is that the subject of the disciplinary society could still have "agency" or at least hope to, an agency provided by the allowance of relative autonomy to institutions and their ideologies. They could "resist" because there was a disciplinary authority to confront. One of the sad things about being in the "post" world of the control society is that, as Balibar put it, there is no outside, no America one can go to and start again, that is, if we think of "America" here not as a real place but as an allegory for a non-networked space (as it once existed in the minds of continental social contract theorists). After Virginia Tech the proposed solution called for an even further networking of what has been a protected space of privacy in the U.S.: our mental health records. Even more disconcerting, everywhere this collapsing of boundaries and privacy is said to be focused on "health." Here we noted Balibar's important claim that links up with Aronowitz's insights from Columbine and Kosovo: everywhere there is an idealization (an attempt to eradicate violence and promote an ideal) but extreme cruelty bubbles up to replace it. This corresponded to Baudrillard's idea that the media promote this endlessly in their "procession of the Good," and it may even be the mantra of the marketplace itself, as Žižek points out the grand hoodwinking that is humanitarianism a la Bill Gates or Google. Aronowitz's solution is to revert back in time to some kind of practicality. Given the pace of technology and the continued celebration of it as object that either saves us or condemns us, we miss sight of the global inequities it breeds, and how it solicits our consent in the process. Practicality was the ethic of the disciplinary society. Ideality is the ethic of the control one. Recall Galloway's insights about protocol and its relationship to power via Foucault. Protocol is what replaces civil society. When we speak of a civility, following Balibar, we must also take into account the way events and people are networked through what Hardt and Negri called the "non-place of production."

Paulo Virno has re-examined citizen subjectivity by globalization by providing an analysis of the kinds of "intellects" necessary to survive it in post-industrial societies. Much like Stanley Aronowitz's contextualization of mass school shootings through a sociological lens aimed at apprehending the effects of the decline of the middle-class social contract to opt out of violence as a solution, he has looked closely at more benign behaviors the domestic populations might engage in to survive the uncertainty of the times. He has argued that the concept of "people" applies only where a state is the locus of sovereignty, and in an age of globalization, the appellation "multitude" gestures to people who are politically disenfranchised from the state in a novel way. This is not disenfranchisement in the sense of those living in a bounded territory with a strong central power that denies or lacks guarantees for political participation of minority groups, but a disenfranchisement of the majority from even the most basic sense of security that would be provided by a state, whether in the form of employment, health care or relief from terrorism. One key symptom of this disenfranchisement is the lack of public spaces where a niche or comfort discourse can find a home for the individual situated in this multitude. Virno argues that a general intellect is formed to replace these specialized places of refuge (e.g., working class spaces, spaces in civil society), and that people have to become smart. They are "obliged to obtain the status of thinkers," whom for Virno separated themselves from the political community to do their work.

In the U.S., the respected "thinkers" have largely been religious figures and have been in constant contact with the public's existential problems. This is one explanation for the overwhelming belief in religion as a source of public policy compared to other G-8 countries. It might also explain why this spiritual belief gets grafted onto even more violent responses to cruelty in the form of "stand your ground laws" and increasing Second Amendment civil rights activism. These "fictive ethnicities" presuppose that all the answers to current ills caused by failing institutions is to revert back in time to the Bible or the Founders. This may explain many of our perpetrators' attraction to Nietzsche as well as to some form of social Darwinism. They despise the fatal strategies of the people around them. Their disdain for what they consider to be the celebration of mediocrity smarts when they realize that they are going to be continually judged by it, usually indifferently. Almost all of them have been reported to have been bullied extensively at some point in their development, and they cannot get over it. Usually at the point in their lives where they have to confront a big decision (or failure), they begin planning. For Harris and Klebold, college could only seem like more of high school, Weise could not get past the judgment of his teachers and peers and the decline of his community, Cho was close to graduation, the reward for which would have been back home to his parents and no literary career, for Holmes the failure of a test in the neuropsych department, and for Lanza, a mother moving on, looking for special schools for him to attend. For Kazmierczak, it was the death of a mother who blamed him for their separation from one another, and as he learns near the end, her unwillingness to forgive him for it. They were unable to make connections that felt meaningful to them. As Kass recalls, it's important to realize that Harris and Klebold felt like outcasts.

Yet most people do find connection using virtual technologies, and researchers have noted that immersive ones (the so-called Web 2.0 revolution, whether the Internet, file sharing, blogging, etc.) forge relationships through propiquinity; that is, their relationships are increasingly based upon electronic proximity, "where the social anchor has replaced the geographic grid as a way of identifying where we are in relation to someone" (Braman 2005, 19). They also use connective technologies to enhance norms of social practice offline, as well as connect politically in ways that they cannot in physical spaces, particularly in Asia and Africa. However, in the U.S. where the dominant political solution is self-care, virtual technologies that promote new forms of social behavior are often considered suspect for a range of potential ideas: there is concern with how youth interact in these spaces, contagion with adult communities, the still reigning notion of mimetic violence (that kids are driven to copy violent images and ideas from virtual technologies and film and television because they are so "real" in their effects), and obsession with how they learn anti-social behaviors from them or develop aloof personalities. Japan seems to have taken its own tack with this phenomenon in popular explanations for otaku (literally "you") youth who seclude themselves in online worlds that are seemingly more pleasurable than real ones. Again, we see an expanding sense that civil society (at least as configured under the form of the nation-state) now retreats, breaks down or is increasingly inhabited by those ideal persons outlined in the introduction. This works well with consumer expansion. The perpetrators do not communicate their acts in a way that their societies can understand. Still looking for discursive proof of a motive, the public finds such acts "senseless" and is satisfied with the media recycling of comforting narratives that we have seen, by and large, do not explain the process that leads these persons to their acts.

As a consequence of rejecting the notion of discursive ideology, one is required to also reject the theoretical concept of alienation that goes with it as a second order simulation (Baudrillard). To believe that contemporary generations can be alienated from productive forces (or the inverse, completely in league with them) misses the forest for the trees: they, unlike their parents or grandparents, have no concept of the political. If that conception no longer exists, how can one be alienated from it? The example of the City of Boston transportation bomb scare in 2007 demonstrates this gap in understanding between generations. Two media artists, working on the marketing campaign of the Adult Swim series *Aqua Teen Hunger Force*, placed a series of battery-powered LED placards throughout the Somerville and Cambridge neighborhoods of Boston. These placards depicted characters from the *Aqua Teen* show. Both Boston police and fire department officials mistook them for IEDs (improvised explosive devices) and shut down most of the city's transportation. In the aftermath, it was younger Bostonians and others who pointed out that the characters resembled LiteBrite figures rather than bombs, and most figured it was part of a guerilla advertising campaign (it was, to feature the show's forthcoming film). As one analysis has shown, we have an emerging gap between patriots and this "new" generation that is seemingly "detached" from others. William Rivers Pitt makes this alarmingly clear with his "fear" of generation 9/11. In writing of about the Boston public transportation scare,

> The event also exposed a dissonance in our collective thinking, especially among the aforementioned younger set. For them, and to use their favorite word, the 21st century absolutely sucks. A twenty-one year old today was seventeen years old when we invaded Iraq, fifteen years old when September 11th happened, and fourteen years old when the Supreme Court decided to take over the duties and responsibilities of electing our public officials. Since then, they have been subjected to bogus terror scare after bogus terror scare, to lies without count about threats beyond measure, to a war seemingly without end that serves only itself. (Pitt 2007)

What Pitt misses is that the two members of Generation Y featured in the media following the Boston transportation scare were engaged in resistance against the entire edifice of public security and surveillance. Refusing to answer media questions at an interview following the revelation that it was not a true bomb scare, the two young advertisers/artists held a press conference where the only questions they would answer from journalists had to involve 1970s American men's haircuts! That is, they were not even prepared to take fear inspired by confusion seriously. Journalists were apparently "shocked" by their blasé attitude toward the scare, an event which eventually caused Sen. Edward Kennedy to propose a senate bill that would criminalize false terror/bomb scares, cost the Cartoon Network millions of dollars to compensate the Boston police and transportation departments, as well as call for the resignation of the network's head. Sociologists continue to attempt to name Generation Y in accordance with traumatic national events, academics search their student bodies for evidence of civic fortitude or cynicism or claim their souls lack longing (Bartlett 2003), and then there are David Brooks's *NY Times* musings on students' pragmatism through one of the following: a rejection of politics, distrust of politicians or emphasis on utopian futures. Certainly they are "detached," but not from reality or even history; no one can any longer be said to be attached to any of these things in their absence. Reality is now different.

Rejecting the interpretive tradition of alienation is a first step toward understanding the role of the virtual in general and gaming in particular for immersed publics. What this means practically is to reject the tradition of interpretation that intimately or outwardly argues that virtual technologies somehow separate humans from a known truth about their social relations, one that is unchanging, immutable and if apprehended properly, transformative. Immersion, if done right, according to Michael Heim, cuts off several senses in order to isolate one in particular, usually sight and imagination. For clarification, it should be noted that it is slightly different from distraction, which emphasizes that a person is focused on an object or environment and then has their attention divided by another (usually passing) idea or object. This has great implications for surveillance societies. If control is premised on being seen, then being immersed is more about indifference or lack of awareness to those who monitor you in physical space, and it is not yet clear that most people understand how cyberspace is monitored. While surveillance cameras and satellites in physical spaces go unattended and still exert control over people's behavior, immersion in virtual spaces retains its aura of lawlessness. As an example of the effect of forms of immersion on adolescents, the indie film *The Chumscrubber* brilliantly demonstrates how a teenager continuously tries to tell everyone around him that a child (the spectral object of the control society) has been kidnapped, and the only way the police finally hear this revelation is in replaying a video tape with the character parodying the revelation. In this film, the allegory for new generations in confrontation with mediatized forms of security is presented in brilliant poignancy—they cannot even respond to a political and policing establishment that is indifferent to their participation except as extras to their own dramatic agendas: a divorcee who wishes to remarry, the divorcee's intended who is searching for himself in the ethereal, the housewife who immerses herself in healthy living and vitamins, and her husband the psychiatrist who uses his son (the main protagonist) as a guinea pig for his new book on adolescent psychology and keeps him drugged to avoid any nasty side effects, the grieving mother whose son has committed suicide and the divorced parents who have a strict "don't ask, don't tell" policy approach to child rearing. The main moment that I refer to in the film comes when the drugged son of the psychiatrist named Dean has information about a child who has been kidnapped by other teenagers ("bad ones") in the neighborhood. Since the sheriff cannot hear an adolescent, he speaks instead to the father who interprets the entire situation through the thesis of his latest book (one that he practices promoting to national audiences in front of the hallway mirror). Labeled "at the station" in this scene, the father accompanies him, the main protagonist, to his "mediation" with law enforcement where he proceeds to tell the truth about everything he knows including the blackmailing problem with other kids who are asking him to get drugs from his dead friend's house. He explains that a kid has been kidnapped by the blackmailers, but the cop refuses to believe him because there are no reports of kids being kidnapped. The father psychiatrist intervenes to "make sense out of this" for the cop, and it is clear that he will make sense of it through the lens of psychiatric disorder, of delusion, of pharmacological side effect. As they leave the room, Dean realizes that the kid who has been kidnapped is the son of the sheriff by looking at "Charlie's" picture on the sheriff's desk. He picks up the pictures and holds it out to the camera that's been taping the entire interview and smiles.[1]

It is only after reviewing the videotaped interview that the policeman concludes that there has indeed been a kidnapping, and it is of his very own son, Charlie! Throughout the film we are treated to glimpses into this son's life, that of his ex-wife who is attempting to remarry and himself, a noncustodial father with circumscribed access to his son's whereabouts. In the mother's concern to remarry (almost desperately to an unsuitable man), she loses sight of her son and does not know he is even missing—a persistent theme is that parents do not know anything about their children other than what their imaginations dictate to be the case. Any attempt to question parental agency (or lack thereof) in these cases is considered conservative, and often rejected out of hand.

Unfortunately, most contemporary media and public discussion has focused on WMDs (weapons of mass distraction) in the media rather than the pivotal role played by a new immersed subjectivity. For them, virtual subjectivity is just regular old humanist subjectivity enhanced by digital technologies (Hayles's fear), and it is true that they are marketed this way by advertisers who naturally seek to seduce more and more consumers to their products, regardless of age or income barriers. But there is a whole subterranean consciousness that is both enabled and blunted by nonlinear pathways to information, digitally generated worlds, and otherness. One study released by British researchers has highlighted the use of virtual technologies as means of exhilaration and escapism. The British Board of Film Classification (BBFC) found that gamers believe they are engaged in escapism (much like one would do with a novel or film), but that they believe the games exhilarate that escapism, and take it out of ordinary life.

Most theories of gaming and technology privilege the human side of the binary over the non-human by arguing in some form that humans are separated from the environment that would restore their wholeness by technologies of control and discipline. For some these are harnessed by other humans to use them in a form of exploitation in the Marxian tradition, and all of the remedies found in popular culture are the means to hide the maladjustment from those who sell their labor in this system. Whether it was jazz music, cinema or football, one critical thinker or another has attempted to argue that people are immersed in these (usually passive) activities that provide vicarious satisfaction from the gaping holes and contradictions in their lives left by technologies. This ranges from the "man-machine complex" of Ellul that anticipates "total integration" of humans into the slavish demands of technology (Ellul 1967), Kroker's "panic discourses," and in the game milieu the dominant idea of games or play as separate from "reality," free, secluded, order-creating and community oriented (Galloway 2006 on Huizinga, 19–23). Play that is evinced in games that give rise to culture because they are competitive, involve chance, mimicry and potentially induce panic or vertigo (Callois in Galloway 2006, 23–28). In particular, video games have been interpreted as "half-real" in that a game "does not as much attempt to implement the real-world activity as it attempts to implement a specific stylized concept of a real-world activity" (Juul 2005, 172). As an IT gamer, Juul presents video games as media that enhance or substitute for the real thing but they are not seen as threats to reality or the humans who inhabit it; they simply extend its parameters and empower its users. In other theoretical genres, games are viewed as expressions of play that, in working out societal contradictions, are therapeutic to the players and still others see games as a means to learn new ways of resisting modes of domination that exist within the structures of reality as relived in gaming through such simulation or stylized concepts. Video game criticism is the new literary theory or cinematic studies putting an Adorno against a Benjamin or producing new versions of Lukàcs theory of realism in literature.

Galloway makes clear, however, that there is a real difference between gamic vision and the spectatorship of cinema. For him, gamic vision implies action, whereas the viewing of images implies passivity. As was argued in Chapter 6, the war on terror and the war in Iraq are not games that the U.S. public was actually playing. Instead the public was invited to watch as subjectivity on the sidelines, and when the embedded reporting was successful, the public was able to sublimate or rationalize their civic choices.

These conditions transform war into something like a spectator sport. As with sports, nothing ultimately is at stake: neither national survival, nor the fate of the economy. War affords the pleasures of a spectacle, with the added thrill that it is real for someone, but not, happily, for the spectator (Ignatieff 2000, 191). For others who identify with the players too readily, watching the game for them was like a snuff film, as Galloway puts it, while explaining the difference between the subjective shot and the POV (point of view) shot apropos of Hitchcock's *Rear Window*:

> There is nothing sinister about POV shots, but subjective shots signify something dark and murderous, and so when Hitchcock elects to use a subjective shot, he comes up with a formally affected image, emanating from the eyes of a murderer. In this sense, it is easy to see how the subjective shot is a close cousin of the snuff film, connected as they are through the coupling of predatory vision and the impotence of gaze. (Galloway 2006, 53)

Teleportation is, as media artist Eduardo Kac describes it, "an unknown state" where one can base new social relationships on "propiquinity," but also can base new forms of collective security or responsibility. As Kac sees it, responsibility can go "cosmopolitan" since knowable human imposed boundaries can be suspended for the purposes of maintaining a collective project, such as watering and caring for a plant (*Eighth Day*). Collective problems are posed in a Neo-Deweyan way using telecommunicative experience. Rather than the traditional pragmatic experience conditioned by nature or culture, as Dewey held, telecommunications technologies allow for new kinds of immersive experiences, and in the case of artistic production, new kinds of creative experience.

In control societies, the search for the self has become delinked from an actual awareness of the existence of the polity that that particular self would find its place in and then practice its corresponding civic duties. It is not ethically guaranteed. In decentralized societies, according to Galloway, control exists through flexibility, as evidenced in the way choice is framed as liberty: menus of all types frame the choices of consumers, seducing them through the promise of expanded options while limiting them to a discrete set of actions.

> "electronic interaction has the danger of promoting instead interpassive experiences that catalog all possibilities within a preestablished restrictive system of choices." (Kac 2005, 114)

> "Whether involving an exchange between two interlocutors or not, telepresence seems to create this space of reciprocity absent from mass media. The space created by telepresence is reciprocal because the decisions (motion, vision, operation, etc.) made by the 'user' or 'participant' affect and are affected by the remote environment." (Kac 1993)

Scientists, Kac notes, were eager to pursue telepresence because it could "equate robotic and human experience," so that they could create, he says using Baudrillard's phrase, an "operational double" in order to achieve the "feeling of being there." However, Kac insists that his interest in telepresence was different because he saw in it a way to "produce an open and engaging experience that manifests the cultural changes brought about by remote control, remote vision, telekinesis, and real-time exchange of audio-visual information," as he says of "challenging the teleological nature of technology" (ibid., 1993). Yet, as Katherine Hayles warned us in the last chapter, we can view telepresence in its unique features as a challenge to our thinking about this continuous script being written by civil society mass killers. First though, we must add some meaning to this experience, some content to this script, and we can then begin to see them as transpolitical acts (we may not like them) that challenge both the media's fascination with them as an index for ratings (the so-called antihero fascination promoted by the media and demanded by fans and critics) that actively seek to subvert the media gauging the public's will to know "why?" and indict civil society for failing to contain them. We are no longer in the realm of individuals who try and fail to join communities that then exact revenge on them by choosing a school, we are in a telepresent reality, a place where motive does not matter.

I end this book with an attempt to politicize spatial constructions of civility in regions that are heavily dependent on information-based and image-based communications systems. Technologies now network humans; governments rarely need to impose order. As was argued in the last chapter, images now assume a vital function in the construction of citizen subjectivity. The media provide an environment primarily hyperreal, and this is achieved by a series of stages described by Baudrillard and attributed to the status of the image: "In the first case, the image is a good appearance: the representation is of the order of sacrament. In the second, it is an evil appearance: of the order of malfeasance. In the third, it plays at being an appearance: it is of the order of sorcery. In the fourth, it is no longer in the order of appearance at all, but of simulation" (Baudrillard 1994b, 6). As we examine the media events such as school shootings, we find hyperreality or Third Order simulation emerges as the primary mode of representation where specific examples include:

- reduplication of the "real" through technologies (Xerox, photography, film, programming)
- remediation of it (YouTube, file-sharing, blog posts, faked or leaked Facebook posts)

This was (and is) specifically found in the practice of video autobiography where school violence perpetrators pre-record poses and parodies of still images for them to be viewed by the networked public. No one any longer leaves a note at the scene. The same is said for suicide bombers and the authors of other "inexplicable" acts of atrocity. The public is lured into the desire to know what motivated such an act, to know something about this person, or the group they come from (there is always presumed to be a second shooter). In this way the "real" is reduplicated over and over again as the images of the video clips are replayed by the media. Moreover, the images of the authors of these acts become self-referential as they may be taken into other contexts to explain rage or dissatisfaction. In addition, such reduplication of autobiography transforms what Goffman described as the personal management of the *concealed* stigmas of *discreditable* people (see discussion in Chapter 3) into something of a cottage industry where these hidden stigmas are revealed in a public and managed way unanticipated by modern sociologists: as marks of infamy. In these autobiographical moments the stigmatized person has moved beyond norms of personal identity where shame and the management of spoiled identity is the central focus to a final videotaped statement or presentation of self that disrupts the everyday life and routine of "normals" (Goffman).

- mimetic behaviors (school shootings as serial media events—no motive)
- methectic play (school shootings as a game where each new player adds to the script)

School violence perpetrators are writing a continuous "hidden script" where each new event attempts to outdo another, or demonstrates that the shooter learned something from the media coverage of past events. They refer to past events, shared sentiments of alienation, heroism and martyrdom, as Cho specifically did in his videos. At the same time, they issue a challenge to future protagonists generating new scripts in public to be acted upon at a later date. The only motive that can be attributed to such events is to take up where past events left off: killing more people than the last event, perfection in the execution of the event (Cho chooses classrooms during official class hours, chains the doors shut, choice of hall with easy classroom access), making up for past event mistakes, and fooling the public and police authorities by using their surveillance codes against them (Cho stages a domestic violence scene at Ambler Johnston in order to mail the video autobiography to NBC in New York—something Harris and Klebold could only have dreamed of doing with their infantile demands of crashing helicopters into the city of New York). They choose poses from popular film, wear commando regalia, use the same type of weapon, tape bullets to the chest (Kip Kinkel), and augment the weapon to increase the number of rounds. The only motive in these events is to continue the script, and to improve upon it by shaming the authorities in the process by demonstrating their ineffectiveness at anticipating the shooter's grand strategy. The latest iteration of this script has been the ending characterized by a shootout. The perpetrators no longer turn the gun on themselves as the police close in on them, they return the gunfire, knowing they will die. Possibly believing, in some gruesome way, that it is honorable.

- democratic and widespread opposition to the idea of false representation (there is no real to represent, the hyperreal masks this)

First, there is no real motive in the modern sense of the term. Motive implies that shooters are exacting revenge against a particular person or groups (their peers) based on shared norms of social interaction. If shooters wanted something tangible from the public, they would make demands and live to see those demands met in future interactions. School and other mass shooters beyond Columbine want to make fantasies of revenge real through simulation of past events. Motive suggests something personal or hidden that we can reveal by investigating their personal lives and family history; by contrast, the desires of these perpetrators are public ones made real by mimicking previous acts of violence.

Second, the media is a willing accomplice to such motiveless crimes. Any motive that is given in the media is immediately rejected as baseless or injected there as a "reality principle" by a second media outlet that will motivate further speculation to keep the signifying chain attached to school shootings in play (this is the precise function of remediation). The media's goal is to keep the coverage going as long as it needs for ratings; social/symbolic agreement on a motive would spell the end of the media event (Edelman 1988, 3). This cannot happen until all possible motives have been exhausted and imagined (Cho as mentally ill, gay, a problem immigrant, creepy, evil, etc.; Harris and Klebold as popular, unpopular, gay, and mentally ill). At the same time that we cannot decide upon any one of these explanations as definitive of the event's motive, we also cannot eliminate them as possible explanations; this is evidence of the rejection of illusion as explanation and recognition that there is no "real" behind the interpretations only a masking of the absence of that reality prolonged in satellite feeds, blogs and screened images.

- causes of events attributed to objects and behaviors, not human intentionality; idea is to eliminate human error from social and political life. (Era of surveillance, U.S. school surveillance forms model for airport surveillance.)

The death of intentionality is the death of humanism, an ideology that privileges human agency over all others. Humans are equal to objects, and at times their subjects. Human motivations are explained by surveillance procedures; by an extended logic of perception. If a person uses an object, frequents a place, or acts in a certain way, those things give rise to suspicion of him or her as a person of interest. Motive about revenge for interpersonal reasons is increasingly less of a target by law enforcement and institutional authorities, unless a crime already committed falls neatly into the simulated design attributed to such events (e.g., Cho's domestic scene). Interpersonal reasons, past psychological traumas or failures, and bullying cannot be mined from large quantities of public data nor can they be captured in images to communicate to the public. What can be *seen* is privileged as a source for motive, or can be imagined to be seen (and in this latter case, it would have already been seen). Being seen is now more important than being heard; discursive explanations for events that approach signification are inadequate to cultures "weaned on the screen." For some, who claim that we are now "equal in submission," we can see how the old phrase about children being "seen and not heard" has been applied to everyone (man, woman and especially child) in the effort to give the child a "voice" or "rights."

- marks out the claim that there is no original; end of aura, end of artistic inspiration, end of singular existence, democratization of divinity

School shooters, like suicide bombers, do nothing unique. Every aspect of their acts is planned using available media or by citing predecessors. They see themselves as secondary to a cause greater than themselves, and their acts are preoccupied with the behavior of normal society, of indicting it and interrupting its casual flow. Taking up such a divine calling is a democratic endeavor, and personal identity is placed under erasure by acts of martyrdom; this is their appeal. Recall that Cho often referred to himself as "?". Kazmierczak erased every aspect of himself from the act, choosing to merge completely with the methectic ritual. Attacking democracy and its public spaces of free assembly is the best way to achieve it for one's cause. This is not representation because there is nothing left to represent in the aftermath of a suicide bombing or a school shooting, except a defense of that which was challenged (all the accoutrements of democratic culture: rights, security, protection, civility, etc.). So far, those publics challenged have used such defenses to drive a wedge between themselves and would-be suicides. As the gulf widens between those who have representation yet have gone cold to it and those who reject it in suicidal protest, the genetic and nuclear promise of life beyond nature is held out as the future.

- not representational but genetic and nuclear (Rubenstein 1989); societies are built around a code, a semiotic system that provides the necessary signifiers for understanding what constitutes "life" at a given time.

Territory is generated by the map or model, it no longer precedes it. This is Baudrillard's language but we can update it: spaces, especially political and social ones, are increasingly networked by software designed to exploit.

To return for a moment to the example of *WoW*, a player of this game belongs precisely to a control (rather than a disciplinary) society insofar as she creates content, scans and sorts information, manages guilds, and laboriously grinds her way to more experience points. (Jagoda 2013)

In order to save the reader from confusion, it is necessary to state this clearly. Violent video games do not motivate mass shootings, neither do video games proper. They are, however, as Galloway says, a figurable instance of how ideology works at present. The interface in these cases is between the civil society and the perpetrator who remakes the space of civil society into his game. The rules are set by him. He is in control.

In the virtual, which as Bergson insists, has *always* played a role in human life from the way that it can be imagined without detached technology by reference to the brain. From the perspective of Virilio, the virtual is that which enhances our physical spaces but is often controlled by technological forces and used in ways that demoralize our collective perceptions, increase disparities in power and make senseless killing possible. For Baudrillard, "we no longer have the good old philosophical sense of the term, where the virtual was what was destined to become actual, or where a dialectic was established between those two notions. The virtual is now what takes place of the real; it is the final solution of the real in so far as it both accomplishes the world in its definitive reality and marks its dissolution. At this point, it is the virtual who thinks us; no need now for a subject of thought, a subject of action; everything happens by technological mediation"

(Baudrillard 2003, 39–40). For Galloway, the regimes of power are challenged by virtual modes deployed in gaming. To him, gaming is conceptualized as a new form of literature, capable of bringing out latent forms of resistances to codes imposed by one-way virtual programming. People who game learn the vulnerabilities of codes and exploit them in a fashion similar to the détournement of culture by stylizing such resistances to make them more real (or in some cases, personalize the revenge). Gaming not only allows for tactics and strategy to be deployed but something akin to grand strategy emerges in the last chapter of the book, where gamers can reprogram games to resist dominant modes of interactivity. Much was made of Eric Harris's reprogramming of *DOOM*, and Larkin provides an extended analysis of it, by placing it within what Galloway would call the social realist vision of paramilitary culture:

> Eric Harris was quite skilled at playing video games. The games themselves can be reprogrammed by players. Harris apparently reconfigured *DOOM* so that when victims were killed, they cried out, "Lord, why is this happening to me?" (Hubbard 1999), an apparent allusion to evangelical Christians, toward whom both Klebold and Harris evinced a great deal of animus. (Larkin 2007, 170)

Larkin further cites from Brooks Brown's book (a former friend of Harris and Klebold and a central figure in the investigation that followed Columbine) which revealed that Harris would also reprogram both *DOOM* and *Quake* so that the "protagonist was overwhelmed by the enemy," and he was criticized by friends for making the game too difficult to play. Here is an example of Harris using the game to inject his version of social realism into it; as Galloway contends, it must achieve "congruence" between the game and the social reality of the gamer. Harris reprogrammed *DOOM* to have this "fidelity of context" (that apparently others did not share or appreciate) between the game and his social reality at Columbine High School, caught between the unending assault alleged by Larkin at the hands of the jock elite, as well as the judgment by activist evangelicals at the school as his "Lord, why is this happening to me?" program attests. As was noted in the introduction, publics have developed numerous ways to explain school violence that rely on simple, causal logic, such as the Columbine thesis, to reiterate Galloway's definition: "The problem of the Columbine theory is, to put it bluntly, one of directionality. Realism in gaming is about the extension of one's own social life. The Columbine theory claims the reverse, that games somehow exert realistic effects back onto the gamer" (Galloway 2006a, 78). Using Galloway's definition, we can see that while some games may appeal to the social reality of the gamer (for example, Palestinians playing a game that allows them to strategize about the

West Bank), making the claim that FPS games, even when they capture the ideals and mission of the U.S. military, as in our case with Harris and the Marines, can never be an exercise in social realism (which is Galloway's interpretation of what might be a gateway to some kind of agency). Rather when the fidelity of context is missing they are nothing more than fantasmatic, which is to say, for most of their users, harmless. However, if we leave the terrain of video games and reach beyond them to the entire political edifice of what Galloway calls "informatics," we can see two major problems with contemporary social and political life in the United States and other post-industrial countries: one, it is characterized by control and two, by inertia. These two problematic states are the result of our nearly total reliance on media and mediated existence, what Baudrillard, a few paragraphs up, revealed as the situation where "it is the virtual who thinks us; no need now for a subject of thought, a subject of action; everything happens by technological mediation." Baudrillard is completely pessimistic about this mediation, offering that it is the total procession of the "good" (at least that is how we valorize it) that can eliminate "evil." Baudrillard sees this as an illusion; we are simply covering over our lack of a proper (rational or even moderate) relationship to the "real" with hyperreality, or the virtual.

It comes back to haunt that society in the deeds of these men. As was said at the end of Chapter 3, we are in the real.

Epilogue

I have attempted to tell a story about mass attacks and the violence they communicate. Most of it has been told from the side of the perpetrator. This is because, as Enns notes, perpetrators were nearly always once victims themselves, "The victim who kills out of revenge and in the name of claiming dignity and humanity can be the most vicious killer of all" (Enns 2012, 119). American culture has a pronounced affinity for "law and order" solutions to problems of violence. Moreover, it has a law and order interpretation of violence—victims must always be innocent, and the blame goes to one specific type of person. In this story, I refer not to the actual victims (they have their own meaning and interpretation) but to the American public as it constructs itself as victim each time one of these events takes place. When I wrote my first book, the newspaper headline that stuck in my craw was "Why?". As I wrote this book, one of my favorite articles about this violence was about Virginia Tech. Its title is "The Thirty-Third Victim," and it refers to the perpetrator, Seung-Hui Cho. Jones's analysis echoed my own regarding Columbine and incidents prior to it:

> Cho's identities as criminal gunman, Hokie victim, evil monster, pathetic reflection of American young manhood, or unassimilated foreigner were tried on and sloughed off over the first weeks after the shootings. Like the spontaneous memorials, these identities represented both the search for an explanation and an inchoate call to action to prevent more tragedies. Those that contained an indictment of contemporary culture, however, proved to be unsuitable as an identity for the shooter. The media and the mourners needed Cho to stand alone, to adopt an identity against which "we" could all be "hokies" and "we" could all "prevail." (Jones 2009, 74)

Ultimately, the media crowd decided mental illness was the problem, and fixing our mental health system the solution. This has yet to happen. Furthermore, the search for why Cho might have experienced such mental illness (whatever its nature) is still to be sought in some kind of biological cause alone. There is no admission or exploration of the fact that perhaps this violence and mental illness is produced by the environment in which Cho lived, in public culture in the United States, characterized by a fetishism of privacy, racism and fear of being perceived as racist, stigma of non-normalized identity, homophobia, gender paranoia, masculine entitlement (yes, that too) and his own failed attempt at it. We have seen that it is especially hard for first generation Americans. I can not help but think this is the case even more so after 9/11 and the American and European response to it. Beyond Columbine the search for suicidal fame has reached tragic levels, indicating that we do indeed need to look at marginalized peoples and their difficulties in negotiating an increasingly networked and screened existence, but we need not imagine them as innocent to do this, only human, all too human.

Notes

Chapter 1: Introduction—Virtual Violence: Beyond the "Columbine Thesis"

1. Let me be clear: I realized there was probably a group in the school that was called such a thing; however, I had no illusions about its effectivity on bully culture. This group was clearly a disorganized group of friends who liked trench coats and probably bore little resemblance to a proper mafia. In short, it was most likely a running joke at Columbine.
2. This, in spite of the fact that their facial recognition software failed, and they had to release the still images to the public in order to locate them.
3. Scholars point to first and second generation school violences, and make the critical cut off point at Columbine. The key difference is that Columbine established school shootings as a political act, whereas previous shooters were supposedly driven by privations (family problems, cliques, etc.) and wanted interpersonal revenge. Another line is drawn at the Virginia Tech event, where it is said that the violence then transcended national boundaries, and became infinitely shared across the Internet via YouTube, which did not exist until 2005. I reject the first distinction, but also see no reason to include events that occurred decades prior that have no relationship to the ones examined later in the 90s and beyond, such as Marc Lépine's horribly tragic attack on the École Polytechnique in Montreal. While unfortunate, it has no gamic

relationship to the events examined here, and it is doubtful that any of the attackers since the late 90s even knew of Lépine's crimes.

4. Standardized testing is no doubt a failure in the United States, largely because of the way it has been implemented (applying standards of economic efficiency to success). However, it can only deal with one aspect of the crisis that Arendt examines in the essay "The Crisis in Education," that of mass society. It attempts to force a system of meritocracy onto a political and educational structure dominated by the American ideology of equality. In order to have successful standards of any sort it would be necessary to reform the teacher's colleges to make the curriculum more responsive not only to subject matter related expertise, but also to educate teachers about the politics of education so that they could advocate for themselves in their districts and at the national level through new and stronger unions whose goals could be more consistent with present political and economic realities. This may even mean starting new community based schools that operate parallel to and outside of present district politics offering the communities more meaningful forms of education than the present schools can provide. Not charter schools, actual community run schools that do not take directives from federal or state initiatives.

5. Following Sestir & Green (2010), Böckler & Steeger (2012, 316) call this "parasocial interaction" where the user interacts with a media persona, like Cho or Eric Harris, "as if they were an external entity." This interaction provides three necessary elements to the subject: continuity, narration and intimacy.

6. This is a point of contention between Cullen and the rest of the independent journalists and academics who interviewed the Columbine community. Kass argues that Eric's mom had told the recruiter about the Luvox (innocently, she did not want anything to hurt his chances, and appreciated the possibility of tuition benefits for college). The recruiter told her that an applicant had to be off anti-depressant meds for one year. Cullen says that Eric never bothered to follow up with the recruiter as he was so intent on making his psychopathic dreams come true at Columbine. Kass, by contrast, reports that Brooks Brown indicated he mentioned the rejection at school on April 16th but downplayed it, and further another friend told the *National Enquirer* "Dylan and I were the first ones Eric told about the rejection. He asked me 'Where do I go from there? He saw it is as a last option" (147). Here is how Cullen frames it. He too recounts Kathy Harris showing the recruiter the Luvox (at this point, according to Kass, he was probably on 200 mg per day), and the recruiter said he would "check on it" and call back. Here's Cullen, "Like Eric cared. He had been invoking the Marines in his war fantasies all his life, but all he really wanted out of the corps was the prestige of its patch on his shoulder. Eric never depicted himself supporting a squadron, and certainly not taking orders. It was always an army of one or two, and the mission was about him, not country or his corps. Gonzales phoned on Friday or Saturday and left a message to call him back. Eric never bothered" (Cullen 2009, 335). Did Cullen miss the ads for the army over the past decade that

stressed "An Army of One" as an alternative path to college? I'm guessing a survey of recruiters would confirm that the majority of new recruits think about joining exactly the way Cullen describes it.

7. Balibar makes a twist on Hegel's "morality of culture" which is produced in the civil society by the state's influence by calling the contemporary version "the normality of morals." To be moral is to appear "normal." None of these kids were ever able to be seen as normal in the Goffmanesque sense of the term; they were irreparably stigmatized; first by peers, then, usually by psychiatric, legal or crime control institutions.

8. For a precise definition of how this profiling happens in more theoretical terms, see Mary Ellen O'Toole (2012). On pages 184–86 she explains how the FBI behavioral analysis unit "make a distinction between motive for the crime and justification for the crime," which go like this: "Justification is what the public wants to know in order to make sense of the crime. They want to be able to say, "Ok, I understand now why someone would go into a school and shoot and kill ten people." There will never be a reasonable justification for what Jeffrey Weise did that day. However, the motive for the crime is entirely different. The motive is the offender's emotional and psychological reasons for committing the crime, which can be either conscious or subconscious." See the difference? Neither do I.

9. Although there are many others in Germany, they do not rise to the mediated level of these three. In addition, later ones "after 2006" did "preoccupy themselves" with former offenses, like Columbine. One of them (the German researchers avoid naming their subjects and hide their identities in data) "admired and closely identified with one of the Columbine shooters and copied his behavior before (e.g., drawing a map of his school for a first-person shooter or making violent videos at school), during (e.g., by his clothing at the day or by details of the planning of his offense) and even after his offense (e.g., leaving proof of his own thoughts and ideas by spreading parts of his diaries) (Bondü, Cornell, & Scheithauer 2012, 82).

10. Johann Galtung, theorist of structural violence, as an example, whose granddaughter survived the Utøya shooting, has become interested in studying them.

11. I also believe that by isolating the focus to social problems leads to researchers including every single unrelated case into their analysis and confusing the situation. When one starts with the political, they can isolate the other cases that do not fit. As we shall see in Chapter 3 more specifically, these cases are "transpolitical" in that they do, as Böckler and Seeger (2012) and Kiilakoski and Oksanen (2011) have argued, participate in the notion of the cultural script that develops over a decade. The case I am making here corresponds only to those transpolitical acts, not to any episode of mass violence, whether rampage or bombing, prior to 1999 (I would even exclude the cases in *Failure to Hold*); Muschert is right, these are "first generation." And any other shooting that does not rise to the level of the ones examined here, i.e., that are peer oriented (the cases of Lanza and Oliveira I will explain later), focused on mass atrocity, extermination, suicide or psychotic break, bombs are usually a feature, diversion/deception, etc.

Chapter 2: The Many Tropes of Columbine

1. Deleuze and Guattari, *Anti-Oedipus*. Trans. 7–8. Bricolage is the mode of production of the schizo.

2. Yes, there are many attempted shootings in the interim period. However, as I argued in my first book, even in Taber, Alberta (which occurred within days of Columbine), the gun was pointed down, the plot was thwarted, evidence of planning was missing. In short, most of these attempts, even Santee, California, were what could be called "copycats." Copycats are failed shootings in the sense that they lack the planning, execution and malevolence of the methectic version where the shooter is playing the game.

3. See Webber 2003a, pp. 17–19 for a discussion of Loukaitis.

4. Leavy and Maloney (2009) argue that the Red Lake shooting resists the media spectacle coverage because of race. I concur with their analysis. This is important, because it goes back to our claim from Galloway about what kinds of images of violence can be represented as such. While I would argue that Weise's act is no less significant in the signifying chain of school shootings, it has been marginalized because it does not "fit" the typical model of spectacular mediatized event. However, Weise cited Columbine in the sense that he asked one of his victims if they believed in God (a nod to Columbine, no matter how incorrect), and wore red-laced combat boots and a trench coat. It doesn't matter; the act is for the spectators, not for the perpetrators. He also shot his victims in the face. To me, this seemed a pretty serious overcoming of protoempathetic identification, as will be described by Protevi later on in this chapter.

5. Kass's critical reading demonstrates this to be untrue. The Klebolds gave a total of one interview in the ten years following Columbine, to Oprah. The Harrises reached out through personal letters a few months after the shooting. Unfortunately, they did the appropriate thing and routed them through the sheriff's office that delayed sending them to the victim's families for a significant time.

6. As Dewey Cornell has argued about the peer relationship: "A more promising strategy for preventing homicidal acts of violence can be found in the findings by both the FBI and Secret Service that most of the attackers communicated or leaked their intentions to others prior to their attack. Many of the students had spent weeks or months contemplating, planning, and preparing to attack, and had often confided their ideas to friends or classmates. In some instances they sought assistance in obtaining a weapon or carrying out an attack, and in other cases they issued warnings to persons they did not want to harm or expressed anger toward those they wanted to kill. All of these behaviors reflected the strong developmental need of adolescents for peer acknowledgment. Similarly, the decision to carry out an attack in the open, public setting of a school reflected the adolescent's need to make a compelling statement to an audience of peers" (Cornell 2011, 45).

7. As Kass puts it, these "basement tapes" were shown to *Time Magazine* and a few others. "In maybe one of the most bizarre paths of a piece of evidence, the tapes were then shown to journalists, victims' families, the Klebolds, and select others such as law enforcement officials," but then lawsuits put them under wraps. As with other forms of information, these tapes have been summarized for the public by those who saw them, mostly the Jefferson County Sheriff's office, so we have reason to be suspicious of how they are interpreted. Kass sees them as a clear suicide note, whereas Cullen offers little in the way of explanation for the suicide portion of the acts (Kass 2009, 137).

8. This is why everyone who writes about Columbine has to cite the only evidence of bullying that came out from one lone idiot who clearly never got the group silence memo: E. Todd (Columbine Defensive lineman) who said, "Columbine is a clean good place except for those rejects. Most kids didn't want them here. They were into witchcraft. They were into voodoo dolls. Sure we teased them. But what do you expect with kids who come to school with weird hairdos and horns on their hats? It's not just jocks; the whole school's disgusted with them. They're a bunch of homos, grabbing each others private parts. If you want to get rid of someone, usually you tease 'em. So the whole school would call them homos, and when they did something sick, we'd tell them, 'You're sick and that's wrong'" (Gibbs & Roche 1999). Aside from Brooks Brown and some anonymous sources interviewed by Larkin and Kass, no one has admitted Harris and Klebold were ever bullied and revealed their identity at the same time.

9. I would give some weight to the argument about the South because it is a traditional political culture, focused on maintaining a hierarchical status quo. It did have a form of a feudal past in the form of slavery and the Southern plantation culture that developed along with it. But again, here the honor is on the side of the powerful, the established. Questioning it is not normal in this political context. Therefore, there's no strain to experience if it's the political and cultural standard. That's why people talk about it being so difficult to change the culture of the South. It doesn't seem like the violence that occurs there ever produces a counter-violence, which is what school violence is, no matter how disproportionate it may seem.

10. The most reliable and well-known research on this subject is by Ferguson (2008).

11. Margaret Price's work on this subject is invaluable. Her critical readings of the reports at Virginia Tech and Northern Illinois make the point that FBI and university (or high school) converge on the topic of mental illness precisely because this argument protects the "normates" or reasoning audiences from implication in the madness. See "Assaults on the Ivory Tower" from *Mad at School.*

12. Protevi also makes a strange off topic comment about how this case differs from others because of "guns and bombs" but never explains why, except to cite Grossman on protoempathy, then makes several long digressions about how soldiers have killed in the past (from heroic Homeric narratives to blind rages) and moves on

from there. I guess this is important if you begin your argument from "seepage," which is the assumption that we domesticated humans living outside the military get infected with this military contagion through our use of video games, well at least some of us, distributed in a population. It is unclear to me, anyway, why shooting someone at point blank range is all that different (in the protoempathetic sense) from using a knife to stab them, which Harris and Klebold mention, or from other weapons attackers have used.

Chapter 3: *Passage à l'acte*: New Thoughts on Civility

1. Tim Weiner, "Parents, Shopping for Discipline, Turn to Tough Schools Abroad," *The New York Times*. 9 May 2003, Sections A-1 to A-10.
2. Every single FBI profile seems to imply that these perpetrators are like our now commonsense understanding of serial killers on television who, unable to stop themselves from fantasizing about an act, have to make it real. But serial killers don't commit suicide, do they?
3. Kass cites an empirical study on the South and West, and while his book was published in 2009, it did not contain references to shootings in Germany or Finland, which had taken place by that time. However, I can see how school violence of this type (especially prior to Columbine) looks like what Paton (2012) and Newman (2004) describe as a reversal of identities. Paton describes the self-presentation of shooters in their videos as a successful series of identifications: first, as loser and marginalized social outcast that they embrace, and second as taking revenge and denying their weakness through violence (Paton 2012, 218). However, Paton also describes the shooter's presentation as alluding to an "unfairness" that relates to "democracy." My response to this is that it is not possible because schools (at least in the U.S.) are not democratic institutions and no one expects them to be. They are socialization chambers more in line with Rousseau than Locke (where revenge is not only allowed, it is a part of natural law). Schools teach conformity; there's just no getting around that. Where would this democratic discourse come from? It may look more like Mika LaVaque-Manty's analysis of the role of dueling in Southern culture, but that emerges from a feudal culture, not an open, liberal capitalist democratic one. See Mika LaVaque-Manty (2006), "Dueling for Equality: Masculine Honor and the Modern Politics of Dignity," *Political Theory* 34(6): 715–740. Furthermore, dueling implies a "respect for the other" missing from either side of the bullying equation in American schools. That is, it implies civility.
4. For a compelling reading of Holmes through this exact lens see Ingar Solty (2012).
5. The judge threw out this defense saying, it was "not a matter of law" and was "a non-justiciable political question not before the court" (Johnson 2013). In other words, a political defense cannot be entered.

Chapter 4: The Failure of the Middle-Class Social Contract

1. CNN "Virginia Tech Health Report: Share Mental Health Data," http://www.cnn.com/2007/US/06/13/virginia.tech/index.html (6/13/07)

2. Two important claims about Hasan still loom in the mediascape but have little validity. One, on the political right, it has been imperative to see this as a terrorist act by foregrounding Hasan's Muslim identity and his contact with Anwar al-Awlaki, a "spiritual leader" executed in a drone attack in Yemen by the Obama government at a later date in 2011. First, Hasan was born in Virginia to Palestinian parents and graduated from Virginia Tech in 1995 and continued on through medical training paid for by the military. He did have personal conflict with the idea of the U.S. government killing Muslims and his role in it as a military psychiatrist (he joined before the GWOT). Second, the FBI knew about Hasan's contact with al-Awlaki and concluded it was part of a larger study he was undertaking through his military post. The contacts did not warrant further investigation by the FBI. It did not help that al-Awlaki praised Hasan's acts later, nor did it help that Hasan took up the idea of "protection of others" as a defense in his trial (which was thrown out by the military judge). Had Hasan been seen by the government as engaging in *treason*, not terrorism, he would have been tried in a federal court (remember this is the Obama administration, not the Bush one).

3. Here we might truly have what Henry Jenkins has labeled an effect of "convergence culture" where old and new media collide, but it might more persuasively be called where "old and new" imaginaries collide.

4. For more on this see "Amok und zielgerichtete Gewalttaten in Deutschland" ("Amok and goal-oriented acts of violence in Germany") by Jens Hoffmann, Karoline Roshdi and Frank Robertz. Thanks to Ingar Solty for this reference.

5. I will problematize this notion in the next chapter. It is commonplace for those who wish to see these killings stop to argue that the media, in covering the perpetrator, asking why, etcetera, contribute to the idea that these individuals are "antiheroes" that is, "loveable rogues" who "force us to forgive their occasional misdeeds or repulsive behavior because they are flawed but inherently loveable" (Donnelly 2012, 24). They are incorrect.

6. We can see this is the apartheid that Balibar speaks of in every society.

7. This insight will be important when we look at more kinds of "fans" that emerge following the James Eagan Holmes shooting and the Boston Marathon bombing by the Tsarnaev brothers.

8. The most extreme example of this offer has been made by Rudy Guliani as mayor of New York. On and on go the media discussing how he "cleaned up" New York, but did he? Or did he create a situation where he contained the poor and disenfranchised

from the moderately wealthy? For more on this see Michael Warner, 2005. *Publics and Counterpublics.* New York: Zone Books.

9. This is key: the American public is the most important public for this analysis because its understanding of the conflict in Kosovo and beyond was limited to an "us" versus "them" mentality about Serbs as the aggressors to the peaceful Croats and Muslims. There was no public understanding of the history of the conflict (for example, Croat alliances with Nazis during World War II, or of Tito's style of rule). Aronowitz's argument about moral suasion is important because it means American leadership took sides in a conflict that was presented as having only two when in reality it had more like five or six. This means partisanship without sensible moral suasion provided a model of behavior to the American public that degraded its sense of justness and fairness.

10. Indeed this is how Solty (2012) defines the relationship between Christians in the U.S., those of the working class type (evangelical) versus more established and wealthy (Presbyterians).

11. Nowhere more in evidence than in the Clinton endorsement of the 1996 Welfare "reform" Act.

12. The Health and Human Services Report on Virginia Tech urges the government to remove the stigma associated with mental illness. One can suspect that the more practical option will be to resignify it as something to celebrate or as something to medicate, coinciding the desires of pharmaceutical companies to expand market activity. Perhaps we'll even be treated to new (saner) versions of Tom Cruise's argument that physical activity can cure depression and other illnesses.

13. As was the case with Goth subculture after Columbine when whole new retail chains emerged to sell Goth clothing and paraphernalia.

14. This is not to say that these people do not really exist or that that cannot make a small difference in people's lives, as they do. It is to note how these stories have already been so overdramatized as to become scripts that people can slip into when they rationalize taking these career paths. When they are disappointed that the story does cohere the way they were instructed to imagine (via the visual culture of film) their inevitable conclusion is that there's something wrong with reality because it doesn't match cinematic fantasy (when in fact, it never did meet such lofty expectations).

15. Studies in the decline in consumer satisfaction reveal such real-time social disparity, as does the continued cultural fascination with both real increases in cases of autism and in ones that are attributed to digital culture. See Douglas Coupland's *JPod* for an interesting fictional depiction of the effect on software programmers. Important here is an entire section of the novel where one programmer begins designing a "hugging machine" that will apply pressure to people who can no longer interact with other people effectively in physical proximity. Anne Allison's depiction of hikikomori in Japan, a subclass that does not leave their rooms, defined as a person who goes a year or longer without communicating with family or friends (Allison 2006, 82).

16. By April 27, gaming blogs had caught on to the strategy of pundits at blaming video games, where they revealed that *Washington Post* coverage deleted references to Cho (in the space between online and print) playing *Counterstrike*. Interestingly, online posts do not have to list "corrections" if they have not appeared in print yet. This means people will take the online version as truth, since no one reads papers anymore. As the blogger who discovered this argued, "Oh wait, there is just one more thing. According to the search warrant results, hosted on CNN and referenced by Gay Gamer, authorities found no videogame consoles in the killer's dorm room. There is still the possibility that there could be computer games stored on Seung-Hui Cho's PC (though roommates reported as never seeing play a game), but for now we can rule out gaming consoles" (Yam 2007).

17. See Chapter 5 for an analysis of spite as the "sign of the times" in Ortega's formulation.

18. Larkin, at the end of his thorough and thoughtful research on Columbine suggests "peace" education. I would be wary of this as it has not had much success in other countries where peace (like Finland) is valued, so it would be difficult in a U.S. or German or Brazilian context. Even more disturbing is the way that solutions focusing on peace may only exacerbate the problem, as we've seen so far it is one of idealizing, following Balibar. To put more stress on an ideal or peaceful outcome may only add to the grievance. In addition, a solution of peace presumes that the conflict itself is the result of relatively autonomous actors who will feel like their choices and responses would be valued in some way; in the control society there are no longer independent choices.

19. In watching the coverage of the Virginia Tech shootings, it was troubling to find that all the "experts" called on to situate the crisis for the public were either nearby on the East Coast, or they were stand-by (often retired) FBI agents with little or no understanding about university culture or school shootings. The public assumes these experts are chosen for their knowledge, yet it seemed they were chosen for their proximity and availability.

20. Jay, Mike. "Tim Robbins." *The Charlie Rose Show*, 13 October 2003.

21. As we saw in the Introduction and shall see in Chapter 6, in the contemporary era, we find a newfound insistence on the maxim that "children should be seen and not heard" through the control society's deployment of surveillance technologies.

22. For an excellent report on this see *The Merchants of Cool*, a documentary about how marketing companies seek out consumer models by gender and age (*The Merchants of Cool*, 2001). For teenage boys they are called "Mooks" and girls its "Midriffs." Advertisers use these market researchers for two main purposes: to search for innovation and creativity to market and to construct an ideal "type" to market these innovations to adolescents based on insecurities about "coolness."

23. In the contemporary era, shame and the perception of unfairness always presuppose one another. If the person or nation does not feel it has been judged unfairly it would

not feel shame (this is what theorists of shame do not understand). Without ties to moral systems that can explain why an act is shameful and what remedies can make up the debt incurred by the unjust action, shaming for its own sake necessarily leads to *ressentiment*, as Nietzsche argued.

24. Keenan evokes a Croatian scholars' adoption of Baudrillard's concept of the "transparency of evil" to capture this phenomenon where this analysis is contained to the former Yugoslavia; it is still considered seemingly inappropriate by many American academics to use Baudrillard's work to understand American popular culture or militancy. Let me be clear, however; Baudrillard's intention is not about finding collective responsibility for human suffering, as many in the liberal tradition presuppose and then proceed to flunk him for failing to do so convincingly. Nor is it to provide a revolutionary framework by which to overcome and emancipate citizens from capitalism or oppression. Further, his texts can only be read as an endorsement of nihilism by readers who presume there is a strategy of overcoming based in rationalism, progressive time or "reality." Baudrillard is best read as ironic, using Nietzsche's style of aphorism to refrain from or fall short of any endorsement of prescriptive political analysis. His theoretical insight is to describe an overall logic of a system of "good" and "evil" that is maintained by the governments and economies of the West, and the virtual values they espouse (bourgeois affectations and a rejection of irony). In democracies, it is the populations that must justify the system since it is presumed to represent them, but how do they sort out the differences between themselves and others in their midst who do not share the value system they espouse?

25. Talovic and the Ft. Dix 5.

Chapter 5: Of Rogues and Fans

1. This is exactly what Adam Lanza did when he arrived at Sandy Hook Elementary; he simply shot through the windows, entered the building and shot the guard.

2. Again, I am unable to effectively compare the cases in Germany, Finland and even Norway, Brazil and Canada here. However, I would like to point out that medicating mental illness is a form of stigma itself. It aims at alleviating symptoms but not curing or making the illness compatible with the rhythms of the larger society. Individuals do not function within a set of rules, identifications and cultures by taking a pill. The medication either stabilizes them to the point where they can take that culture seriously (without harm) or it numbs them to it. Without the secondary civil society mediation, the idea of medicating away mental illness is already an admission of failure at integration.

3. This coverage is disingenuous. In a culture where stalking is not taken seriously either by the public or by law enforcement, to later judge the students for not pressing charges is an example of American culture's double standard when assessing women's

safety. It is symptomatic of other kinds of double standards and inequities that have only increased in the past few years. Wherever there is a social problem, the individual who alerts the authorities to its presence will be made personally responsible for taking it seriously.

4. Furthermore, any university that does not receive any form of federal aid does not have to comply with the Clery Act. As schools and universities become increasingly reliant on private foundations and alumni donations, they are also increasingly independent from compliance with federal legislation, especially of the type that seeks to ensure the protection of women and minorities, ensure diversity and provide students with the kinds of security their parents assume will be there. The public is so far removed from understanding these laws and the fact that any progressive legislation that's aimed at providing security for vulnerable populations is tied to the federal government and not ensured at campuses where private funding and higher tuition provide such supposedly higher quality education. It is patently wrong to believe that if you pay more, you get more for your students. What the Clery Act does accomplish is the groundwork for collecting statistics on violent crimes so that researchers and agencies can actually demonstrate to the public that such a phenomenon exists and presents a substantial problem to the public. Related to this point, any alerting system that caused such panic presupposes an evacuation plan that all faculty, staff and students are trained in executing. College and university campuses are very often situated in remote locations with only a few roads surrounding them, many students are prohibited from having a car, and the public transportation systems may be unreliable. All these considerations make it highly unlikely that even if there were an evacuation plan, very few would have the means to make it off campus without encountering even more anxiety-causing obstacles in the form of traffic jams, people on foot and bike, treacherously navigating dangerous roads with little concern for immediate safety, crowded buses and very unfortunate problem that thousands would be "left behind" to be further managed by campus security. In the situation at Virginia Tech, it was best to not alert the campus to prevent such widespread panic, which may have caused even more problems for the campus police to have to respond to while attempting to apprehend the shooter. It was more responsible to have the campus community calm and carrying out their normal routines, the only way the university could possibly track thousands of people is if they stayed on their schedules, rather than ditched them in a panic.

5. Virginia Tech had apparently met with a campus security organization to adopt a text message alerting system where students could be instant messaged in the event of a campus emergency. While this system might reach more students than email, it still does not account for the number of phones and services a student might go through in the span of year. Furthermore, most students only inform the university of their permanent phone contacts, which include their parents' home phones, information of little use in an emergency except to unnecessarily frighten families. The anxiety

and hysteria over the lack of alerting system in this case is symptomatic of the American need for an agent of responsibility even though the very nature of the college experience militates against such surveillance and encourages the privacy that helps to develop the individual into a fully functioning adult citizen. Given these realities, the flip side of mass security is an individualized form of self-care and protection that has made the idea of students carrying guns seem like a plausible option to the public.

6. The autopsy reported no psychiatric drugs were present in Cho's system at the time of the killings. Also, Virginia Tech Report noted that one reason people were able to save themselves through barricades at Norris Hall was because the autopsy report noted that Cho had "weak musculature" (*Mass Shootings at Virginia Tech* 2009 94).

7. I would like to underscore here that in mentioning this I do not mean to pathologize it. Indeed, most young people discuss Columbine and other shootings in this way.

Chapter 6: Remote Projection and Militarized Subjectivity: A Different Iteration

1. Or, as Robert Kagan insists, "[sic] the very fact of the Soviet empire's collapse vastly increased America's strength relative to the rest of the world. The sizeable American military arsenal, once barely sufficient to balance Soviet power, was now deployed in a world without a single formidable adversary. The 'unipolar' moment had an entirely natural and predictable consequence: It made the U.S. more willing to use force abroad" (Kagan 2002, 26).

2. "Reification under modernity was always 'I'm just doing my job'—leave me alone in my penance, I'm just 'working for the weekend.' But reification in the information age has an entirely different emphasis: 'Just let me do my job.' In this mode there is a heightened ownership of one's labor within an ethic of self-worth and spiritual achievement. It is an appeal: let me. Real life is an anti-labor blockade, an interruption. The goal is not to uncouple from the sphere of labor, but instead to enter it entirely and sincerely" (Galloway 2012, 107). This is especially interesting given the way "support" figured in relation to the troops.

3. In interactivity, according to Virilio, one learns to "love at a distance" without corporeality (Virilio 1997, 112). For Eduardo Kac, virtual artist, telepresence allows people to find community again in the shared acting upon a specific object in geographic space (Kac 2005).

4. In a reading of Saito's theory of the "beautiful fighting girl" the Japanese analog to the American (insert culture/national online identity) YouTube/gamer fanatic, Casey Brienza suggests that it is the superhero. Our dropped out subject, like the Otaku (literally "you"), but the one million youth who are shut-ins online in imaginary worlds may be the "standard bearer for postmodernity" (Azuma) in that since no meaningful relationships can be forged outside consumerism, they are invented

online. Brienza writes, "in lieu of the desire to possess that enervates the experience of the Japanese otaku, for the American otaku it is the desire to become. Perhaps the superhero is the image of the child in Lacan's theoretical mirror, uniting fiction and reality through the ordinary, imperfect man's anticipatory (yet of course never fulfilled) desire to become the extraordinary, perfect superhero? This is but a possibility. Nevertheless, it is safe to conclude that if the superhero is indeed desireable, then Saito's theory can be exported in a productive manner that he himself did not anticipate" (Brienza 2012, 227).

Conclusion

1. https://i.ytimg.com/vi/W7yyYbzBywI/hqdefault.jpg

Bibliography

Abad-Santos, Alexander. 2012. "The NRA vs. Really Old Video Games: Important Updates for Wayne LaPierre." *The Atlantic Wire*, December 21.

Abdel-Nour, Farid. 2003. "National Responsibility." *Political Theory* 31, no. 5 (October): 693–719.

Abel, David. 2013. "Conspiracy Theories, Innocence Claims Find Audience." *The Boston Globe*, July 27.

Abu-Assad, Hany, dir. 2005. *Paradise Now*. Warner Independent Pictures, DVD.

Adam Lanza's Father: 'Evil' Sandy Hook Shooter Would Have Killed Me 'in a Heartbeat' 2014. *Huffington Post,* March 10. Accessed June 13, 2016. http://www.huffingtonpost.com/2014/03/10/peter-lanza-interview-adam-lanza_n_4933912.html

Ahmed, Sara. 2004. "Affective Economies." *Social Text* 79, 22(2): 119–39.

———. 2004. *The Cultural Politics of Emotion*. New York: Routledge.

Aksoy, Mete Uiaş. 2011. "Hegel and Georges Bataille's Conceptualization of Sovereignty." *Ege Academic Review* 11(2): 217–27.

Allen, Nick. 2008. "Finland School Shooting: Gunman Had Contact with 2007 School Killer." *Telegraph.co.uk*, September 24.

Allison, Anne. 2006. *Millennial Monsters: Japanese Toys and the Global Imagination*. Berkeley and Los Angeles, California: University of California Press.

Althusser, Louis. 1971. *Lenin and Philosophy and Other Essays*. Translated by Ben Brewster. New York and London: Monthly Review Press.

"American Coup D'etat: Military Thinkers Discuss the Unthinkable." 2006. *Harper's Magazine*, April.

Ames, Mark. 2008. "Northern Ill. University Massacre: A Story of Bleakness & Madness." *The Exile*, February 20.

Andersen, Audrey. 2012. "Anders Behring Breivik Phoned Police to Surrender but Carried on When They Failed to Return Call." *Telegraph.co.uk*, April 23.

Anderson, Curt. 2006. "Florida Homeless Beatings Put Light on Hidden Problem." *Chicago Sun-Times*, January 20.

Andersson, Mette. 2012. "The Debate about Multicultural Norway before and after 22 July 2011." *Identities: Global Studies in Culture and Power* 19(4): 418–27.

Appadurai, Arjun. 2006. *Fear of Small Numbers: An Essay on the Geography of Anger.* Durham, NC: Duke University Press.

Apter, Emily. 1999. *Continental Drift: From National Characters to Virtual Subjects.* Chicago, IL: University of Chicago Press.

Arendt, Hannah. 1958. "The Crisis in Education." *Partisan Review* 25(4): 493–513.

———. 1961. *Between Past and Future: Six Exercises in Political Thought.* New York, NY: Viking Press.

———. 2000. "Reflections on Little Rock." In *The Portable Hannah Arendt*, edited by Peter Baehr, 231–47. New York, NY: Penguin.

Aronowitz, Stanley. 2000. "Essay on Violence." In *Smoke and Mirrors: The Hidden Context of Violence in Schools and Society*, edited by Stephanie Urso Spina, 211–27. Lanham, MD: Rowman and Littlefield.

Aronowitz, Stanley, and Jonathan Cutler, eds. 1998. *Post-Work: The Wages of Cybernation.* New York, NY: Routledge.

Arreguín-Toft, Ivan. 2005. *How the Weak Win Wars: A Theory of Asymmetric Conflict.* Cambridge, MA: Cambridge University Press.

Asprem, Egil. 2011. "The Birth of Counterjihadist Terrorism: Reflections on Some Unspoken Dimensions of 22 July 2011." *Pomegranate* 13(1): 17–32.

Baker, Kevin. 2003. "We're in the Army Now: The G.O.P.'s Plan to Militarize Our Culture." *Harper's Magazine*, October.

Bakken, Ryan. 2005. "Teen 'Seemed Lost in Life.'" *The Seattle Times*, March 22.

Balibar, Étienne. 2001. "Outlines of a Topography of Cruelty: Citizenship and Civility in the Era of Global Violence," *Constellations* 8(1): 15–29.

———. 2002. *Politics and the Other Scene.* Translated by Christine Jones, James Swenson, and Chris Turner. London; New York: Verso.

———. 2009. "Violence and Civility: On the Limits of Political Anthropology." Translated by Stephanie Bundy. *Differences: A Journal of Feminist Cultural Studies* 20(2/3): 9–35.

———. 2012. "What Democratic Europe? A Response to Jürgen Habermas." *Social Europe Journal* 7(1): 9–11.

———. 2012. "Civic Universalism and Its Internal Exclusions: The Issue of Anthropological Difference." *Boundary 2* 39(1): 207–29.

Barnes, Fred. 2005. "A War Without Heroes?" *The Weekly Standard*, December 26.

Bartlett, Robert C. "Souls without Longing." *The Public Interest*, December 2003, 101–14.

Bataille, Georges. 1979. "The Psychological Structure of Fascism." *New German Critique* 16: 64–87.

Bataille, Georges, and Jonathan Strauss. 1990. "Hegel, Death and Sacrifice." *Yale French Studies* (78): 9–28.

Baudrillard, Jean. 1988. *America*. Translated by Chris Turner. London; New York: Verso.

———. 1994a. "No Reprieve for Sarajevo." Translated by Patrice Riemens. *Canadian Journal of Political and Social Theory* 17(3): 1–6.

———. 1994b. *Simulacra and Simulation*. Trans. Sheila Faria Glaser. Ann Arbor, MI: University of Michigan Press.

———. 2001. *Impossible Exchange*. Translated by Chris Turner. London; New York: Verso.

———. 2003. *Passwords*. Translated by Chris Turner. London; New York: Verso.

———. 2005. *The Intelligence of Evil or the Lucidity Pact*. Translated by Chris Turner. New York: Berg.

Baumann, Nick. 2011. "Exclusive: Loughner Friend Explains Alleged Gunman's Grudge Against Giffords." *Mother Jones*, January 10.

Bean, Henry, dir. 2001. *The Believer*. Fireworks Pictures.

Belau, Linda. 2003. "Killing the Object: Psychosis and the Criminal Act." *Cardozo Law Review* 24(6): 2229–54.

Benjamin, Walter. 1978. "Critique of Violence." In *Reflections: Essays, Aphorisms, Autobiographical Writings*, edited by Peter Demetz, translated by Edmund Jephcott, 277–300. New York: Schocken Books.

Bergson, Henri. 2004. *Matter and Memory*. Translated by Nancy Margaret Paul and W. Scott Palmer. Mineloa, NY: Dover Publications.

Berlant, Lauren. 1993. "The Theory of Infantile Citizenship." *Public Culture* 5(3): 395–410.

Blacksburg, Erfurt. "Littleton: A Chronicle of the Worst Rampages Ever." *Spiegel Online*, April 17, 2007.

Blanchot, Maurice. 1986. *The Writing of Disaster*. Translated by Ann Smock. Lincoln, NE University of Nebraska Press.

Böckler, Nils, and Thorsten Seeger. 2012. "Revolution of the Dispossessed: School Shooters and Their Devotees on the Web." In *School Shootings: International Research, Case Studies, and Concepts for Prevention*, edited by Nils Böckler, Thorsten Seeger, Peter Sitzer, and Wilhelm Heitmeyer, 309–41. New York, NY: Springer.

Böckler, Nils, Thorsten Seeger, Peter Sitzer, and Wilhelm Heitmeyer. 2012a. "School Shootings: Conceptual Framework and International Empirical Trends." In *School Shootings: International Research, Case Studies, and Concepts for Prevention*, edited by Nils Böckler, Thorsten Seeger, Peter Sitzer, and Wilhelm Heitmeyer, 1–24. New York, NY: Springer.

———, eds. 2012b. *School Shootings: International Research, Case Studies, and Concepts for Prevention*. New York, NY: Springer.

Boldt-Irons, Leslie Anne. 2001. "Bataille and Baudrillard: From a General Economy to the Transparency of Evil." *Angelaki* 6(2): 79–89.

Boltanski, Christophe. 2006. "Stop, or I'll Shoot! We're Here to Help You." *Libération*.

Bondü, Rebecca, Dewey G. Cornell, and Herbert Scheithauer. 2011. "Student Homicidal Violence in Schools: An International Problem." *New Directions for Youth Development* 129: 13–30.

Boose, Lynda E. 1993. "Techno-Masculinity and the 'Boy Eternal': From the Quagmire to the Gulf." In *Gendering War Talk*, edited by Miriam Cooke and Angela Woollacott, 67–102. Princeton, NJ: Princeton University Press.

Boym, Svetlana. 2001. *The Future of Nostalgia*. New York: Basic Books.

Braman, Sandra. 2005. *Information Technology, National Identity, and Social Cohesion*. A Report of the Project on Technology Futures and Global Power, Wealth, and Conflict. Washington, D.C.: Center for Strategic and International Studies, April.

Brandenburg, Heinz. 2005. "War Stories as Political Strategy." In *Bring 'Em On: Media and Politics in the Iraq War*, edited by Lee Artz and Yahya R. Kamalipour. Lanham, MD: Rowman & Littlefield.

"Breivik: 'When Nato Drops Bombs in Libya or Other Locations They Calculate on Less than 10% Civilian Casualties; … That Was My Aim Too.'" *Twitter*, April 19, 2012. https://www.theguardian.com/world/2012/apr/19/anders-behring-breivik-trial-live quoting Breivik.

Brienza, Casey. 2012. Taking otaku theory overseas: Comics studies and Japan's theorists of postmodern cultural consumption. *Studies in Comics*, Vol. 3 Issue 2, pp. 213–229.

Britton, Sheilah, and Dan Collins, eds. (2003). *The Eighth Day: The Transgenic Art of Eduardo Kac*. Tempe, Arizona: Institute for Studies in the Arts, Herzberger College of Fine Arts, Arizona State University.

Bronson, Rachel. 2002. "When Soldiers Become Cops." *Foreign Affairs*, 81(6): 122–132.

Brown, Janelle. 1999. "*DOOM, Quake* and Mass Murder." *Salon*, April 23, 1999.

Brown, Jennifer. 2012. "James Eagan Holmes' Defense Will Be Complex, Difficult." *The Denver Post*, July 23.

Brown, Ryan P., Lindsey L. Osterman, and Collin D. Barnes. 2009. "School Violence and the Culture of Honor." *Psychological Science* 20(11): 1400–1405.

Brown, Wendy. 2006. "American Nightmare: Neoliberalism, Neoconservatism, and De-Democratization." *Political Theory* 34(6): 690–714.

Buell, John. 2004. "Terror, Evil, and the New Cold War." *The Humanist* 64(4): 7–11.

Bunch, Joey. 2010. "Twins in Suicide Pact Had Contact with Columbine Survivor in 1999." *The Denver Post*, November 21.

Burns, Gary. 2009. "Here It Comes Again, That Feeling." *Popular Music & Society* 32(1): 111–12.

"Bush Calls Virginia Tech Shooting 'Terrible Tragedy.'" FoxNews.com, April 16, 2007.

Bush, George W. 2005. Office of the Presidency. Weekly radio speech. March 26.

Byrd, Jodi A. 2007. "'Living My Native Life Deadly': Red Lake, Ward Churchill, and the Discourses of Competing Genocides." *American Indian Quarterly* 31(2): 310–32.

Cabral, Paulo. 2011. "Twelve Die in Rio School Shooting." *BBC News*, April 7.

Campbell, Tara C. 2011. "Did Video Games Train the School Shooters To Kill? Determining Whether Wisconsin Courts Should Impose Negligence or Strict Liability in a Lawsuit Against the Video Game Manufacturers." *Marquette Law Review* 84(4): 811–44.

Carter, Bill. 2007. "Package Forced NBC to Make Tough Decisions." *The New York Times*, April 19, 18.

Cartwright, Zack. 2016. "The Most Powerful Explanation for the Orlando Killings" U.S. Uncut. Accessed June 15, 2016. Retrieved from: http://usuncut.com/politics/powerful-explanation-orlando-shooting/

Carvalho, Edward J. 2010. "The Poetics of a School Shooter: Decoding Political Signification in Cho Seung-Hui's Multimedia Manifesto." *Review of Education, Pedagogy & Cultural Studies* 32(4–5): 403–30.

Cassata, Donna. 2006. "Clark: U.S. Needs New Plan on Terror War." 2 pp. April 1, *Associated Press*.

Caze, Marguerite La. 2004. "Not Just Visitors: Cosmopolitanism, Hospitality, and Refugees." *Philosophy Today* 48(3): 313–24.

Clabaugh, Gary K., and Alison A. Clabaugh. 2005. "Bad Apples or Sour Pickles? Fundamental Attribution Error and the Columbine Massacre. The Cutting Edge." *Educational Horizons* 83(2): 81–86.

Clark, Wesley K. 2002. *Waging Modern War: Bosnia, Kosovo, and the Future of Combat*. New York, NY: Public Affairs.

Cmiel, Kenneth. 1999. "The Emergence of Human Rights Politics in the United States." *The Journal of American History* 86(3): 1231–50.

Cohen, Jodi S., and Stacy St. Clair. 2010. "He Went from Scholar to Gunman: A Report Says the Shooter in a 2008 Rampage Wanted to Punish His Old College. *Los Angeles Times*, March 22, Main News Home edition, 3.

"Columbine Jocks Safely Resume Bullying." 1999. *The Onion*, September 8.

Connell, R. W. 2002. "Studying Men and Masculinity." *Resources for Feminist Research* 29(1): 43–55.

Connell, R. W. 2001. *The Men and the Boys*. Berkeley and Los Angeles, CA: University of California Press.

Connolly, Ceci. 2005. "Native Americans Criticize Bush's Silence." *The Washington Post*, March 25.

Connolly, Ceci, and John F. Harris. 2005. "Rampage in Minnesota Mirrors Other Cases: Motive Unclear, but Student Was Considered Troubled." *The Washington Post*, March 25.

Connolly, William E. 2002. *Neuropolitics: Thinking, Culture, Speed*. Minneapolis, MN: University of Minnesota Press.

——. 2004. "The Complexity of Sovereignty." In *Sovereign Lives: Power in Global Politics*, edited by Jenny Edkins, Veronique Pin-Fat, and Michael J. Shapiro. New York: Routledge.

Cornell, Dewey G. 2011. "A Developmental Perspective on the Virginia Student Threat Assessment Guidelines." *New Directions for Youth Development* 129: 43–59.

Coston, Bethany M., and Michael Kimmel. 2012. "Seeing Privilege Where It Isn't: Marginalized Masculinities and the Intersectionality of Privilege." *Journal of Social Issues* 68(1): 97–111.

Coupland, Douglas. 2003. *Hey Nostradamus!* New York: Bloomsbury Publishing.

———. 2011. *JPod*. New York: Random House.

Cox, Lauren. 2009. "Fort Hood Motive: Terrorism or Mental Illness?" *ABC News*, November 9.

Cullen, Dave. 1999. "Inside the Columbine High Investigation." *Salon*, September 23.

———. 2004. "The Depressive and the Psychopath," *Slate*, April 20.

———. 2009. "The Reluctant Killer." *The Guardian*, April 24.

———. 2009. *Columbine*. New York: Twelve.

———. 2012. "Mean Kids: *The Bully Society*, by Jessie Klein." *The New York Times*, April 27.

———. 2013. "Is Boston Like Columbine?" *Slate*, April 19.

D'Addario, Daniel. 2013. "'Place Beyond the Pines' Director on Movie Violence: 'I Don't Think It's Beautiful. I Don't Think It's Art. I Don't Think It's Cool.'" *Salon*, March 26. http://www.salon.com/2013/03/26/place_beyond_the_pines_director_on_movie_violence_i_don%E2%80%99t_think_it%E2%80%99s_beautiful_i_don%E2%80%99t_think_it%E2%80%99s_art_i_don%E2%80%99t_think_it%E2%80%99s_cool/

Daly, Michael. 2013. "The Boston Marathon Suspects Are Killers, Not Combatants." *The Daily Beast*, April 21.

Davey, Monica. 2005. "Behind the Why of a Rampage, Loner with a Taste for Nazism." *The New York Times*, March 23.

Debarbieux, Éric, and Catherine Blaya. 2002. *Violence in Schools and Public Policies*. Paris: Elsevier.

DeFoster, Ruth. 2002. "American Gun Culture, School Shootings, and a 'Frontier Mentality': An Ideological Analysis of British Editorial Pages in the Decade After Columbine." *Communication, Culture & Critique* 3: 466–84.

Delamont, Sara. 2008. "Review of *Comprehending Columbine*." *Sociological Review* 56(1): 166–167.

Deleuze, Gilles. 1992. "Postscript on the Societies of Control." *October* 59: 3–7.

Deleuze, Gilles, and Felix Guattari. 1994. *Anti-Oedipus: Capitalism and Schizophrenia*. Seventh printing. Minneapolis, MN: University of Minnesota Press.

Der Derian, James. 2001. *Virtuous War: Mapping the Military-Industrial-Media-Entertainment Network*. Boulder, CO: Westview Press.

———. "War as Game." 2003. *Brown Journal of World Affairs* X(1): 37–48.

Derrida, Jacques. 2001. *On Cosmopolitanism and Forgiveness*. Translated by Mark Dooley and Michael Hughes. New York: Routledge.

——. 2004. "The Last of the Rogue States: The 'Democracy to Come,' Opening in Two Turns." *South Atlantic Quarterly* 103(2/3): 323–41.

——. 2005. *Rogues: Two Essays on Reason.* Translated by Pascale-Anne Brault and Michael Naas. Stanford, CA: Stanford University Press.

Deutsch, Kenneth L., and John Albert Murley, eds. 1999. *Leo Strauss, the Straussians, and the American Regime.* Lanham, MD: Rowman & Littlefield Publishers.

Dewan, Shaila, and Marc Santora. 2007. "Officials Knew Troubled State of Killer in '05" *The New York Times*, April 19, A1.

DiBlasio, Natalie. 2013. "7-Eleven Robbery Not Related to Boston Bombing Suspects." *USA Today*, April 22. Accessed April 30, 2013. http://www.usatoday.com/story/news/nation/2013/04/19/7-eleven-robbery-boston/2097915/

Donnelly, Lizzy. 2012. "Pirates!... Floating Nightmares or Loveable Rogues?" The Cambridge Student, Dec. 3. http://www.tcs.cam.ac.uk/?p=0015521.

Doren, James. 2005. "Filing Cabinet Saves Girl From Red Lake Gunman." *London Times Online*, March 23.

Dority, Barbara, and Fred Edwords. 2004. "Humanism versus the Militarization of America." *The Humanist* 64(6), 12–17.

Dwyer, Jim. 2003. "A Nation at War: In the Field—V Corps Commander; A Gulf Commander Sees a Longer Road." *The New York Times*, March 28. Accessed March 30, 2003. http://www.nytimes.com/2003/03/28/world/nation-war-field-v-corps-commander-gulf-commander-sees-longer-road.html

Edelman, Murray Jacob. 1988. *Constructing the Political Spectacle.* Chicago, IL: University of Chicago Press.

Eide, Elisabeth. 2011. *Down There and Up Here: Orientalism and Othering in Feature Stories.* New York: Hampton Press.

——. 2012. "The Terror in Norway and the Multiculturalist Scapegoat." *Journal of Contemporary European Studies* 20(3): 273–84.

Elazar, Daniel J. 1970. *The Metropolitan Frontier and American Politics: Cities of the Prairie.* New York, NY: Basic Books.

——. 1972. *American Federalism: A View from the States.* Second Edition. New York, NY: Crowell.

Ellul, Jacques. 1967. *The Technological Society.* Translated by John Wilkinson. New York: Vintage Books.

Enns, Diane. 2012. *The Violence of Victimhood.* University Park, PA: The Pennsylvania State University Press.

Esposti, Emanuelle Degli. 2011. "Gunman Kills up to 20 Children in Brazilian School Shooting." *The Telegraph*, April 7. Accessed April 5, 2013. http://www.telegraph.co.uk/news/worldnews/southamerica/brazil/8435279/Gunman-kills-up-to-20-children-in-Brazilian-school-shooting.html

"European Press Reactions: Blaming Charlton Heston." *Spiegel Online*, April 17, 2007.

Ezekiel, Raphael S. 2002. "An Ethnographer Looks at Neo-Nazi and Klan Groups: The Racist Mind Revisited." *American Behavioral Scientist* 46(1): 51–71.

Farrell, Laura C., and Robert S. Littlefield. 2012. "Identifying Communication Strategies in Cases of Domestic Terrorism: Applying Cultural Context to the Fort Hood Shooting." *Journal of Homeland Security & Emergency Management* 9(1): 1–18.

"Fast Facts: Major School Shootings of Past 10 Years." FoxNews.com, April 16, 2007.

Feldman, Matthew. 2012. "Bloodlands: Critical Geographical Responses to the 22 July 2011 Events in Norway." *Environment and Planning D-Society and Space* 30: 191–206.

Ferguson, Christopher J. 2008. "The School Shooting/Violent Video Game link: Causal Relationship or Moral Panic?" *Journal of Investigative Psychology & Offender Profiling*. Jan–Jun, Vol. 5 Issue 1/2, pp. 25–37.

Flynn, Christopher, and Dennis Heitzmann. 2008. "Tragedy at Virginia Tech: Trauma and Its Aftermath." *The Counseling Psychologist* 36(3): 479–89.

Forliti, Amy. 2005. "Family of Red Lake Victim Upset over Media Limits." *Associated Press*, March 23.

Forman, Murray. 2004. "Freaks, Aliens, and the Social Other: Representations of Student Stratification in U.S. Television's First Post-Columbine Season." *The Velvet Light Trap* 53: 66–82.

Foucault, Michel. 1978. *The History of Sexuality, Vol. 1: An Introduction*. Translated by Robert Hurley. New York: Pantheon Books.

———. 2003. *"Society Must Be Defended": Lectures at the Collège de France, 1975–1976*. Translated by David Macey. New York: Picador.

———. 2005. *The Hermeneutics of the Subject: Lectures at the Collège de France 1981–1982*. Translated by Graham Burchell. New York: Palgrave Macmillan, 2005.

Fountain, Henry. 2006. "The Camera Never Blinks, but It Multiplies." *The New York Times*, April 23. Accessed April 23, 2006. http://www.nytimes.com/2006/04/23/weekinreview/the-camera-never-blinks-but-it-multiplies.html

Fountain, Jane E. 2001. *Building the Virtual State: Information Technology and Institutional Change*. Washington, D.C.: Brookings Institution Press.

Fox, James Alan, and Jenna Savage. 2009. "Mass Murder Goes to College An Examination of Changes on College Campuses Following Virginia Tech." *American Behavioral Scientist* 52(10): 1465–85.

Francione, Gary L. 2004. "Animals—Property or Persons?" In *Animal Rights: Current Debates and New Directions*, edited by Cass R. Sunstein and Martha C. Nussbaum, 108–20. New York; Oxford: Oxford University Press.

"Fruitless Lead Caused Fateful Delay." *CBS News*, February 11, 2009.

Frymer, Benjamin, Matt Carlin, and John M. Broughton, eds. 2011. *Cultural Studies, Education, and Youth: Beyond Schools*. Lanham, Maryland: Lexington Books.

Fukuyama, Francis. 2006. *The End of History and the Last Man*. New York: Free Press.

Gadamer, Hans-Georg. 2007. *The Gadamer Reader: A Bouquet of the Later Writings*. Edited by Richard E. Palmer. Evanston, IL: Northwestern University Press.

Galloway, Alexander. 2004. *Protocol: How Control Exists after Decentralization*. Cambridge, MA.: MIT Press.

——. 2006a. *Gaming: Essays on Algorithmic Culture*. Minneapolis, MN: University of Minnesota Press.

——. 2006b. "Warcraft and Utopia." Edited by Arthur Kroker and Marilouise Kroker. *CTheory*, February 16. http://www.ctheory.net/articles.aspx?id=507.

——. 2010. "The Anti-Language of New Media." *Discourse* 32(3): 276–84.

——. 2011a. "What Is New Media? Ten Years after the Language of New Media." *Criticism* 53(3): 377–84.

——. 2011b. "Are Some Things Unrepresentable?" *Theory, Culture & Society* 28(7–8): 85–102.

——. 2012a. "A Response to Graham Harman's 'Marginalia on Radical Thinking.'" *An Und Für Sich*, June 3. https://itself.wordpress.com/2012/06/page/6/

——. 2012b. *The Interface Effect*. Cambridge, UK; Malden, MA: Polity.

——. 2013. "The Poverty of Philosophy: Realism and Post-Fordism." *Critical Inquiry* 39: 347–66.

Galloway, Alexander R., Geert Lovink, and Eugene Thacker. 2008. "Dialogues Carried Out in Silence: An E-Mail Exchange." *Grey Room* 33 (November 10): 96–112.

Galtung, Johann. 1969. "Violence, Peace, and Peace Research." *Journal of Peace Research* 6(3): 167–91.

——. 1990. "Cultural Violence." *Journal of Peace Research* 27(3): 291–305.

——. 2012. "Breivik: Living in the Historical Present (Part II)." TRANSCEND Media Service, June 18.

Garcia, George I., and Carlos Gmo. Aguilar. 2008. "Psycho-analysis and Politics: The theory of ideology in slavoj zizek." *International Journal of Zizek Studies*, 2(3), no pages.

Gardell, Mattias. 2011. "Terror in the Norwegian Woods." *Overland*, 205: 4–11.

Gardner, Amy, and David Cho. 2007. "The Virginia Tech Shooter: Isolation Defined Cho's Senior Year." *The Washington Post*, May 6. Accessed May 6, 2007. http://www.washingtonpost.com/wp-dyn/content/article/2007/05/05/AR2007050501221.html

Gasset, José Ortega y. 1972. *Meditations on Hunting*. Translated by Howard B. Westcott. New York: Scribner.

Gell, Aaron. 2013. "How the Bad Guys Won." *Salon*, July 16. Accessed July 16, 2013. http://www.salon.com/2013/07/16/how_the_bad_guys_won/

"George W. Bush: The President's Radio Address." *The American Presidency Project*, March 26, 2005.

Gibbs, Nancy, and Timothy Roche. 1999. "The Columbine Tapes." *Time Magazine*, December 20.

Goffman, Erving. 1963. *Stigma: Notes on the Management of Spoiled Identity*. New York: Simon & Schuster.

——. 1986. *Frame Analysis: An Essay on the Organization of Experience*. Northeastern University Press.

Goldstone, Richard J. 2002. "Whither Kosovo? Whither Democracy?" *Global Governance* 8(2): 143–47.

Goodman, Amy. 2016. "When It Comes to Orlando Massacre, Domestic Violence is the Red Flag We Aren't Talking About," *Democracy Now*, last modified June 14, 2016, accessed June 15, 2016 http://www.democracynow.org/2016/6/14/when_it_comes_to_orlando_massacre

Goodman, David. 2002. "No Child Unrecruited." *Mother Jones*, December.

Gordon, Michael R., and Bernard E. Trainor. 2006a. *Cobra II: The Inside Story of the Invasion and Occupation of Iraq*. New York: Pantheon Books.

——. 2006b. "Dash to Baghdad Left Top U.S. Generals Divided." *The New York Times*, March 13.

Gottfried, Mara, and Shannon Prather. 2005a. "Classmates Recall Shooter's Violent Drawings, Frightening Behavior." *St. Paul Pioneer Press*, March 23.

——. 2005b. "Shooter Long Feared by Others: 'He Wore Black a Lot and Painted His Face.'" *Pittsburgh Post-Gazette*, March 23.

Graham, Caroline, and Ian Gallagher. 2012. "Gunman Who Massacred 12 at Movie Premiere Used Same Drugs That Killed Batman Star Heath Ledger and Messaged Web Lovers to Ask … Will You Visit Me in Prison?" *Mail Online*, July 23.

Greenfield, Beth. 2013. "Boston Bombing Suspect Dzhokhar Tsarnaev's Disturbing Female Fan Club." *Yahoo! Shine*, May 13.

Greil, Marcus. 2002. "The Believer." *Film Comment*.

Griffith, David. 2006. *A Good War Is Hard to Find: The Art of Violence in America*. Brooklyn, NY: Soft Skull Press.

Griggers, Camilla Benolirao. 2009. "The Writing on the Screen: A Meditation on the Virginia Tech Shooting Spree: Age-Appropriate Use of Violent First-Person Computer Games." *Semiotica* 177(1–4): 189–96.

Grossman, Dave. 1996. *On Killing: The Psychological Cost of Learning to Kill in War and Society*. Boston, MA: Back Bay Books.

Grossman, Dave, and Loren W. Christensen. 2004. *On Combat: The Psychology and Physiology of Deadly Conflict in War and in Peace*. Illinois: PPCT Research Publications.

Haddad, Samir. 2004. "Derrida and Democracy at Risk." *Contretemps* 4: 29–44.

Haq, Husna. 2013. "Was Adam Lanza an Anders Breivik Copycat? Why Experts Are Skeptical (+video)." *The Christian Science Monitor*. http://libproxy.lib.ilstu.edu/login?url=http://search.ebscohost.com/login.aspx?direct=true&db=pwh&AN=85694382&site=eds-live&scope=site2/19/2013.

Hardt, Michael, and Antonio Negri. 2001. *Empire*. Cambridge, MA: Harvard University Press.

Harknett, Richard J., and JCISS Study Group. 2000. "The Risks of a Networked Military." *Orbis* 43(4): 127–43.

Hayles, N. Katherine. 1999. *How We Became Posthuman: Virtual Bodies in Cybernetics, Literature, and Informatics*. Chicago: IL: University of Chicago Press.

———. 2002. "Flesh and Metal: Reconfiguring the Mindbody in Virtual Environments." *Configurations* 10(2): 297–320.

Healy, Jack, and Serge F. Kovaleski. 2012. "Before and After Massacre, Puzzles Line Suspect's Path." *The New York Times*, July 21.

Heim, Michael. 1998. *Virtual Realism*. New York: Oxford University Press.

Hendrix, Grady. 2007. "Violent Disagreement." *Slate*, April 20.

Hewitt, Giles. 2005a. "Devastated Tribal Community Has Troubled History." *AFP*, March 23.

———. 2005b. "Motive the Big Question in U.S. High School Shooting." *AFP*, March 23.

Hoffmann, Jens, Karoline Roshdi and Frank Robertz. 2009 "Amok und zielgerichtete Gewalttaten in Deutschland" ("Amok and goal-oriented acts of violence in Germany"). *Kriminalistik* 63(4): 196–204.

Hofstadter, Richard. 2008. *The Paranoid Style in American Politics*. New York: Vintage.

Honneth, Axel. 2010. "Dissolutions of the Social: On the Social Theory of Luc Boltanski and Laurent Thévenot." *Constellations: An International Journal of Critical & Democratic Theory* 17(3): 376–89.

Huerter, Regina. 2000. The Culture of Columbine. Colorado Commission Interview, December 1.

Huffstrutter, P. J., and Elizabeth Mehren. 2005. "Nazi Site Intrigued Shooter; Minnesota Community Struggles to Understand What Dark Forces the 16-Year-Old to Kill." *Los Angeles Times*, March 23.

Huizinga, Johan. 1971. *Homo Ludens: A Study of the Play-Element in Culture*. Boston, MA: Beacon Press.

Hutchinson, Bill. 2013. "Newtown Killer Adam Lanza's Suspected Online Posts Show Fascination with Mass Murder, Weapons: Report." *NY Daily News*, July 1.

Ignatieff, Michael. 2000. *Virtual War: Kosovo and Beyond*. New York: Chatto & Windus.

"In Pictures: Virginia Shootings." *BBC News*, April 17, 2007.

Ingold, John, and Sadie Gurman. 2013. "James Holmes Refuses to Enter a Plea at Aurora Theater Shooting Arraignment." *The Denver Post*, March 13.

Jagoda, Patrick. 2013. "The Next Level: Alexander R. Galloway's 'The Interface Effect.'" *Los Angeles Review of Books*, January 25.

James, Aaron. 2012. *Assholes: A Theory*. New York, NY: Random House LLC.

"James Holmes' Neighbor: Loud Music Played at House of Aurora 'Dark Knight Rises' Shooting Suspect." *ABCactionnews.com*, July 20, 2012.

Jameson, Fredric. 1976. "On Goffman's Frame Analysis." *Theory and Society* 3(1): 119–33.

———. 1977. "Class and Allegory in Contemporary Mass Culture: *Dog Day Afternoon* as a Political Film." *College English* 38(8): 843–59.

Jameson, Frederic. 1991. *Postmodernism, or, the Cultural Logic of Late Capitalism*. Duke University Press.

Jay, Mike. 2003. "Tim Robbins." *The Charlie Rose Show*, October 13.

Johnson, Annie, and Nathan Thornburgh. 2007. "Witness: The Dormitory Murders." *Time*, April 20.

Johnson, M. Alex. 2013. "Fort Hood Gunman Nidal Hasan Banned from Arguing He Was Defending the Taliban." *US News on NBC News*, June 14.

Johnson, Peter. 2007. "Oakeshott's Porcupines: Oakeshott on Civility." *Contemporary Political Theory* 6(3): 312–29.

Johnston, David, and Scott Shane. 2009. "U.S. Knew of Suspect's Tie to Radical Cleric." *The New York Times*, November 10.

Jones, Kathleen W. 2009. "The Thirty-Third Victim: Representations of Seung Hui Cho in the Aftermath of the 'Virginia Tech Massacre.'" *The Journal of the History of Childhood and Youth* 2(1): 64–82.

Jüttner, Julia. 2006. "German School Shooting: Armed to the Teeth and Crying for Help." *Spiegel Online*, November 21.

Jüttner, Julia, and Anne Seith in Winnenden. 2009. "School Massacre in Germany: 'A Totally Normal Teenager.'" *Spiegel Online*, December 3.

Juul, Jesper. 2005. *Half-Real: Video Games between Real Rules and Fictional Worlds.* Cambridge, MA: MIT Press.

———. 2013. "Video Games Make Us All Losers!" *Salon*, July 13.

Kac, Eduardo. 1998. "Teleporting: An Unknown State." Accessed April 9, 2003. http://www.ekac.org/teleporting.html.

———. 2005. *Telepresence & Bio Art: Networking Humans, Rabbits, & Robots.* Ann Arbor: University of Michigan Press.

Kagan, Robert. 2002. "Power and Weakness" *Policy Review*, June/July, Issue 113, pp. 3–28.

Kaldor, Mary. 1999. *New and Old Wars: Organised Violence in a Global Era.* First Edition. Stanford, CA: Stanford University Press.

Kalish, Rachel, and Michael Kimmel. 2010. "Suicide by Mass Murder: Masculinity, Aggrieved Entitlement, and Rampage School Shootings." *Health Sociology Review* 19(4): 451–64.

Kass, Jeff. 2009. Columbine: A True Crime Story : A Victim, the Killers, and the Nation's Search for Answers. Denver, CO: Ghost Road Press.

———. 2010a. "Columbine and Australia." *The Huffington Post*, November 22.

———. 2010b. "Columbine and the End of Journalism: A Daily Blog Series, Part II." *The Huffington Post*, April 16.

———. 2011. "Columbine and Brazil School Shooting." *Huffington Post*, April 8.

———. 2012. "Connecticut and Columbine Shootings." *Examiner.com*, December 15.

———. 2012. "Five Myths about Mass Shootings." *The Washington Post*, July 30.

Kass, Jeff, and Angie C. Marek. 2005. "What Happened After Columbine." *U.S. News & World Report*, April 4.

Keenan, Thomas. 2004. "Mobilizing Shame." *The South Atlantic Quarterly* 103(2–3): 435–49.

Kellner, Douglas. 2007. "Media Spectacle and the 'Massacre at Virginia Tech.'" *Fast Capitalism* 3(1). https://www.uta.edu/huma/agger/fastcapitalism/3_1/kellner.html

——. 2012. "The Dark Side of the Spectacle: Terror in Norway and the UK Riots." *Cultural Politics* 8(1): 1–43.

Khader, Jamil. 2012. "Rampage School Shootings: Reframing the Discourse." *Jadaliyya*, December 24.

Kiilakoski, T., and A. Oksanen. 2011. "Soundtrack of the School Shootings: Cultural Script, Music and Male Rage." *Young* 19(3): 247–69.

"Killer Was 'Lost in Life,' Pitiless in Death." *National Post (Canada)*, March 23, 2005.

Kimmel, Michael. 2002. "Gender, Class and Terrorism." *The Chronicle of Higher Education*, February 8. Accessed March 3, 2004. Found at: http://chronicle.com/article/Gender-ClassTerrorism/6096

Kissane, Karen. 2012. "Breivik Considered Suicide before Arrest." *The Sydney Morning Herald*, April 21.

Klein, Jessie. 2012. *The Bully Society: School Shootings and the Crisis of Bullying in America's Schools*. New York, NY: NYU Press.

Kojève, Alexandre. 1980. *Introduction to the Reading of Hegel: Lectures on the Phenomenology of Spirit*. Edited by Allan Bloom. Translated by James H. Nichols. First Edition. Ithaca, NY: Cornell University Press.

Kolenic, Anthony J. 2009. "Madness in the Making: Creating and Denying Narratives from Virginia Tech to Gotham City." *Journal of Popular Culture* 42(6): 1023–39.

Kroker, Arthur, Marilouise Kroker, and David Cook. 1989. *Panic Encyclopedia: The Definitive Guide to the Postmodern Scene*. Montréal: New World Perspectives.

Labi, Nadya. 1998. "The Hunter and the Choir Boy," Time, 6 April, 2–3.

Lacan, Jacques. 1977. "The Mirror Stage as Formative of the Function of the I as Revealed in Psychoanalytic Experience." In *Écrits: A Selection*, translated by Alan Sheridan, 1–7. New York, NY: W. W. Norton & Co.

Larkin, Ralph W. 2007. *Comprehending Columbine*. Philadelphia, PA: Temple University Press.

——. 2009. "The Columbine Legacy Rampage Shootings as Political Acts." *American Behavioral Scientist* 52(9): 1309–26.

LaVaque-Manty, Mika. 2006. "Dueling for Equality Masculine Honor and the Modern Politics of Dignity." *Political Theory* 34(6): 715–40.

Leavy, Patricia, and Kathryn Maloney. 2009. "American Reporting of School Violence and 'People Like Us': A Comparison of Newspaper Coverage of the Columbine and Red Lake School Shootings." *Critical Sociology* 35(2): 273–92.

Lee, Christopher, and Shankar Vedantam. 2005. "Minnesota Rampage Leaves 10 Dead." *The Washington Post*, March 22.

Lee, Terry. 2002. "Virtual Violence in *Fight Club*: This Is What Transformation of Masculine Ego Feels Like." *Journal of American & Comparative Cultures* 25(3–4): 418–23.

Lennard, Jeremy. 2005. "Ten Dead in US School Shooting." *The Guardian*, March 22.

Lennard, Natasha. 2013. "Making Sense of Adam Lanza." *Salon*, February 19. Accessed February 24, 2013. http://www.salon.com/2013/02/19/making_sense_of_adam_lanza/.

——. 2013. "The Hedge Fund Managers Profiting off Sandy Hook." *Salon*, March 18. Accessed 3-20-2013. http://www.salon.com/2013/03/18/the_hedge_fund_managers_profiting_off_sandy_hook/.

Leonard, Andrew. 2013. "'Gamers' Are Not the Enemy." *Salon*, March 18. Accessed March 20, 2013. http://www.salon.com/2013/03/18/gamers_are_not_the_enemy/.

Lester, Cheryl. 2006. "From Columbine to Red Lake: Tragic Provocations for Advocacy." *American Studies* 47(1): 133–53.

Lewin, Tamar. 2007. "Laws Limit Colleges' Options When a Student Is Mentally Ill." *The New York Times*, April 19.

Lind, Michael. 2013. "How Conservatives See Liberals." *Salon*, March 4. Accessed March 5, 2013. http://www.salon.com/2013/03/04/how_conservatives_see_liberals/.

Lipka, Sara. 2012. "In Reversal of Penalty for 2007 Shootings, a Somber Vindication for Virginia Tech." *Chronicle of Higher Education* 58(32): A-24.

"List of Deadliest Campus Shootings in United States." FoxNews.com, April 16, 2007.

Littlefield, Robert S., Jennifer Reierson, Kimberly Cowden, Shelly Stowman, and Cheryl Long Feather. 2009. "A Case Study of the Red Lake, Minnesota, School Shooting: Intercultural Learning in the Renewal Process." *Communication, Culture & Critique* 2(3): 361–83.

Lukács, Georg. 1971. *History and Class Consciousness: Studies in Marxist Dialectics*. Translated by Rodney Livingston. Cambridge, MA: MIT Press.

Lupica, Mike. 2013. "Lupica: Morbid Find Suggests Murder-Obsessed Gunman Adam Lanza Plotted Newtown, Conn.'s Sandy Hook Massacre for Years." *NY Daily News*, March 25. Accessed March 30, 2013. Found at: http://www.nydailynews.com/news/national/lupica-lanza-plotted-massacre-years-article-1.1291408

Luttwak, Edward. 2006. "American Coup D'etat," *Harper's*. https://harpers.org/archive/2006/04/american-coup-detat/

Lysiak, Matthew, and Bill Hutchinson. 2013. "Emails Show History of Illness in Adam Lanza's Family, Mother Had Worries about Gruesome Images." *NY Daily News*, April 8. Accessed April 15, 2013. Found at: http://www.nydailynews.com/news/national/emails-reveal-adam-lanza-family-illness-gruesome-images-article-1.1310276

Macdonald, Andrew. 1996. *The Turner Diaries: A Novel*. Second Edition. New York: Barricade Books.

Mack, Andrew. 1975. "Why Big Nations Lose Small Wars: The Politics of Asymmetric Conflict." *World Politics* 27(2): 175–200.

Malm, Andreas. 2012. "Bloodlands: Critical Geographical Responses to the 22 July 2011 Events in Norway," *Environment and Planning D-Society and Space* 30: 191–206.

Martin, Brett. 2013. *Difficult Men: Behind the Scenes of a Creative Revolution: From* The Sopranos *and* The Wire *to* Mad Men *and* Breaking Bad. New York: Penguin Books.

Martina, Michael. 2013. "World's Top 5 Arms Exporters: China Replaces UK in Weapons Trade." *Huffington Post*, March 18.

Martinez, Steve. 2005. "LNSG Condemns Modern Society in School Shooting." *Nationalist News Network*, March 22. Accessed March 22, 2013. http://www.huffingtonpost.com/2013/03/18/worlds-top-5-arms-exporters_n_2899052.html

Marx, Karl. 1999. *Marx on Suicide*. Translated by Eric A. Plaut, Gabrielle Edgcomb, and Kevin Anderson. Evanston, IL: Northwestern University Press.

Måseide, Per Helge. 2012. "The Battle about Breivik's Mind." *The Lancet* 379, no. 9835 (June): 2413. doi: 10.1016/S0140-6736(12)61048-4.

Mass Shootings at Virginia Tech: Report of the Virginia Tech Review Panel, August 2007. https://governor.virginia.gov/media/3772/fullreport.pdf.

"Massacre Gunman's Deadly Infatuation with Emily." *The Evening Standard*, April 17, 2007.

Massumi, Brian. 2002. *Parables for the Virtual: Movement, Affect, Sensation*. Durham, NC: Duke University Press.

Matarese, Susan M. 2001. *American Foreign Policy and the Utopian Imagination*. Amherst, MA: University of Massachusetts Press.

McDonough, Katie. 2013. "Adam Lanza's Morbid Spreadsheet and 'Gamer Code.'" *Salon*, March 18.

McIntyre, Mike. 2005. "Death Toll in Killer's School Rampage Lessened by Heroic Teen's Sacrifice: 'Brave Warrior' Died After Taking Bullets for Two Classmates." *Ottawa Citizen*.

———. 2005. "Tragic Home Life May Have Fuelled Rampage: Tales of Courage Surface as Reserve Mourns Dead." *Windsor Star (Ontario)*.

McKinley Jr., James C., and James Dao. 2009. "Fort Hood Gunman Gave Signals Before His Rampage." *The New York Times*, November 9. Accessed March 3, 2012. Found at: http://www.nytimes.com/2009/11/09/us/09reconstruct.html?_r=0

Merrow, John. 2005. "Army Recruiters: 'Counseling' High-Schoolers to Death." *Education Digest* 70(6): 4–7.

Meyer, Jeremy P., and Allison Sherry. 2012. "James Holmes Referred to University of Colorado Threat-Assessment Team, Sources Say." *The Denver Post*, August 2.

Mingus, William, and Bradley Zopf. 2010. "White Means Never Having to Say You're Sorry: The Racial Project in Explaining Mass Shootings." *Social Thought and Research* 31: 57–78.

Moore, Mark H., Carol V. Petrie, Anthony A. Braga, and Brenda L. McLaughlin. 2003. *Deadly Lessons: Understanding Lethal School Violence*. Case Studies of School Violence Committee. Washington, D.C.: National Research Council and Institute of Medicine, Division of Behavioral and Social Sciences and Education, The National Academic Press.

Moore, Michael. *Bowling for Columbine*. United Artists, 2002.

Moreno, Sylvia. 2005. "A Very Quiet Sense of Shock: Small Community Struggle to Cope." *The Washington Post*, March 22.

Mueller, John, and Mark G. Stewart. 2013. "Hapless, Disorganized, and Irrational." *Slate*, April 22.

Muschert, Glenn W. 2007. "Research in School Shootings." *Sociology Compass* 1(1): 60–80.

Muskal, Michael. 2013. "Newtown Massacre: Warrants Detail Adam Lanza's World of Weapons." *Los Angeles Times*, March 28.

Neveu, Brett. 2007. *Eric LaRue*.

Neveu, Brett. 2007. *Harmless*.

Newman, Katherine S. 2012. "School Shootings: Why They Do It." *The Baltimore Sun*, August 28.

Newman, Katherine S., Cybelle Fox, David J. Harding, Jal Mehta, and Wendy Roth. 2004. *Rampage: The Social Roots of School Shootings*. New York: Basic Books.

Ng, Christina. 2013. "Experts Doubt 'Truth Serum' for Accused Aurora Shooter." *ABC News*, March 13.

Nguyen, Tommy. 2003. "School Recruiters Meet Resistance." *The Christian Science Monitor*, December 19.

NIU Report of the February 14, 2008 Shootings at Northern Illinois University. http://www.niu.edu/feb14report/Feb14report.pdf

Nolan, Christopher. *Batman Begins*. Warner Bros. Pictures, 2005.

———. *The Dark Knight Rises*. Warner Bros. Pictures, 2012.

Northern Illinois University Board of Trustees. *Report of the February 14, 2008 Shootings at Northern Illinois University*. Northern Illinois University, March 18, 2010.

"Norway's Johan Galtung, Peace & Conflict Pioneer, on How to Stop Extremism That Fueled Shooting." *SHOAH*, July 29, 2011.

O'Hanlon, Michael. 2000. *Technological Change and the Future of Warfare*. New York: Brookings Institute.

O'Leary, Mary E. 2013. "Newtown Search Warrants: Sandy Hook School Was Lanza's 'Life,' Witness Says." *New Haven Register*, March 28.

O'Toole, Mary Ellen. 2012. "Jeffrey Weise and the Shooting at Red Lake Minnesota High School: A Behavioral Perspective." In *School Shootings: International Research, Case Studies, and Concepts for Prevention*, edited by Nils Böckler, Thorsten Seeger, Peter Sitzer, and Wilhelm Heitmeyer, 177–88. New York, NY: Springer.

Orange, Richard. 2012. "Anders Behring Breivik Spent a Year Playing *World of Warcraft* Role-Playing Game Online." *Telegraph.co.uk*, April 16.

Parachini, John. 2003. "Putting WMD Terrorism into Perspective." *The Washington Quarterly* 26(4): 37–50.

Parenti, Christian. 2003. "Stretched Thin, Lied to & Mistreated: On the Ground with US Troops in Iraq." *The Nation*, October 6.

"Parents Meet Father of Gunman in Sandy Hook Massacre." *New York Times*. March 22, 2013, AP, no author, http://www.nytimes.com/2013/03/23/nyregion/parents-of-newtown-shooting-victim-meet-with-adam-lanzas-father.html

Park, Chan-wook. *Oldboy*. Show East, 2003.

Paton, Nathalie E. 2012. "Media Participation of School Shooters and Their Fans: Navigating between Self-Distinction and Imitation to Achieve Individuation." In *School Shootings: Mediatized Violence in a Global Age*, edited by Glenn W. Muschert and Johanna Sumiala, 203–30. Studies in Media and Communications 7. Bingley, UK: Emerald Group Publishing Limited.

Patton, Jason W. 2000. "Protecting Privacy in Public? Surveillance Technologies and the Value of Public Places." *Ethics and Information Technology* 2(3): 181–87.

Pearson, Michael. 2013. "Obama: No One's Listening to Your Calls." *CNN*, June 9.

Pease, Donald E. 2002. "The Patriot Acts." *Boundary 2* 29(2): 29–43.

———. 2003. "The Global Homeland State: Bush's Biopolitical Settlement." *Boundary 2* 30(3): 1–18.

Pilkington, Ed. 2013. "US Military Struggling to Stop Suicide Epidemic among War Veterans." *The Guardian*, February 1.

Pitt, William Rivers. 2007. "The 21st Century Sucks." *Truth-Out.org*, February 8.

Porteus, Liza. 2007a. "Federal Officials: At Least 32 Dead After Virginia Tech University Shooting." FoxNews.com. April 16. Accessed 4-18-2007. http://www.foxnews.com/story/2007/04/16/federal-officials-at-least-32-dead-after-virginia-tech-university-shooting.html

———. 2007b. "Virginia Tech Campus Reels From Shooting That Leaves 33 Dead." FoxNews.com. April 17.

"Portraits of Suspect, Victim in Minnesota Shootings." *Associated Press*, March 23, 2005.

Posin, Arie. *The Chumscrubber*. Dreamworks, 2005.

"Post from the US: Europe, Please Stop Moralizing." *Spiegel Online*, April 18, 2007.

Post, Tim. 2004. "Tribe Offers to Talk About Sharing Casino Revenue." *Minnesota Public Radio*, August 26.

Poulsen, Kevin. 2007. "The Creative Writing Essay That Got Allen Lee Arrested." *Wired* April 30. Accessed May 1, 2007. https://www.wired.com/2007/04/allen_lees_essa/.

Poupart, Lisa M. 2003. "The Familiar Face of Genocide: Internalized Oppression among American Indians." *Hypatia* 18(2): 86–100.

Povinelli, Elizabeth. 2002. The Cunning of Recognition: Indigenous Alterities and the Making of Australian Multiculturalism. Durham, NC: Duke University Press.

———. 2005. "A Flight from Freedom." In *Postcolonial Studies and Beyond*, edited by Ania Loomba, Suvir Kaul, Matti Bunzl, Antoinette Burton, and Jed Esty, 145–65. Durham, NC: Duke University Press.

Povinelli, Elizabeth A. Powell, Larry, and William R. Self. 2011. "The Rhetoric of Sacrifice in the 'Rantings' of the Virginia Tech Killer." *Journal of Communication & Religion* 34(1): 24–36.

Prendergast, Alan. 2000. "The Missing Motive." *Westword*, July 13.

———. 2004. "Quagmire Without End, Amen." *Westword*, February 26.

———. 2006. "Hiding in Plain Sight." *Westword*, April 13.

———. 2012. "The Columbine Shootings Continue to 'Inspire' Hollywood." *Westword*, March 20.

Price, Margaret. 2011. *Mad at School: Rhetorics of Mental Disability and Academic Life*. Ann Arbor: University of Michigan Press.

Protevi, John. 2009. *Political Affect: Connecting the Social and the Somatic*. Minneapolis, MN: University of Minnesota Press.

Quadrennial Defense Review Report. Department of Defense, United States of America, February 6, 2006.

"Red Lake in Shock After Gun Rampage by 'Teenaged Angel of Death.'" *AFP*, March 22, 2005.

Reitman, Janet. 2013. "Jahar's World." *Rollingstone.com*, July 17.

Rettner, Rachael. 2013. "Kids with Autism Don't Copy 'Silly' Actions." *Yahoo! News*, April 8.

Rimer, Sara. 2004. "Unruly Students Facing Arrest, Not Detention." *The New York Times*, January 4.

Rivera, N. R. Kleinfield, Ray, and Serge F. Kovaleski. 2013. "Obsessions of Adam Lanza, Newtown Killer, in Detail." *The New York Times*, March 28.

Roach, Carol. 2010. "Psychological Profile of a School Shooter." *Yahoo! Voices*, July 19.

Robertz, Frank J. 2007. "Deadly Dreams." *Scientific American Mind*. August: 53–59.

———. 2012. "On the Relevance of Phantasy for the Genesis of School Shootings." In *School Shootings: International Research, Case Studies, and Concepts for Prevention*, edited by Nils Böckler, Thorsten Seeger, Peter Sitzer, and Wilhelm Heitmeyer, 105–30. New York, NY: Springer, 2012.

Rose, Nikolas. 2000. "Government and Control." *Br. J. Criminol.* 40(2): 321–39.

Ross, Winston. 2013. "The Dzhokhar Tsarnaev Admiration Society." *The Daily Beast*, April 22.

Rubenstein, Diane. 1989. "The Mirror of Reproduction: Baudrillard and Reagan's America." *Political Theory* 17(4): 582–606.

Rubenstein, Diane S. 1992. "The Anxiety of Affluence: Baudrillard and Science Fiction of the Reagan Era." In *Baudrillard in the Mountains: Modern Communications and the Disappearance of Art and Politics*, edited by William Stearns and William Chaloupka, 65–81. New York: St. Martin's Press.

———. 2010. "Transpolitics." Edited by Richard G. Smith. *The Baudrillard Dictionary*. Edinburgh: Edinburg University Press.

Rutten, Tim. 2011. "Rutten: The Maniac Challenge." *Los Angeles Times*, July 27.

Ryan, Marie-Laure. 2001. *Narrative as Virtual Reality: Immersion and Interactivity in Literature and Electronic Media*. Baltimore, MD: John Hopkins University Press.

Saletan, William. 2013. "Unfit to Bear Arms." *Slate*, April.

Sarche, Jon. 2005. "Generations of Broken Hearts: Minnesota Shootings Carry Echoes of Columbine." *Associated Press*, March 22.

Sarre, Rick. 1996. "The Public, the Police and Australian Gun Policy." In *Seminar 8, Centre for the Study of Violence and Reconciliation*.

Schulzke, Marcus. 2010. "Defending the Morality of Violent Video Games." *Ethics and Information Technology* 12(2): 127–38.

Seltzer, Mark. 2008. "Murder/Media/Modernity." *Canadian Review of American Studies* 38(1): 11–41.

Senior, Jennifer. 2009. "The End of the Trench Coat Mafia." *The New York Times*, April 19.

Sestir, Marc, and Melanie C. Green. 2010. Social Influence. October, Vol. 5 Issue 4, pp. 272–288. DOI: 10.1080/15534510.2010.490672.

Shafer, Jack. 2010. "Who Said It First?" *Slate*, August 30.

Shapiro, Michael J. 1989. "Representing World Politics: The Sport/War Intertext." In *International/Intertextual Relations: Postmodern Readings of World Politics*, edited by James Der Derian and Michael J. Shapiro, 69–96. Lexington, MA: Lexington Books.

Shon, Phillip. 2012. "'Asian Really Don't Do This': On-Scene Offense Characteristics of Asian American School Shooters, 91–07." *Asian Journal of Criminology* 7(3): 251.

Sibaja, Marco. 2011. "2 Arrested in Rio in Connection to School Shooting." *The Guardian*.

Siddique, Haroon, and Helen Pidd. 2013. "Anders Behring Breivik Trial, Day Four— Thursday 19 April." *The Guardian*, June 26.

Singer, Mark. 2011. "From Oklahoma City to Oslo." *The New Yorker Blogs*, July 26.

Slifkin, Anne R. 2002. "John Walker Lindh." *The South Atlantic Quarterly* 101(2): 417–24.

Solty, Ingar. (2012) "Dear Left: The NRA Is Right—The Mass Shooter as High-Achiever: Historical-Materialist Considerations on the Resistible Fall of James Holmes and the Pathologization and Culturalization of the Cinema Massacre in Aurora, Colorado." *Socialism and Democracy* 26(3): 1–13.

Staal, Jonas, and Vincent W. J. van Gerven Oei, eds. 2009. *Follow Us or Die*. New York, NY: Atropos Press.

Stanglin, Doug. 2013. "Adam Lanza's Mom Was Alarmed by His Gruesome Images." *USAToday.com*, April 8, 2013.

Steinberg, Stefan. 2006. "School Shooting and Suicide in Germany." World Socialist Web Site (22 November), http://www.wsws.org/en/articles/2006/11/germ-n22.html

Steinhauer, Jennifer. 2007. "Korean-Americans Brace for Problems in Wake of Killings." *The New York Times*, April 19.

"Student Describes Shooting Spree." *BBC News*, April 16, 2007.

Sumiala, Johanna, and Minttu Tikka. 2011. "Reality on Circulation—School Shootings, Ritualised Communication, and the Dark Side of the Sacred." *ESSACHESS—Journal for Communication Studies* 4(2): 145–59.

Swaine, Jon. 2012. "Connecticut School Shooting: Adam Lanza Was Assigned Psychologist." *Telegraph.co.uk*, December 17.

Syson, Neil. 2012. "I'd Do It Again … to Stop Towns like Luton." *The Sun*, April 18. Accessed April 24, 2012. Found at: https://www.thesun.co.uk/archives/news/538109/id-do-it-again-to-stop-towns-like-luton/

"Terrorism or Tragic Shooting? Analysts Divided on Fort Hood Massacre." FoxNews.com, November 7, 2009.

The Merchants of Cool. Frontline (PBS), 2001.

"The Pekka Eric Auvinen Manifesto." *Odd Culture*, March 26, 2013.

"The World From Berlin: School Shootings 'Can Happen Anywhere.'" *Spiegel Online*, December 3, 2009.

"They're Blaming Us Again." *Democratic Underground*, 2005.

Thomas, Jim. 2008. "Nietzsche at Northern: An Existential Narrative of Confronting the Abyss." *Social Psychology Quarterly* 71(2): 109–13.

Thorsborne, Margaret. 2000. "School Violence and Community Conferencing: The Benefits of Restorative Justice." APAPDC Online Conference. 15 May. http://www.justiciarestaurativa.org/www.restorativejustice.org/articlesdb/articles/483

Tonso, K. L. 2003. "Reflecting on Columbine High: Ideologies of Privilege in 'Standardized' Schools." *Educational Studies* 33(4): 389–403.

"Transcripts of *The Basement Tapes* of Eric Harris and Dylan Klebold." *Wikisource*, 1999.

Tronto, Joan C. 2011. "Affected Politics." *Political Theory* 39(6): 793–801.

UNESCO Survey Highlights Correlation Between Media Violence and Youth Perception of Reality. Paris, France: UNESCO Press Online, February 19, 1998. http://www.unesco.org/webworld/fed/temp/communication_democracy/un_release.htm#1998

"US University Shooting Kills 33." *BBC News*, April 17, 2007.

van Gerven Oei, Vincent W.J. 2011. "Anders Breivik: On Conjuring the Obscene," *Continent*, 1(3): 213–223.

Vann, David. 2008. "Portrait of the School Shooter as a Young Man." *Esquire*, August.

———. 2011. *Last Day on Earth: A Portrait of the NIU School Shooter.* Athens, GA: University of Georgia Press.

Vasini, Marco. 2009. "Cops Don't Know Va. Tech Gunman's Motives." *CBS News*, February 11.

Vidal, Gore. 2001. "The Meaning of Timothy McVeigh." *Vanity Fair*, September 1.

"Virginia Shootings: Eyewitness Accounts." *BBC News*, April 16, 2007.

Virilio, Paul. 1997. *Open Sky.* Translated by Julie Rose. London; New York: Verso.

———. 2000. *A Landscape of Events.* Translated by Julie Rose. Cambridge, MA: MIT Press.

———. 2000. Strategy of Deception. Translated by Chris Turner. London; New York: Verso.

———. 2002. *Ground Zero.* Translated by Chris Turner. London; New York: Verso.

———. 2005. *Negative Horizon: An Essay in Dromoscopy.* Translated by Michael Degener. New York: Continuum.

Virno, Paolo. 2004. *A Grammar of the Multitude: For an Analysis of Contemporary Forms of Life.* Translated by Isabella Bertoletti, James Cascaito, and Andrea Casson. Los Angeles: Semiotext(e).

Wacquant, Loïc. 2001. "The Advent of the Penal State Is Not a Destiny." *Social Justice* 28(3): 81–87.

Wallis, John W., and James Astor. 2012. "'I've never murdered anyone in my life. The decisions are up to them': Ethical Guidance and Cultural Pessimism in the *Saw* Series." *Journal of Religion and Popular Culture.* 24(3): 352–364.

Walker, Mike. 2013. "What the 'Russian Facebook' Tells Us About Dzhokhar Tsarnaev's Ties to Chechnya." *Slate*, April 22.

Walton, Stephen J. 2012. "Anti-Feminism and Misogyny in Breivik's 'Manifesto.'" *NORA: Nordic Journal of Women's Studies* 20(1): 4–11.

Waltz, Kenneth N. 1954. *Man, the State, and War: A Theoretical Analysis.* New York, NY: Columbia University Press.

——. 1979. *Theory of International Politics.* New York, NY: McGraw Hill.

Wasik, Bill, Jane Avrich, Raph Koster, and Thomas De Zengotita. 2006. "Grand Theft Education: Literacy in the Age of Video Games." *Harper's Magazine*, September.

Watson, Justin. 2002. *The Martyrs of Columbine: Faith and the Politics of Tragedy.* New York: Palgrave Macmillan.

Webber, Julie A. 2001. "Why Can't We Be Deweyan Citizens?" *Educational Theory* 51(2): 171–89.

——. 2003a. *Failure to Hold: The Politics of School Violence.* Lanham, MD: Rowman & Littlefield.

——. 2003b. "Post-Columbine: Youth Violence as a (Trans)national Movement." In *Education as Enforcement: The Militarization and Corporatization of Schools*, edited by Kenneth J. Saltman and David A. Gabbard, 184–201. New York, NY: Routledge, 2003.

——. 2004. "Schooling and the Security State." In *Defending Public Schools: Education under the Security State*, edited by David Gabbard and E. Wayne Ross. Westport, CT: Greenwood Publishing Group.

——. 2005. "Outline of a Generic Will: Global Arrogance, Social Movements, and the Net." In *Beyond Global Arrogance*, edited by Janie Leatherman and Julie Webber, 29–54. New York: Palgrave.

——. 2013. *The Cultural Set Up of Comedy.* Bristol, UK: Intellect.

Weiner, Tim. 2003. "Parents, Shopping for Discipline, Turn to Harsh Programs Abroad." *The New York Times*, May 9.

Weiss, Meredith L., and Michael J. Bosia. (2013). *Global Homophobia: States, Movements, and the Politics of Repression.* Urbana, IL: University of Illinois Press.

Wernick, Andrew. 1999. "Bataille's Columbine: The Sacred Space of Hate." *CTheory*, November 3. http://www.ctheory.net/articles.aspx?id=119

What James Holmes Was Wearing When Police Found Him in His Car. YouTube Video, from HistoricalRecordsVLT., September 30, 2012, https://www.youtube.com/redirect?q=http%3A%2F%2Fwww.youtube.com%2Fwatch%3Fv%3DE8Pz7x-nQf1k&redir_token=JdVpC0bc08kstpk9ixu2WNYbeP98MTQ1Mjk2OD-c2OUAxNDUyODgyMzY5, 2012.

Wilgoren, Jodi. 2005. "Eerie Parallels Are Seen to Shootings at Columbine." *The New York Times*, March 23.

——. 2005. "Shooting Rampage by Student Leaves 10 Dead on Reservation." *The New York Times*, March 21.

Williams, Dmitri. 2007. "Book Review: Alexander Galloway's *Gaming: Essays on Algorithmic Culture*." *International Journal of Communication* 1: 74–76.

Williams, Kayla, and Michael E. Staub. 2006. *Love My Rifle More than You: Young and Female in the U.S. Army*. New York, NY: W. W. Norton & Company.

Winokur, Mark. 2003. "The Ambiguous Panopticon: Foucault and the Codes of Cyberspace." *CTheory*, March 13. http://ctheory.net/ctheory_wp/the-ambiguous-panopticon-foucault-and-the-codes-of-cyberspace/

"Worst U.S. Shooting Ever Kills 33 on Va. Campus." 2007. MSNBC.com and NBC News, April 17.

Wright, Evan. 2004. *Generation Kill*. New York, NY: Putnam.

Wyatt, Edward. 2006. "Anti-U.S. Attack Videos Found on YouTube." *The New York Times*, October 6.

Xenos, Nicholas. 2004. "Leo Strauss and the Rhetoric of the War on Terror." *Logos* 3, no. 2: 1–19.

Yam, Marcus. 2007. "No Video Games Found in Cho Seung-Hui Dorm Room; Games Not to Blame for Tragedy." *DailyTech*, April 20.

Yost, Pete, Lara Jakes, and Rodrique Ngowi. 2013. "Bombing Suspect Goes Silent after Being Read Miranda Rights." *Salon*, April 25.

Zaretsky, Mark. 2013. "Police Not Challenging Report Adam Lanza Planned Newtown Massacre on Spreadsheet." *Litchfield County Times*, March 13.

———. 2008a. *In Defense of Lost Causes*. London; New York: Verso.

———. 2008b. *Violence: Six Sideways Reflections*. New York: Picador.

Žižek, Slavoj. 2009. *First as Tragedy Then as Farce*. New York: Verso.

Žižek, Slavoj (ed.). 2003. *Mapping Ideology*. Verso.

Zucchino, David. 2010. "Police Officers Describe Fort Hood Gunfight." *Los Angeles Times*, October 2.

Index

C

Y

Z

Violence Studies

Felix Ó Murchadha, *General Editor*

The Violence Studies series aims to publish work that explores violence in the diverse areas of human life from the bedroom to the battlefield and in its different modes of appearance from language to social and economic structures to the infliction of physical harm. This series is particularly, though not exclusively, directed toward scholars in the areas of philosophy, literature, sociology, and cultural studies. It seeks to encompass a wide range of theoretical approaches and disciplinary orientations investigating the phenomena of violence and how they are expressed and codified in literature, cultural and political practice, and in the forms of human society. It also welcomes works that explore the ways in which violence is inflicted on the non-human world of animals and the environment. We are especially interested in books exploring the intersections of violence and religion, violence in language and rhetoric, as well as studies on the issues of gender, power and ideology as they relate to questions of violence. This series welcomes both individually authored and collaboratively authored books and monographs as well as edited collections of essays and conference proceedings.

For additional information about this series or for the submission of manuscripts, please contact:

Peter Lang Publishing
Acquisitions Department
29 Broadway, 18th Floor
New York, New York 10006

To order other books in this series, please contact our Customer Service Department:

800-770-LANG (within the U.S.)
(212) 647-7706 (outside the U.S.)
(212) 647-7707 FAX

Or browse online by series at:

www.peterlang.com